THE PAPACY

THE PAPACY

•PAUL JOHNSON•

Edited by Michael Walsh

BARNES & NOBLE BOOKS
NEW YORK

This edition published by Barnes & Noble Publishing, Inc.,
by arrangement with Orion Publishing Group

2005 Barnes & Noble Books

M 10 9 8 7 6 5 4 3 2 1

ISBN 0-7607-7534-6

First published in 1997 by
George Weidenfeld & Nicolson Ltd

This paperback edition first published in 1998 by
Orion Publishing Group

British Library Cataloguing-in-Publication Data
A catalogue record for this book is available from
the British Library

Picture research by: Joanne King
Designed by: Peter Laws
Typeset in: Sabon
Printed and bound in Singapore

CONTENTS

'UPON THIS ROCK I WILL BUILD MY CHURCH'

PAUL JOHNSON

WE MAY DISPUTE the truths of Christianity. We may deny the primacy of Roman Catholicism within the Christian communion. We may reject the dogma of Papal Infallibility. But we cannot dispute that the papacy itself, purely as a human institution, is unique. The historian bows his head in humble respect at its antiquity, continuity and durability, and observes in awe its endless splendours and shadows as they flicker across the centuries. It has now survived two entire millennia with its essential functions intact. It is granitic in its capacity to endure. 'Thou art Peter, and upon this rock I will build my Church.' The Church is still there. The pope is still the rock on which it leans for guidance and leadership. The papacy is the last of the ancient autocracies, the only one where the autocrat himself has preserved his essential powers intact. Caesars and tsars, kaisers and Holy Roman Emperors, mikados and sultans and Moguls have vanished or shrunk into mere constitutional functionaries, no

St Peter's Square and its environs.

more significant today than the high priests of the Israelites or the pharaohs of ancient Egypt. But the pope is still there, and a larger congregation than every before – over one billion people of all races – acknowledges his spiritual sovereignty.

What are the characteristics which have ensured this lonely survival from the first century AD? Leaving aside the factor which Catholics would claim is the most important of all – the support and guidance of the Holy Spirit, springing from the fact that the pope is Christ's vicar on earth – they are three-fold. The first is unity of place. Rome means the papacy, and the papacy is essentially Roman. There is an early tradition that St Peter reached Rome in 42 AD. He is accounted, again by tradition, the first Pope and Bishop of Rome, reigning there twenty-five years and dying there, as a martyr, in 67 AD. He has had 262 successors, not counting anti-popes, and the overwhelming majority of them were elected in Rome, reigned there and died there. Indeed no less than 124 of them were actually born in Rome, and counted themselves Roman through and through.

It is true that popes have not always reigned from Rome. Between 1309 to 1377 the papacy directed the Church from Avignon, of which the dramatic papal palace there is a reminder. But this absence from Rome was always referred to as 'the Babylonian Captivity', and when Pope Gregory XI (reigned 1370–78) finally brought the papacy back to Rome, it was soon as though it had never left. It is true that some popes were never able to get to Rome and others were forced to flee it. Urban IV (1261–4), Clement IV (1265–8) and Celestine V (1294) never actually set foot in Rome as pope. John XXI (1276–7) – John XX, curiously enough, never existed, though there have been two John XXIIIs, one an anti-pope – never got to Rome either, being elected in Viterbo and killed there when the ceiling collapsed. Some popes failed to control Rome and paid for their failure with their lives. Thus John X, Leo VI, Stephen VIII, John XI and John XII, all of them tenth-century

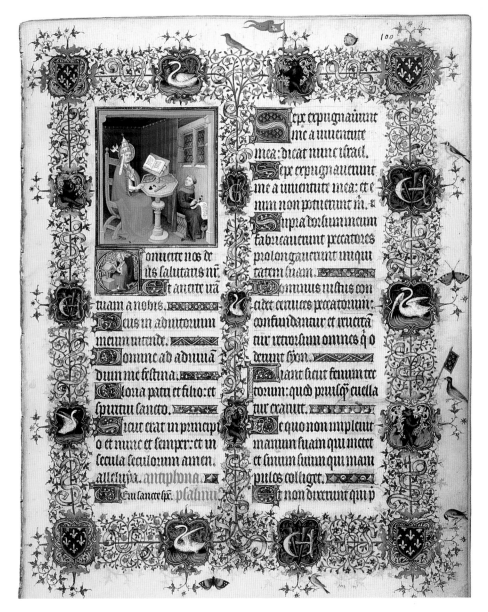

Pope Gregory I, 'the Great' (590–604). Frankish illuminated manuscript, fifteenth century, from the Duc de Berry's Hours.

popes, were deposed in Rome and were murdered or died in prison. Benedict VI was strangled, John XIV was starved to death in a dungeon, Lucius II (1144–5) was killed in battle. A score of popes were driven from the city and died outside the protection of its walls – the archetype of them being the great Gregory VII (1073–85), who died in Salerno, his last words reputed to have been 'I have loved justice and hated iniquity, therefore I die in exile'. But for a pope to be outside Rome was always a form of exile, an anomaly. During most of the two millennia, the popes have actually ruled Rome, as independent princes, the majority of them enjoying peace and security, long years of piety and honour, in which they ceaselessly adorned and embellished the Eternal City.

This Roman continuity was enhanced by the fact that, though the popes have left their mark on every corner of Rome, for most of two thousand years they have concentrated their activities in two particular areas of it. The tradition that St Peter was actually buried beneath the present St Peter's basilica is a very old and strong one and appears to be confirmed by archaeological evidence. The actual spot is just below the high altar and Bernini's magnificent 100-foot baldacchino, under which only the pope himself may say mass. When the Emperor Constantine embraced the faith in the early fourth century, he gave to the pope, as Bishop of Rome, an ancient palace he had received as part of his wife's dowry. This had belonged to the noble Laterini family, and the Lateran became the site both of the papal palace and the magnificent church of St John Lateran, which remains the official Cathedral Church of Rome, 'omnium urbis et orbis ecclesiarum mater et caput'.

However, St Peter's burial place had been the site of an equally ancient church, founded by Constantine himself around 330 AD. At least two papal palaces were built nearby on what had been the 'Mons Vaticanus', where Nero had watched circuses and animal sacrifices. When the popes returned to Rome after the exile in Avignon, the Lateran Palace was a fire-damaged ruin, so they decided, once and for all, to make their home where the first of them had died a martyr. Since 1377, therefore, the Vatican has been the pope's principal place of residence, a covered passage leading from it to the Castel San' Angelo, the huge round fortress where the popes could shelter in time of danger (itself built over the tomb of the Emperor Hadrian). The first conclave to elect a pope was held in 1378. Thereafter, no less than nine popes contributed to the buildings which now constitute the Vatican. Meanwhile in 1506 Pope Julius II laid the foundation stone of the present St Peter's

Christ gives the key to St Peter. Fresco (1482) in the Sistine Chapel by Perugino (c. 1448–1523).

*Plan of the city of Rome.
Miniature (1415/16) by
Gebrüdern Limburg
(active 1401–16) on
parchment.*

basilica. The vast church was the work of, in succession, Bramante, Raphael, Peruzzi, Sangallo and Michelangelo, and was finally consecrated by Urban VIII in 1626. Thus for two thousand years, the papacy and the popes have been firmly centred along a Roman axis, the two poles of which are the Vatican on the left bank of the Tiber, and the Lateran in the heart of the ancient Roman city. For most of the last half-millennium, the popes have rarely set foot outside Rome, except (since the seventeenth century) to spend the heat of the high summer at Castel Gandolfo, a lofty and umbrageous residence in the Alban Hills, eighteen miles to the south-east of the city. Not until the reign of the late pope, John Paul II, did the pope become peripatetic, and even he remained as he said 'a Roman of the Romans', paying official visits to over 200 of the churches in his diocese.

The second source of papal strength is its internationalism. It may be asked: why so, since so many of the popes have been Italians? It is true that a majority of the popes have come from Italy. This was not always so, however, especially in early times. Nine popes were from Palestine, Syria and the near East, no less than seventeen were Greek, three were Africans, two Goths, two from Sardinia, one was Hungarian, one English, one Portuguese, six German and seventeen French (this list includes some anti-popes). The last non-Italian pope before the present Polish one was Hadrian VI from Utrecht in the Netherlands, who reigned 1522–3. Then there were forty-four Italians in succession. But it has to be remembered that, during these long centuries, Italy was never a nation in the sense that England or France or Spain or even Germany were nations. Italy was a world in itself, a collection of city–states, each of which traced its origins back to the international confraternity of the Roman Empire, the global society *par excellence*. Rome, in particular, saw itself as a city bound by no national confines but stretching out its hands to the entire world. It still, for all liturgical and most administrative purposes, spoke and wrote the language of the old Republic and Empire, the lingua franca of antiquity and the Middle Ages, Latin. Italians, and especially Romans, regarded themselves as in some meta-physical sense supra-national, still representing the global perspective of the empire which, in their eyes, had never died. The papacy always embodied this cosmopolitan spirit. The popes addressed their messages *urbi et orbi*, 'to the City and to the world'. Some of their transactions and documents recalled the methods of their Roman predecessors. Thus their weightier written mandates were termed 'bulls', from the Latin bulla, seal, the documents being sealed in the earliest times with the pope's signet-ring, just as the Emperors had done, though from the sixth century they had seal-boxes in red or signets stamped in wax – a practice followed by the Holy Roman Emperors.

Consistent with their supranationality, the popes fiercely opposed the emergence of a unified Italian state, not only

Sculpted papal crown and keys to Heaven. St Peter's Square, Rome.

because it absorbed the wide Italian territories ruled by the Holy See but because it snatched from the papacy the very capital, Rome itself. That was one of the reasons why Pope Pius IX (1846–78), who had excommunicated the new King of Italy, summoned the first Vatican council, to proclaim the most controversial of dogmas: if the pope was no longer a major territorial ruler, at least he was infallible when he spoke on faith and morals, *urbi et orbi*. To this great council came 764 'fathers of the Church' from all five continents, including 113 from America, 83 from Asia, 14 from Africa and 13 from Australia, besides 265 from all the other European countries outside Italy. In addition to 50 cardinals, 10 patriarchs, 130 archbishops and 522 bishops, there were the 30 generals or heads of the great orders of monks, friars and priests which likewise operated in virtually every country in the world. The popes flaunted their internationalism in the face of the narrow nationalism of their Italian masters, and refused to recognize the new Italian state until, in the fullness of time, the Lateran Treaty of 1929 'finally and irrevocably' settled the Roman question. The pope recognized Italy and, in return, Italy recognized 'the sovereign independence of the Holy See in the

The main door of St Peter's Cathedral, Soria, Castille, showing the seated image of St Peter as pope, in the Plateresque style. Sixteenth century.

international field' and the Holy See's 'sovereign jurisdiction' in the Vatican City.

Thus the papacy's independence of Italy was secured and the popes remained players on the international chessboard: not major ones, indeed – they had not been that since the sixteenth century – but influential enough. When Stalin asked, 'How many divisions has the pope?' it was he, not the Holy See, who seemed lacking in realism, and the regime he represented, seemingly all-powerful but lasting a mere seventy-five years in all, appears now a mere episode in the long

Death carries off the pope, the emperor, a cardinal and a king. Illuminated manuscript (1492).

centuries of the papacy's existence. Shorn of its territories (except the Vatican City) the papacy in fact has acquired a kind of supra-national status, marked by the fact that the pope's nuncios or ambassadors are in many countries automatically recognized as doyens or deans of the diplomatic corps. Pope John Paul II, the first non-Italian pope since the sixteenth century, underlined the papacy's internationalism by visiting scores of countries in all the continents, some repeatedly, and by taking every opportunity in Rome itself of addressing visitors in up to a score of languages. Most papal masses and other ceremonies in Rome today are conducted in part in a variety of tongues. There are bishops, priests and nuns from all over the world living and working in Rome, and the Vatican administration itself, like the United Nations, is recruited globally. At the same time there is a pervasive element of Latin in the documents with which the papacy transacts its business. It never, and rightly, forgets its origins in Imperial Rome. Therein lies much of its tenacity and strength.

A third reason why the papacy has survived is the variety and capacity of its long sequence of rulers. Plenty of popes have been saints (and martyrs). Plenty have also been astute lawyers, forceful men of state, skilful diplomats – a few even warriors. St Peter himself, of course, was a humble fisherman and some of the early popes came in similar manner from complete obscurity – indeed, we know little more than their names. As the papacy struggled into the limelight of history, its pontiffs, like other rulers, tended to come from the aristocracy, though it is notable that even Leo the Great (440–61), the first pope to establish the authority of the Holy See over a vast swathe of the civilized world, emerged from a shadowy background. By contrast, however, Gregory the Great (590–604) was the son of a senator and himself the Prefect of the City, rich enough in lands to found and endow seven monasteries. Thereafter, many popes came from landed families, often from old noble lines in Rome itself. But the keynote was variety. Gregory VII (1073–85), who began the great reforms of the eleventh century, and forced the Emperor Henry IV to prostrate himself in submission at Canossa, was a Tuscan of very humble background who came to Rome as a child and rose entirely by his own efforts and brilliance in the service of the Church. That was the pattern for many medieval popes who began as monks, usually Benedictines. On the other hand, Innocent III (1198–1216), perhaps the most magisterial of all the pontiffs, came from a noble family, the Scotti, and his full name was Lotario de' Conti di Segni. He became one of the most learned lawyers of the age, thus rising rapidly in the papal administration and becoming a cardinal, though when he was elected pope he was still a layman, not yet in priest's orders.

Many medieval and renaissance popes came from distinguished and ancient Roman families, like the Colonnas, or, like Nicholas III (1277–80), built up their own. He transformed the Orsini from parvenus into princes by distributing lands as fiefs of the Papal States among relatives. Some, like Sixtus IV (1471–84), the General of the Franciscans, were famous preachers. One, Eugenius IV (1431–47) had been an anchorite. Others were learned; Callistus III (1455–8) a Spaniard from Valencia, was an outstanding doctor of laws. His successor, Pius II (1458–64), was even more remarkable. Anaeus Silvius de' Piccolomini, from a poor but ancient noble Sienese family, distinguished himself as a humanist and poet, as the author of a famous love-story, Eurylaus and Lucretia, as the writer of a celebrated work on the theory of papal councils, and as a reformed rake, before becoming pope and instantly organizing a crusading war against the Turks. He is the only pope, so far, to write his autobiography. A number of popes reached the chair of St Peter through family connections. Thus Alexander VI (1492–1503), the disreputable Borgia pope from Spain, was the nephew of Callistus III, Pius III (1503) was the nephew of the Piccolomini pope, and Julius II (1503–13) was the nephew of Sixtus IV the preacher. Julius and Sixtus were both from the della Rovere family, poor nobles from Savonna, who became rich through Church benefices. Julius was the grandest and most imperious of the renaissance popes, enlarging and fortifying the papal domains, conducting coalitions and wars, and making the papacy respected and even feared. Like some other great popes, he was Janus-faced, or rather sacred and profane according to your line of vision. His reliance on indulgences for finance was the occasion of Luther's protesting theses which began the Reformation, and his bellicosity was fiercely attacked by the great Erasmus. On the other hand, he patronized Raphael, Michelangelo and Bramante, he was responsible for the sublime decoration of the Sistine Chapel, built by his uncle, and no pope did more to create objects of beauty for the glorification of God and the delight of posterity.

On the whole, and despite some weak individuals like Alexander VI, and one or two bad patches, notably the tenth century, the popes have been earnest, holy, prayerful and well-meaning men, doing their best to preserve the authority and dignity of their See, often under fearful conditions. Of course, some have been too old to be anything except venerable.

S.EVTYCHIANVS
creatus die 4.Iunij
5 mens.6.dies 4.
mbris ann.283.Vac

Tuscus Marini filius
ann.275.Sedit an
Pasfus die 8.Dece
Sedes dies 9.

S.CAIVS Dalmata
die 17 Decembris
12.mens 4.dies 5.
rilis ann.296.Vac.

Caij filius,creatus
ann 283.Sedit ann
Pasfus die 22.Ap-
Sedes dies 11.

S.MARCELLINVS
lius creat.die 3.Maij
7.mens 11.dies 23.
rilis ann.304.Vac.

Romanus,Proiecti fi-
an.296.Sedit ann.
Pasfus die 26.Ap-
Sed mens 6.dies 25.

S.MARCELLVS.I.
filius creatus die 21
Sedit ann.5.mens.1
Iannarij an.309.Vac

Romanus,Benedicti
Nouembris ann.309
dies 23.Pasfus die 16.
Sedes dies 20.

BONIFACIVS.II
buldi filius,creatus
530.Sedit ann.1
Octobr.an 531 Vac

Romanus,Sigis-
die 17.Octobr.an
dies.2.Obijt die 17
Sed

IOANNES.II.Ro
creatus circa fin.an
mens. Obijt die
Vac.Sedes dies 6

mana,Proiecti filius
531 Sedit ann 2.
26.Iunij ann 535

Though the average age of popes up to the modern period was about fifty-five, according to my calculations, five were eighty or over at their election. (By contrast, Benedict IX, 1032–48, was only fifteen when he became pope and he abdicated at the age of twenty-seven.) Pius VI (1775–99) was unlucky enough to coincide with the French Revolutionary wars and died Bonaparte's prisoner, in Valence, at the age of eighty-two. Boniface IX (1389–1404) got the tiara at the age of thirty, but that was very unusual. Most candidates in the last half-millennium have become pope in their late fifties, sixties or even seventies. The longest-reigning pope, Pius IX, was quite young, fifty-four, when elected, and had all kinds of radical ideas, quickly extinguished by the disastrous 'Year of Revolutions', 1848, and lived on for a total of thirty-one years and seven months, dying a confirmed reactionary. But fourteen popes reigned for only a month, or less. One or two excellent popes have come from abject poverty. Sixtus V (1585–90) was the son of a washerwoman. Pius X (1903–14), the last pope to be canonized a saint, was born in a tiny cottage in the Alpine foothills, his father being a humble process-server earning pennies a day, his mother a seamstress. He too lived to be an outstanding reactionary, author of the famous or notorious decree *Lamentabile*, which condemns sixty-five 'Modernist Errors'. It is a fact that the most 'progressive' popes have tended to be well-born, while the 'popes from the people' have been traditionalists and anti-reformers.

But it is difficult to generalize about the popes. In a sense, they are a cross-section of serious, sober-minded and God-fearing humanity, ranging from the bookish Alexander VIII (1689–91), who added some splendid manuscripts to the Vatican Library, and the scholarly Clement XI (1700–21), who likewise endowed the library and added other treasures to the Vatican's riches, to Pius XI (1922–39), another professor and librarian but also known as a daring mountaineer and patron of Catholic Alpinists, and the late pope, John Paul II, who had been a passionate climber and skier but at the same time a

poet and profound student of some of the most difficult philosophical systems in intellectual history.

In view of the antiquity of the papal office, and the grandeur of the claims made by the pontiff to be the divinely appointed authority on faith and morals for the entire human race, the pope is still surrounded by ceremonial magnificence of a kind which most royal courts have now abandoned. It is true that the pope is no longer carried about Rome on a swaying mobile platform borne by his chamberlains – as were the potentates of antiquity – and that Paul VI (1963–78) abolished many of the pontifical splendours and deprived the cardinals of their unforgettable broad scarlet hats with dangling tassels. So we see no more the unique spectacle of the pope progressing in state surrounded by his Sacred College, as the cardinals are known, in their traditional garb. But much remains. The pope still wears the pallium, the circular band of white wool with two hanging strips marked with six purple crosses, which was part of the Roman imperial insignia and symbolizes 'the plenitude of the pontifical office'. And he still, on rare occasions – as when he defines a new dogma – puts on the imposing tiara, or triple crown, which signifies his spiritual superiority over all other earthly sovereigns. In some respects, the liturgical splendours of the papacy have actually increased. Not only is St Peter's Basilica, which with a length of 619 feet is the largest church in Christendom (and the last resting place of no less than 130 popes), the setting for religious ceremonies on a scale which cannot be matched anywhere else, but in recent years the popes have celebrated the great feasts of the Church at an outside altar on St Peter's steps, with the great facade of the church as background, and the towering colonnades of the square as encircling arms. It is possible to see half a million people, densely packed in the vast square, their ranks stretching to the banks of the Tiber, listening intently as the pope consecrates the bread and wine at mass.

Yet austerity and humility, as well as majesty, are the hallmarks of the papacy, as they always have been. There is an

Various popes from a collection compiled in the nineteenth century.

ancient tradition that St Peter, condemned to be crucified, asked to be nailed to the cross upside down, so that he might not be thought to compare himself to his divine master. The great majority of the popes have striven to conduct themselves in this spirit. The Vatican Palace has many grand corridors and salons adorned by Raphael and other great painters. But the papal apartments are austere, even chilly and (one fears) often lonely. Once a year, in Holy Week, the pope washes the feet of some poor old men of the city, and he hears confessions of ordinary Romans in the basilica, though which confessional box he occupies is kept a secret. In some respects, granted the immense size of his global congregation, he is surprisingly accessible. In addition to many private and semi-private audiences, he gives public audiences to countless organized groups in the modern audience-hall which has been built in the grounds of the Vatican. There, the present pope listens to his visitors and speaks to them in many languages, sings hymns with them joyfully, jokes and embraces the disabled, the sick and the aged. There is great humanity in the modern papacy as, one suspects, there always has been, since the days when the simple fisherman first spoke 'to the City and the world'. But there is something else as well: the true charisma or 'gift of grace' which the pope receives by virtue of his office, and which he radiates. A pope may be old and frail. He may be of limited intelligence or possess human weaknesses. He may even be, as a few popes undoubtedly have been, unworthy of his office. But he is also, as the Catholic Church has believed for two millennia, and as a billion Catholics throughout the world today still believe, Christ's vicar on earth. This tremendous belief, so ancient and intense, imposes itself almost physically, so that it is impossible to see the pope performing his liturgical functions in the dramatic setting of St Peter's, without being aware of it. There stands the 263rd pontiff at the high altar, and behind him, in the imagination, stretch the long line of all his predecessors, back to St Peter himself, whom Jesus Christ personally chose and invested with office. This is in truth an Apostolic Succession, and in this volume we see how it has worked itself out over two thousand years.

Inside the Vatican.

CHAPTER ONE

THE ORIGINS OF THE PAPACY

C. 33–440

THE REVD PROFESSOR W. H. C. FREND

'IN AS MUCH THEN as the primacy of the Apostolic See is assured by the merit of St Peter, prince of the episcopal order, by the rank of the city of Rome, and also by the authority of a sacred synod, lest presumption endeavour to attempt any unauthorized act contrary to the authority of that See, then at length will the peace of the Churches be everywhere maintained, if the whole body acknowledges its ruler.' (Constitution of Valentinian III, AD 445)

The western emperor's turgid Latin demands that obedience to the Roman primacy, founded on association with St Peter and Rome's status as the capital city of the empire, must be observed by all Churches. The decree was a binding law in the west, but carried less weight among the eastern Churches. These were governed collectively by the patriarchates of Rome, New Rome (Constantinople), Antioch and Alexandria, among which Rome enjoyed a primacy of honour only. In matters of belief and practical Church government eastern and western Christendom were already going their separate ways. How did this happen, and how did the papacy gain such undisputed authority over the Churches in the west?

The first we hear of Christians in Rome is in Acts 2:10, where 'strangers from Rome' were among those in Jerusalem who experienced the first Pentecost, probably in AD 30 or 33. What happened in the next thirty years is a matter of conjecture. The last documentary evidence relating to Peter is in Paul's First Letter to the Corinthians 3:22 and 9:5, written around AD 54, that Peter had preached to the Christian community in Corinth. Thereafter we have to rely on Church tradition. In 57 Paul wrote to the Christians in Rome, as a community who could follow his detailed theological arguments. He regarded Rome not as the centre of the Christian Church, but as a springboard for his proposed mission to Spain (Romans 15:24), and there is no mention of Peter. It would seem likely that the Church in Rome grew up among the house-churches and Christian synagogues associated with the friends and disciples of the apostle Paul.

In AD 64, however, disaster befell this community. Tacitus, writing in about 115, relates how the Emperor Nero (54–68) was blamed by the

The apostles Peter and Paul disputing with Simon Magus before Emperor Nero.
(An apocryphal story taken from the Acts of Peter.) Fresco by Filippino Lippi,
1457–1504, in the Brancacci Chapel, Santa Maria del Carmine, Florence.

giving advice and sometimes warning. Clement rebukes the Corinthians for their conduct towards their presbyters. Peter and Paul are then mentioned, and significantly their deaths are associated with 'a great multitude of the chosen' who were done to death 'through jealousy' in ways much like those described by Tacitus.

Peter and Paul, however, do not appear to have been monarchical bishops handing on office to their successors. Where Clement speaks of the ministry, he speaks, like Paul in his Letter to the Philippians (1:1), of two ranks. There are bishops or presbyters appointed 'by the apostles or subsequently by other eminent men', and deacons. Presbyter-bishops seem therefore to have been the rulers of the Churches of both Rome and Corinth; evidently this remained so in Rome for some twenty years.

Parallel to this tradition one must take into account the letter written around 107 by the Confessor Ignatius, Bishop of Antioch, on his way to Rome as a prisoner. He regards the Church there as 'deserving its renown', and he associates Peter and Paul with the Church. They gave orders as apostles, he is a convict and can only plead. About a dozen years later Hermas, a humble member of the Church in Rome, but one with prophetic gifts, alludes to 'the elders who are in charge of the Church', but makes no mention of the apostles.

One can only set these traditions side by side. They are not easy to reconcile. In any case, by 150 the situation was changing. Episcopacy had gradually come to prevail over other forms of Church government. Already in the first decade of the second century churches in Syria and Asia (western Asia Minor) were governed by single bishops, such as Ignatius and Polycarp, Bishop of Smyrna. Inevitably the same system would develop elsewhere, including Rome. The leader of one of the synagogues or house-churches in the city would emerge as ruling bishop or presbyter. The first bishop whose actions suggest monarchical status is Anicetus (c. 155–66), with whom one also finds the first evidence of doctrinal questions being discussed between Rome and other Churches.

In this case it concerned the date of Easter.

An illuminated letter E depicting St Peter as the first Bishop of Rome, from a manuscript antiphon by Don Simone Camaldolese (fl. 1381–1426).

people of Rome for setting fire to the city, perhaps as part of a clearance operation designed to make room for a new and magnificent building programme. The emperor blamed the Christians, at that time unpopular and 'hated for their abominations'. Many were rounded up and killed. The story in Acts ends with Paul preaching in Rome between 60 and 62, 'in free custody' awaiting trial, but of Peter records are silent.

In the last years of the first century a letter was written from the Church of Rome to the Church of Corinth by a Christian named Clement. A dissension in the Church of Corinth had resulted in the removal of some of its ruling presbyters. It is the first of a number of letters that passed between major Christian communities during the second century,

THE ORIGINS OF THE PAPACY

Already the Roman community was proving a magnet to Christians from other parts of the empire, with different interpretations of Christianity. A large group came from Asia. Here Easter was celebrated on 14 Nisan, following Jewish dating, regardless of the day of the week. In Rome, however, the custom was to celebrate on the Sunday following 14 Nisan. It was clearly inconvenient for one group of Christian synagogues to treat as Easter Day the day that another regarded as Good Friday; there would be rejoicing in one church, fasting and penance in another. In 154 or 155 the aged Polycarp came to Rome to discuss the problem with Anicetus. They failed to agree, but remained in communion.

During Anicetus' pontificate we see the first clear evidence for the cult of Peter in Rome, and the association of a particular spot with his death. During the first half of the second century a cemetery for relatively wealthy Greek-speaking Romans had begun to grow on the south side of the Vatican hill. By *c.* 160 a small shrine had been constructed. Was this the reputed burial place of Peter? The earliest tomb on the site cannot be dated earlier than the reign of Vespasian (69–79). Why it was only after nearly a century that the Roman Christians selected this spot as the burial place of Peter (and Paul) is a mystery. Yet association with Peter remained strong enough for Constantine later to choose the site for his new basilica.

In the 160s and 170s the Church was becoming conscious of its identity as an apostolic foundation. A Jewish-Christian traveller named Hegesippus 'recovered the list of the succession [of bishops, i.e. of Rome] until Anicetus'. Succession lists were drawn up to demonstrate that episcopal government had been the practice there and elsewhere, including Corinth, from the beginning.

At the end of the second century, in the last years when the Church in the Mediterranean areas was still solely Greek-speaking, respect for the Roman Church was being consolidated. The main interest of Irenaeus, Bishop of Lyons (178–*c.* 200) was to refute gnostic and Marcionite teaching. One question concerned tradition. Was there a gospel handed down from the apostles 'and guarded by the succession of elders', or was there a secret tradition emanating in the first place from revelations to apostles and handed down through a succession of gnostic teachers? Irenaeus replied that 'the apostles instituted bishops in the Churches and the succession of those men to our own times'. He went on that 'it would be very tedious in a volume such as this to reckon up the succession of all the Churches', so he

Constantine I, Emperor 306–337. Colossal statue sculpted for the Basilica of Constantine, c. 330.

Three scenes from the legend of Constantine: Pope Silvester's dispute with the Jews, Constantine crowns Silvester and the Baptism of Silvester. Early fourteenth-century painting on the choir screens in Cologne Cathedral. This is unhistorical, as Constantine was baptized at Easter 337 by Eusebius, Bishop of Nicomedia. Silvester had died in 335.

will choose 'the very great, the very ancient and universally known Church founded and organized by the two most glorious apostles Peter and Paul'. He then lists the succession of Roman bishops from Linus, Peter's successor, to Eleutherus, 'the twelfth place from the apostles', as evidence that 'in this very order and succession the apostolic tradition in the Church and the preaching of the truth has come down even to us'.

These passages show how far the Roman Church had progressed during the second century from presbyter-bishops to monarchical episcopacy, and to a position of influence based on a tradition of apostolic foundation and the fact of being the Church in the empire's capital. True doctrine, however, depended on apostolic authority and tradition wherever found, and in this the Churches in Asia, represented by Polycarp, shared eminence with Rome.

In 189 Victor became the first Latin-speaking Bishop of Rome. The recent emergence of a Latin-speaking Church centred on Carthage would affect profoundly the growing unity of the Greek-speaking Churches. Within the fairly wide boundaries of orthodoxy the tendency of these had been inclusive. Letters written by their leaders in the period 160–70 inform, advise and warn, but do not threaten. Carthaginian Christianity, however, breathed a new spirit of exclusiveness. Throughout the third century the Roman and North African Churches would represent different ideas of the nature of the Church. The standpoint of the Roman bishops, however, particularly of Callistus (217–22), would affect Rome's relations with the eastern, Greek-speaking Churches throughout the Trinitarian controversies of the next century.

Victor (189–99), a North African, found himself embroiled with immigrant Christians from Asia, and also, more seriously, with the Asian Churches over the still unresolved date of the celebration of Easter. A synod at Rome (the first recorded) under his presidency requested similar synods to be held throughout the Christian world to accept the Roman dating. Many Churches agreed with him, but the bishops of the province of Asia – where there was the largest community of Christians – were opposed. Their leader, Polycrates of Ephesus, told Victor that they kept 'the date consecrated by the great luminaries, the apostles John and Philip'. Victor then threatened to excommunicate all the Asian Churches; but he had overreached himself. Irenaeus and other bishops stepped in with 'rather sharp rebukes'. The Churches were not excommunicated, and while Rome eventually got its way on the celebration of Easter it was left to the Council of Nicaea in 325 to settle the matter finally.

Immigrants from Asia Minor continued to pour into Rome, bringing their controversies with them. The long delay in the Second Coming had added to the gnostic controversies, and increased discussion concerning the relations of the Person of the Trinity to each other, and in particular of the Son to the Father. The Monarchian controversies in Rome between *c.* 195 and 230 were the result. The majority view among Christian intellectuals was that Christ was the Word (Logos) of God, His instrument in creating the universe and redeeming mankind, but subordinate to Him as being created by Him. The Monarchian opposition, representing many of the Christians of Asia, divided into two groups.

One, represented by Noetus, asserted that if God were One, there could be no difference between God and Christ. 'Christ,' Noetus stated, 'was the Father Himself, and the Father was born, suffered and died.' Noetus was excommunicated in Smyrna, but found support for his views among some in Rome, and the influential Sabellius 'the Libyan'. They regarded Christ as a 'Mode' or aspect of the Father, and were known as Modalist Monarchians. The second group of Monarchians took the opposite view. God was One, but Christ was a man upon whom Godhead as a divine power settled at his baptism, and he was 'adopted' into the Godhead.

This 'Adoptionist' view would have reduced Christ to the status of the greatest of God's prophets. Victor rejected it. His successors Zephyrinus (199–217) and Callistus (217–22), however, were

The third-century catacomb of Callistus, showing grave-niches, Rome.

Heavenly banquet scene from a catacomb, Rome. (Peter and Marcellinus.)

The apostles Peter and Paul, from the tomb of the boy Aurellus, c. 313, Rome.

undecided about the less extreme Modalist teaching of Sabellius, who conceived of God as One, but having three activities as Father, Son and Holy Spirit. Though the Roman Church rejected Sabellius himself it tended to start its approach to the doctrine of the Trinity from the unity of God, whereas the east would start from the basis of duality of God and Logos.

The disciplinary and Christological disputes between Callistus and the presbyter Hippolytus (*c.* 155–236) anticipated the controversies affecting Rome for the next century. Hippolytus is best known for having devised the modern timing of Easter on the Sunday after the first full moon following the spring equinox.

Callistus, responding to the problem of growing numbers in the Church, had relaxed discipline to the extent that forgiveness could be offered to adulterers and other grave sinners after penance. Hippolytus objected, but the Church in Rome was already changing its role from gathered

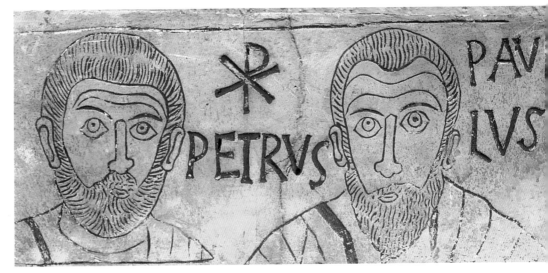

community to school for sinners, whose members were united by the sacraments. On the issue of Christology, however, Hippolytus commanded greater support. He asserted that the oneness and transcendence of God necessitated the existence of the Logos as God's wisdom and power through

Grave-niches from the third century and a seventh-century fresco of Christ the Pantocrator, from the catacomb of Callistus, Rome.

Christian catacomb art. The first steps were being taken to transform the Roman Church to a Latin-speaking body. The controversies of the time had been conducted in Greek, and until the end of the century nearly all the names of the popes in the catacombs were written in Greek characters. However, the important Muratorian Canon, dated *c.* 190, cataloguing the books of the New Testament accepted by the Church in Rome, was written in Latin, as was Novatian's work on the Trinity (*c.* 250). The change of language dragged out over the whole of the third century, which may have prevented Rome from developing a distinctive theology in this period, such as was happening in Carthage, Antioch and Alexandria.

Relations between Rome and Carthage were close but often uneasy. Around 200 Tertullian had defended the tradition of the apostles Peter and Paul preaching in Rome and dying as martyrs there, in his battle against the gnostics. Later, however, he would disagree violently with Callistus for allowing adulterers and fornicators to be admitted to penance, regarding this as besmirching the purity of Christ's betrothed, the Church.

The purity of the Church was hotly debated by Pope Stephen and Bishop Cyprian of Carthage. Cyprian had become a bishop around 248, on the eve of the Decian persecution (249–51). Pope Fabian was one of its first victims, the emperor allegedly remarking that he would rather face a usurper than another Christian bishop; a compliment to the growing influence of the Church. When the persecution ended with the death of Decius in 251, Cyprian supported the election of Cornelius as bishop against Novatian, who rejected forgiveness for those who had lapsed during the persecution. Cyprian and, it would seem, Cornelius, believed that even the worst sinners might eventually be reintegrated into the Church.

Cyprian spoke of Christ having built his Church on Peter; while all apostles possessed equal authority, Peter represented the unity of the Church. This statement does not go as far as what appears to have been a shorter, alternative draft, in which Cyprian writes that though like power had been

whom the world was created. The Logos, however, could only be distinct from the Father, as was clear from the fact of the Incarnation. The resulting schism in the Roman Church was ended only in 235, when Hippolytus was exiled to Sardinia and reconciled there with his fellow exile, Bishop Anteros (235–6).

Despite the schism, the period of the Severan dynasty (193–235) saw the Roman Church consolidate its position in Rome and in the empire. We hear of the first catacomb, with the future Bishop Callistus as its administrator, and the beginnings of

assigned to all apostles, 'a primacy was given to Peter', and 'if a man does not hold fast to this oneness of Peter, how does he imagine that he still holds the faith?' It is still an open question which really represented Cyprian's view.

Harmony reigned between Rome and Carthage through the short pontificates of Cornelius (died in exile in 253) and Lucius (d. 254), but with the accession of Pope Stephen difficulties arose. Scenting a lenient policy at Rome towards clergy who had lapsed, two dismissed Spanish bishops, Basilides of Leon and Martialis of Merida, appealed to Stephen for restoration. He complied. The Spanish Churches appealed to Cyprian, whose council in 254 declared the bishops unworthy of office and justified the right of a congregation to dismiss an unrighteous cleric.

Next year a more serious dispute broke out. Many erstwhile supporters of Novatian sought admission to Cyprian's Church. Most bishops in the province of Africa (North Africa) believed they should be baptized again, for the local form of the creed stated that remission of sins could be granted only inside the Church. Cyprian believed in communion with the See of Peter without, however, accepting its authority over him. Rome did not agree with Cyprian over re-baptism: nothing more exacting should be demanded from any convert than acceptance of laying on of hands, as was the Roman custom.

Stephen threatened excommunication against those who differed. On 1 September 256 Cyprian held a council of African bishops, whom he addressed: 'It remains that each of us declare his opinion, judging no one, nor depriving anyone of the right of communion if he differs from us. For no one of us sets himself up as a bishop of bishops.' Though Stephen was not mentioned directly here, Firmilian, Bishop of Cappadocia (232–72), wrote to Cyprian that Stephen had claimed Petrine authority to excommunicate others, but had succeeded only in excommunicating himself. Stephen was the first pope to use Matthew 16:18–19 ('You are Peter, and on this rock I will build my Church') to justify his see's authority. Yet neither Carthage nor the major sees in the east were prepared to accept papal jurisdiction.

Stephen died on 2 August 257, within a few days of the outbreak of the persecution of the Christians by Valerian (253–60). His successor, Sixtus II, corresponded with the Church of Alexandria to find a *modus vivendi* before he and four of his deacons were arrested and executed on 6 August 258. But when Sixtus had the supposed remains of both Peter and Paul removed from the shrine in the Vatican to a new resting place beneath the Church of St Sebastian on the via Appia, the subsequent cult was connected with both apostles

Third- or fourth-century dove on marble from the catacombs, via Latina, Rome.

and not with Peter alone.

Persecution ceased with the capture of Valerian by the Persians in June 260, and a new pope, Dionysius (260–68), was elected. Until the Great Persecution initiated by Diocletian in February 303, records are almost silent. Despite the use of Latin by Novatian and the Roman presbyters in 250, it was in Greek that Dionysius corresponded around 262 with his namesake in Alexandria over an appeal by Cyrenaican bishops whom Dionysius of Alexandria had accused of Sabellianism. Dionysius of Rome did not assert primacy over the Alexandrians, but clearly took the side of the bishops.

Ten years later we get a glimpse of how the imperial government regarded the see of Rome. The Church of Antioch appealed to the Emperor Aurelian (270–75) to order the expulsion of Bishop Paul of Samosata from the bishop's house, following his condemnation as an Adoptionist heretic. The emperor ordered 'the house to be given up to those to whom the bishops of Italy and of the city of the Romans should assign it'. The order clearly rates the collective authority of the bishops above that of the see of Rome.

Rome's status was, however, enhanced by the great increase in the number of Christians between 260 and 300. There was a vast extension of the network of catacombs along the roads leading out of the city. No fewer than 11,000 graves have been

Damasan inscription commemorating the martyred companions of Pope Sixtus II (6 August 258) from the crypt of the popes, in the catacomb of Callistus, Rome.

identified as belonging to this period in the catacomb of Ad Duos Lauros alone, whose galleries now extended over 2 kilometres (1.24 miles). For the first time dated tombs appear, those of members of wealthy Roman families.

In the Great Persecution, Bishop Marcellinus (296–304) was believed, particularly in Africa, to have collaborated with the authorities, and after his death schism broke out, again about how the lapsed should be treated. A similar issue provoked the Donatist schism in Africa, with more long-lasting results. We find the same tendencies towards schism following persecutions in Rome and Carthage, but possibly in Rome the prestige of apostolic foundation prevented unity from being destroyed for long, and the rigorists getting the upper hand.

Constantine, the first emperor to embrace Christianity, delegated adjudication between the African parties to Pope Miltiades (311–14), himself an African. When Miltiades' verdict was not accepted in Africa, Constantine summoned a full Church council of the western provinces he controlled to meet at Arles on 1 August 314. Caecilian, Bishop of Carthage, was cleared of charges brought against him by his opponent Donatus. The result was reported by Miltiades' successor Sylvester (314–35). While the pope was not invited to confirm the decrees, the language of the council was deferential: 'We salute you with the deference that is your due, most glorious father. Then, we agreed to write to you ... that by you especially our decrees should be brought to the knowledge of all.' The Council of Arles marks a long step forward towards the pope's supremacy in the west.

Constantine entered Rome in triumph after his defeat of Maxentius at the Milvian Bridge on 28 October 312. General religious tolerance was declared. He showered gifts on the Church in Rome, including the palace of the Lateran, and around 322 a vast new basilica began to rise over the shrine now associated with Peter's burial place. Peter was now regarded as the sole founder of the see of Rome.

On 18 September 324 Constantine defeated his co-ruler Licinius and became sole emperor. In the east, too, he was confronted by religious controversy, this time over the subordinationist views of the Trinity held by the Alexandrian presbyter Arius. Constantine was determined that the Church should be united. He had failed to settle the Donatist dispute in Africa ten years before, and would not allow a similar state of affairs in the east. In the spring of 325 he summoned a universal council of the Church at Nicaea to settle all outstanding disputes. The bishops who assembled, however, were all easterners except for Sylvester's two delegates and the now discredited Caecilian of Carthage. The weakness of the western presence was a disadvantage to the papacy, for the decisions of Nicaea favoured the eastern view. The creed and accompanying administrative and disciplinary canons agreed at the council were regarded for the next century as the touchstone of orthodoxy, to which all decisions, whether by Rome or by other bishops, must conform. Rome's immediate authority over an undefined area, probably the prefecture of Italy, was confirmed by the council on the same terms as Alexandria's authority over Cyrenaica and Antioch's (undefined) privileges.

Until the meeting of the Second Ecumenical Council at Constantinople in 381, the scene would be dominated by doctrinal and disciplinary problems arising out of Nicaea. Initiative lay increasingly with the imperial courts, and with Alexandria and Constantinople rather than Rome.

Athanasius, Bishop of Alexandria (328–73), was a firm upholder of the Creed of Nicaea, recognizing that the Son was co-eternal and of the same substance as the Father. Athanasius was also wily and ruthless and was soon accused of oppressing his opponents in Egypt. For this he was condemned in 335 by the Council of Tyre to deposition and exile. Recalled by Constantine II in May 337, he was again expelled two years later. This time he repaired to Rome.

Sylvester's long pontificate was not distinguished, but his gifts to the see laid the foundations of its future wealth, while its association with St Peter attracted throngs of pilgrims. After the brief pontificate of Marcus (335–6), a new, self-confident pope, Julius (337–52) prepared to challenge the eastern bishops in favour of Athanasius.

Julius' letter of October–November 340 to the easterners contains the clearest statement of Roman claims to date. After complaining of the removal of Athanasius and his ally Marcellus of Ancyra as being 'not in accordance with the gospel', Julius continues, 'Are you not ignorant that the custom has been for word to be written first to us, and then for a just sentence to be passed from this place?' The expulsion of the two bishops had offended against the 'constitutions of Paul and the traditions of the Fathers'. He ends, 'What I write is for the common good. What we have received from the blessed

Apostle Peter, that I signify to you.'

Julius appealed to the custom of his Church, the 'constitutions of Paul' and the authority of Peter, and asserted authority over the Church of Alexandria in particular, possibly on the basis of Pope Dionysius' correspondence with his namesake at Alexandria. The letter, however, stopped short of claiming jurisdiction over all bishops, let alone over a council. It was a protest and a plea. Without his agreement the decision against Athanasius and Marcellus would lack universal consent. The eastern bishops replied at once. A council of ninety-seven bishops met in 341, and condemned Athanasius again before setting out creeds that specifically omitted reference to the consubstantiality of Son and Father, as stated at Nicaea.

Two years later the Churches of east and west collided at a council summoned by Constans and Constantius II at Serdica (Sofia) just inside the borders of the western empire. The eastern bishops

Basilica of San Paolo fuori le Mura, on the outskirts of Rome. Neoclassical rebuilding of a fourth-century church founded by Constantine.

The Forum, Rome, westward view.

walked out and anathematized Pope Julius and other bishops 'who held communion with Marcellus, Athanasius and other criminals'. The western bishops approved a canon allowing a bishop who had been condemned by his colleagues to have the case referred to Rome by the bishops who tried the case or by bishops in a neighbouring province. The Bishop of Rome could then, if he thought fit, appoint new judges to re-hear the case. For the papacy it was a step forward, the first sign of an appellate jurisdiction being accorded to Rome. The council also affirmed that there was not only one substance in the Godhead but one individuality – a partial return to Sabellianism – and that anyone who professed three individualities was an Arian.

Schism, however, was avoided until, ten years later, a form of Arianism reasserted itself in the counsels of Constantius II. Like his father, Constantius aimed at religious unity in the empire based on a united Church. He saw that quarrels over

the meaning of words were leading nowhere. There had been bitter arguments with the western bishops under the leadership of the new pope, Liberius (352–66), as Constantius moved towards basing the religion of the empire on a creed that avoided reference to the relations between Christ and God within the Godhead. Liberius opposed the emperor's will. For him Nicaea was the sole creed. Following the Council of Milan, Constantius had him deposed, replaced by the deacon Felix, and exiled to Thrace.

Athanasius remained a thorn in the emperor's flesh, suspected of disloyalty. In February 356 he was forced to flee to the desert. At a small synod held in August 357 at the imperial headquarters at Sirmium (Srem) on the Danube, a creed was drawn up declaring that though Christ was 'begotten of the Father before all ages' he was subordinate to the Father. All mention of 'substance' relating to the Trinity was forbidden. Bishops were compelled to agree to this statement, known as 'the Blasphemy of

Sirmium'. There is some doubt whether Liberius signed the Blasphemy, or whether he assented to the less provocative creed agreed at Sirmium in 351. It seems unlikely that an exception would have been made for him. He returned to Rome in August 358.

Damasus' succession to Liberius in 366 was marked by fighting between his supporters and those of a rival presbyter, Ursinus. On 26 October 366 violence in the basilica of Sicinius (now Santa Maria Maggiore) left 137 dead. Though victorious, Damasus (366–84) was accused of murder. The charge hung over him, damaging his effectiveness, until in 378 he was officially cleared by a Roman council assembled by the Emperor Gratian (367–83), which among other things declared that the Bishop of Rome should not be subject to trial by a secular court. Gratian also extended Rome's appellate jurisdiction to the prefectures of Gaul, that is, the whole of the west outside Africa on the one hand, and Illyricum (the Balkans) on the other.

In 380 the authority of the see of Rome was greatly enhanced as a guarantor of orthodox doctrine. In August 378, the Roman army had been defeated by the Goths at Adrianople and the Emperor Valens had been among the fallen. Early in 379 Gratian hastily summoned the Spaniard Theodosius, a strong Nicene, to be emperor. Delayed by illness in Thessalonica, on 27 February 380 he issued a general edict.

'It is Our Will that all the people who are ruled by the administration of Our Clemency shall practice that religion which the divine Peter the Apostle transmitted to the Roman, as the religion which he introduced makes clear even unto this day. It is evident that this is the religion that is followed by the Pontiff Damasus and by Peter, Bishop of Alexandria, a man of apostolic sanctity: that is, according to the apostolic discipline and evangelic doctrine, we shall believe in the single Deity of the Father, Son and the Holy Spirit under the concept of equal majesty and of the Holy Trinity. We authorize the followers of this doctrine to assume to title of Catholic Christians.'

Catholicism was therefore the creed of Nicaea as interpreted in the west, a numbered but otherwise undifferentiated Trinity, a faith guaranteed by the

bishops of Rome and Alexandria. Theodosius required the unity of the Church as the basis for the security of the empire, though this time built on the creed of Nicaea. That creed, however, was interpreted differently in the east, and once in Constantinople Theodosius saw that a collective decision was necessary. The Second Ecumenical Council of May–July 381 was not attended by representatives of the papacy. Only eastern bishops were invited, and until his death in June it was presided over by Meletius, Bishop of Antioch.

Daniel in the lion's den. Detail from the sarcophagus of Junius Bassus, Rome, 359.

Meletius' interpretation of the Creed of Nicaea had developed through an understanding of the duality of Father and Son, of 'like essence in all things', and therefore by a rather forced logical extension to the acceptance of 'of the same substance'.

The Creed of Constantinople modified that of Nicaea slightly but significantly, in particular that the Holy Spirit was acknowledged as proceeding 'from the Father' – that is, not Father and Son. Constantinople was granted primacy of honour after Rome; Rome was the older city. There was no reference to Rome's superior status being founded on apostolic authority.

Lack of understanding between Rome and the eastern Churches was demonstrated in the autumn of the next year when Damasus' council of 382 excommunicated Bishop Flavian (381–98), whose election as bishop in succession to Meletius was supported throughout the east against an uncompromising Nicene bishop, Paulinus, supported by Rome and the west. On the other hand, Rome's prestige in the west was heightened by the beginning of a new Latin version of the Bible by Jerome, who from 382 to 384 acted as Damasus' secretary. The Psalms were followed by the New Testament before Jerome was forced to leave Rome in 385. The finished work completed in 404, known as the Vulgate, gradually superseded other versions to become the most widely used version of the Bible down to recent times.

Damasus' council gave an early definition of the nature of papal claims. Rome claimed to be 'pre-eminent over the other Churches', on the basis not of synodical decisions but directly on the promise of Christ to Peter. Though 'the fellowship of the most blessed Paul' was mentioned, the three sees whose prerogatives were recognized at Nicaea became a Petrine hierarchy led by Rome.

Damasus' work was continued by his successor, Siricius (384–99). During most of his fifteen-year pontificate Rome was overshadowed by Milan, where Ambrose (373–97) had acquired a degree of pre-eminence which extended to the Balkans to Gaul. Siricius' surviving letters, however, show a confident administrator able to settle any questions submitted him by the western bishops. As early as 10 February 385 he wrote to Himerius, Bishop of Tarragona, who had asked a series of questions regarding discipline: 'We refuse not to reply point by point to your inquiries and to give such answers as we own to the inspiration of the Lord. Our office will not permit us either to shut our eyes or hold our tongue ... We bear the burden of all who are in difficulties; or rather he who bears the burden in us is the Blessed Apostle Peter, who in everything, as we trust, protects and watches over us, the heirs of his administration.' Siricius' style copied that of the imperial chancery, suggesting that he had even loftier ambitions.

Two other letters written in 386, one to the Catholic bishops in Africa and the other to 'Orthodox [bishops] of the different provinces' emphasized his disciplinarian outlook. A Roman synod, assembled solemnly 'at the holy Apostle Peter', ordered that 'under pain of excommunication and the pains of hell' no bishop should dare to ordain without the knowledge of the apostolic see or, in Africa, without that of the primate.

Siricius' successors, Anastasius (399–401) and Innocent I (401–17), maintained his policy. In February 404 Innocent, replying to a request by Victricius of Rouen for regulations concerning discipline, opened by claiming that 'the aid of the holy apostle Peter, through whom both apostolate and episcopate in Christ took their beginning'. He went on, however, to say that quarrels should be settled in accordance with the Nicene synod, the first recorded time that the latter was invoked by the pope as the final authority in matters of Church discipline.

In the early years of the fifth century the Pope's authority was securely based on a Christian populace in Rome. The reign of Theodosius (379–95) had seen the terminal decline of the once powerful pagan aristocracy. The great families were now Christian, and devoted benefactors of the Church.

The barbarian invasions in the west in 406–7 broke papal communication with the Churches in Gaul and Spain. Africa, however, remained unscathed until the arrival of the Vandals in 429. The relative weakness of the Catholic Church in Africa during the whole of the fourth century had prompted it to seek aid from Churches overseas. Thus in 397 the Council of Carthage decided to consult Siricius and Simplicianus (of Milan) on whether there was any impediment against those who had been baptized by Donatists being accepted into the ministry. The council consulted their fellow clergy in Rome and Milan on a basis of equality. In June 401 they further consulted Anastasius of Rome and Venerius of Milan. Anastasius' reply was negative, but on 13 September a full council of the African Church met at Carthage and, while paying elaborate deference to Anastasius' views, agreed to make exceptions where it was to the advantage of Catholic unity.

The bishops took the same line in the doctrinal and disciplinary questions that arose during the decade 415–25. Pelagius had questioned the value of infant baptism and emphasized human free will in a Christian's approach to God. The African Church condemned his ideas, and their conclusions together with a letter from Augustine and four other bishops were forwarded to Pope Innocent early in January 417. Innocent replied graciously enough, thanking the Africans for having remitted the case to his judgement, though they had done no such thing. His reply, however, gave Augustine his chance to utter his famous verdict: '[Reports of] the two councils have been sent to the apostolic see. Rescripts have come from there as well. The cause is finished.'

The cause was not in fact finished. Innocent's successor Zosimus (417–18) first acquitted Pelagius of heresy and then yielded to a large African council meeting in May 418 by allowing Innocent's verdict to stand. The partnership of pope and council in Africa created under the pressure of events seemed to be establishing itself as the accepted government of the Church.

The large number of Catholic bishoprics in Africa provided scope for indiscipline and disputes. Disgruntled clerics sought redress not only from Rome but from overseas bishoprics in general, or from the imperial court. A canon in the Hippo breviary (recording decisions of African councils after 393) laid down that 'bishops must not set out

Bust of Pope Cornelius (251–3) with his tiara, made c. 1350–60 of gold, silver and jewels; 78 cm tall.

across the sea without first consulting their provincial primate', and in 405 Innocent I wrote in exasperation to the African bishops requesting 'that bishops should not travel to overseas destinations for frivolous reasons'. The council agreed. The issue between Rome and Africa was not one of Rome's appellate jurisdiction, but how far a papal decision should prevail over an African conciliar decision, and not least over a presumed decision of the Council of Nicaea.

In 417 or 418 an incident in Sicca Veneria (now Le Kef in western Tunisia) led to acrimony between Carthage and Rome. Apiarius, a local priest, was excommunicated by his bishop, Urbanus, a friend of Augustine, for serious offences. Apiarius sailed for Rome to seek redress from Pope Zosimus. The latter, already nettled by the African council, determined to

*Third-century sculpture of
the Good Shepherd in the
Lateran Museum, Rome.*

teach the Africans a lesson. He sent Apiarius back accompanied by three legates – the first recorded instance of papal legates dispatched to judge a case armed with the pope's authority. They demanded that the right of appeal to Rome should be restored, and threatened to excommunicate Urbanus himself if he did not reinstate Apiarius. They supported their demand for acceptance of the right of appeal to Rome not on apostolic authority, but on 'the canons of Nicaea' (though in fact the rulings were from the less important Council of Serdica). Apiarius was partially reinstated.

The case could have ended there but Apiarius, now at Thabraca on the north coast of Tunisia, repeated his offences. In 426 he was again excommunicated and again appealed to Rome. Once more a legate was sent to Carthage to demand that the decision by the 'apostolic see' should be final. The Africans stood their ground, asking Pope Celestine (422–32) 'not to receive to communion persons excommunicated by us', and reminded him of the genuine Nicene canon committing both lower clergy and bishops to the judgement of their own metropolitan. How this answer was received in Rome is not known.

The case of Antoninus of Fussala in 422–3 nearly forced Augustine to resign his bishopric. Antoninus had been placed in the former Donatist see of Fussala in his early twenties, below the canonical age even for a deacon, because he could speak Punic. He proved corrupt, unscrupulous and tyrannical. A synod at Hippo upheld charges of misconduct and, while permitting him to remain a bishop, confiscated part of his see. Antoninus persuaded the primate of Numidia to sponsor an appeal to Rome. The new pope Boniface (418–22) sent legates to see that justice was done; but they were kept waiting while the Africans again decided against Antoninus. In 426 the tenth Council of Carthage resolved that in future 'no one should dare appeal to Rome'. Nicaea was sovereign. Rome, as guardian of apostolic tradition, was expected to uphold (and not violate) its decrees.

In the east Rome's primacy of honour was acknowledged, not least by John Chrysostom when he appealed to his western colleagues for help in 404 on the eve of his final exile. The real test came, however, in the events leading to the Council of Ephesus in 431. Cyril of Alexandria decided in June 429 to oppose publicly Nestorius' teaching that the Virgin Mary was not Theotokos (Bearer of God) but Christotokos (Bearer of Christ). The long-standing alliance between Rome and Alexandria swung into action. Celestine rejected Constantinople's claim to be second in rank after Rome, and resented Nestorius' sheltering of refugee Pelagians. Alexandria resented Constantinople's assumption of supreme judicial authority in the east. The alliance was to endure through the period of the council, though increasingly to Alexandria's advantage.

Nestorius' sermons and treatises had reached Pope Celestine during 429. Celestine asked Cyril for his opinion. Both Cyril and a council under Celestine's presidency found against Nestorius. On 11 August 430 Nestorius was ordered to withdraw his teaching on pain of excommunication.

Emperor Theodosius II ordered a general council to meet at Ephesus at Pentecost 431. Without waiting for the pope's legates, Cyril opened the council on 22 June, insisting that the nature of the Word was unchanged by the Incarnation, as opposed to Nestorius' emphasis on the two separate natures of Christ. The council adopted Cyril's view as being in accordance with the doctrines of Nicaea; Nestorius was denounced as 'a new Judas', deprived of priestly office and excommunicated.

The pope's legates arrived on 10 July for the second session of the council, and next day Philip, a Roman presbyter, made a declaration on behalf of Celestine: 'It had been well known in every age that the holy and blessed apostle Peter, chief and head and column of the faith and foundation of the Catholic Church received the keys from our Lord Jesus Christ ... [and] evermore lives on and exercises judgement in his successors.' The council took little notice.

The Council of Ephesus marks a stage in the history of the papacy. North Africa, occupied by Vandals, has fallen out of account. Rome is the unchallenged leader of the Church in the west. In the east, while Rome is accorded a primacy of honour and regarded as the centre with which communion must be maintained, ecclesiastical affairs are administered by the great sees of Constantinople, Alexandria and Antioch. The emperor summons councils on doctrinal matters and maintains the discipline of the Church. Two theories of Church government were emerging that have still not been fully harmonized.

The nine-year pontificate of Sixtus III (432–40) saw the acceptance of the Formula of Reunion in 433, healing the rift between Antioch and Alexandria, and the end of Pelagianism as an active force. Only the long-running dispute concerning the allegiance of the see of Thessalonica to Rome or to Constantinople disturbed the harmony. Yet there would further trouble in store for Sixtus' successor Leo I before the decade was out.

FURTHER READING

Bonner, Gerald, St Augustine of Hippo, Norwich 1986

Chadwick, Henry, The Early Church, London 1967

Ehrhardt, A., The Apostolic Succession, London 1953

Frend, W. H. C., The Rise of Christianity, London 1984

Jalland, T. G., The Church and the Papacy, London 1944

Kelly, J. N. D., Jerome: His Life, Writings and Controversies, London 1975

Kidd, B. J., The Roman Primacy to AD 461, London 1936

Merdinger, Jane, Rome and the African Church in the Time of Augustine, New Haven 1997

Pietri, Charles, Roma Christiana: Recherches sur l'Église de Rome ... de Miltiade à Sixte III, Rome 1974

Seppelt, F. X., Geschichte der Päpste, Munich 1954–9

Stevenson, J., revised W. H. C. Frend, A New Eusebius, London 1987

Stevenson, J., revised W. H. C. Frend, Creeds, Councils and Controversies, London 1989

Pope Leo I repulsing Attila from Rome, supported by Sts Peter and Paul, by Raphael Sanzio d'Urbino (1483–1520) in the Vatican.

POPES AND EMPERORS

440–731

PROFESSOR R. A. MARKUS

AFTER MORE THAN a century since the first Christian emperor, the 430s and 440s were the decisive period in the christianization of the city of Rome. Rome's political importance had long been eclipsed by the more recent imperial residences, nearer the troubled areas of military insecurity: Trier and Milan in the west, superseded around AD 400 by Arles and Ravenna respectively; Sirmium and Nicomedia in the east, superseded since Constantine's time by Constantinople. Rome, although a backwater politically and economically, kept its high status in the imaginative landscape of the empire. Especially for members of the old senatorial aristocracy, it remained a symbol of the ancient traditions to which they were still strongly attached. They had seen their political ideals, their pagan religion and their élite culture threatened by the development of the Christian empire since Constantine. For them, 'Rome' summed up what they had lost.

By the 430s all the aristocrats to whom the Christian empire had seemed a dire threat had been converted to Christianity. The old conflicts were gone; by Leo's time, the Roman aristocracy had made common cause with the bishop of their city. The papacy, for its part, espoused the interests of these 'Romans of Rome'. Not long before Leo, during the pontificate of Sixtus (432–40), it had begun to sponsor an architectural revival in the city which was notably classicizing in flavour. Both in its physical appearance and in papal ideology, Rome was reborn as a Christian version of its old self: the 'head of the world' was renewed under the patronage of its apostles Peter and Paul. Its symbolism and its traditions were given new Christian form in the preaching of bishops and the writings of Christian poets and historians, as well as the imagery of the mosaics which came to adorn some of the greater Roman Churches. Leo liked to remind his congregations both of their truly Roman heritage, and of its christianization, especially in the sermons he preached on the feast days of the two Roman apostles. Rome, he said in a sermon, was now 'a holy people, an elect nation, a priestly and royal city; become, through the see of St Peter established here, the head of the world, ruling more widely now

The Pilgrims meet Pope Cyriac before the Walls of Rome, from the St Ursula Cycle, 1490–94. Gallerie Dell'Accademia, Venice. Vittore Carpaccio (c. 1460/5–1523/6)

through divine religion than it ever did by worldly dominion. Though enlarged by many victories, you have spread the authority of your rule over land and sea. What your warlike labours have obtained for you is less than what the Christian peace has brought you.'

The renewal of the city was not only a classical revival in Christian garb; it was also to be a fully Christian, religious renewal. Thus Leo set out to rid the city of heresy, notably Manichaeism, and to transform the old ideals of civic munificence into Christian charity; the duty of almsgiving is stressed in nearly half of his surviving sermons. His liturgical preaching sought to impose a truly religious time system on the Roman calendar, which still contained some of its traditional pre-Christian celebrations. One of the last surviving ancient Roman celebrations, the Lupercalia, continued to be keenly observed by Christian aristocrats, and was tolerated by the popes – even Leo had left it intact. In the 490s it was forbidden by Pope Gelasius I.

The popes' municipal role had grown and become endowed with a moral authority that Leo did his best to enhance. This new standing of the papacy gave it a power which could be deployed on behalf of the citizens. The stories of the embassies of Roman nobility led by the pope to secure Rome's safety from destruction by barbarian leaders such as Attila the Hun (452) and Geiseric the Vandal (455) show the extent to which the papacy's standing in the city, now endowed with an aura of moral authority, had grown to allow it to be the patron and protector of the citizens. Rome was well on the way to becoming a papal city.

When Leo succeeded Sixtus III in 440 in the Roman see, a crucial century lay behind the development of the papacy's position in the Church. Leo consolidated the papal primacy for which Pope Damasus had laid the foundations in the 360s, and Innocent I continued in the early fifth century. Leo rounded off the theoretical justification for the primacy of his see which his predecessors had been promoting. In the language of Roman law he formulated its prerogatives in terms of the heritage of the Roman Church's apostolic founders. Leo raised

Rome's standing among the other major Churches of Christendom. His reputation, and that of his see, was immeasurably enhanced by the fact that for the first time Rome was playing a decisive part in defining the Church's faith.

The bishops of Rome had taken little effective part in the first three councils. Since the Council of Ephesus (431), however, Rome had moved increasingly towards the centre of the stage. Always conservative in doctrinal matters, its bishops were content with the role of arbiters; in a period of intensive doctrinal clarification, they took no active part in theological controversy and kept out of the various intellectual cross-currents created by theologians elsewhere. Indeed, they considered themselves above doctrinal disputes, as guardians of the received faith. A somewhat loose alliance with one or other of the principal rivals in the christological controversies – Antioch and Alexandria – did not prevent the bishop of the Roman see from being seen as above the sway of controversy. As a consequence, in the late 440s, when christological dispute seemed especially intractable and the government saw no way to resolve it that would be generally acceptable or easily imposed, Leo emerged in a very strong position. The conspicuously pious court of Emperor Marcian and Empress Pulcheria looked to the Bishop of Rome as a natural ally. If anyone could further the work of resolving conflict – always the overriding aim of the Christian court – it was Pope Leo. In these circumstances Leo's role at the fourth ecumenical council held at Chalcedon in 451 was almost predictable: his doctrinal letter on the incarnation to Flavian, patriarch of Constantinople, concerning the one person of Jesus Christ in two natures, was adopted by the bishops as an authoritative statement of their faith.

The pope's prestige was at its zenith; but that did not prevent the council enacting a canon which assigned a rank to the see of Constantinople equal to that of the 'old Rome'. The session which approved this canon was not accepted by the papacy. The claim reflected the Byzantine principle that ecclesiastical status should be commensurate with the secular rank of each city, a claim energetically contested by the popes, to whom apostolic origin was the supreme consideration. Later the rivalry between the two sees was to become a source of continuing tension, sporadically flaring into conflict.

The doctrinal agreement reached at Chalcedon did not, however, put an end to the christological conflicts. Opposition remained especially in circles loyal to the tradition of Cyril of Alexandria, and reasserted itself from the 480s. In an attempt to suppress controversy, and encouraged by the Constantinopolitan patriarch Acacius, the Emperor Zeno (474–91) issued an act of union, the Henotikon, in 482. Seen from Rome, this seemed a betrayal of Chalcedon and, at the same time, a high-handed imperial intervention in a matters of faith. Pope Felix III (483–92) condemned and deposed Acacius who, with the emperor's backing, refused to acquiesce. The ensuing 'Acacian schism' between Rome and Constantinople lasted until a change of the reigning dynasty brought a new direction in imperial religious policy, from 519.

Pope Gelasius I (492–6) attempted to define the legitimate spheres for the deployment of secular as against spiritual authority. This move must be seen against the background of doctrinal conflict and protest against the exercise of imperial authority over the Church; an authority seen by the papacy, along with many western churchmen, as unwarranted. Uncompromising and ardently committed to the pursuit of unchallenged authority, in a statement due to become famous in the western middle ages Gelasius defined two agencies 'which govern this world: the sacred authority of the bishops (*pontificum*) and the imperial power'. It was a characteristically western principle, in the tradition of Ambrose of Milan's rebuke administered to the Emperor Theodosius I as a 'son of the Church'. Sacred and secular had always been much more easily differentiated in the western Church than was ever to prove acceptable, or even intelligible, in Byzantine Christianity. Gelasius' principle, however, was forgotten even by western churchmen until conflicts between popes and secular rulers in medieval western Europe gave it a new relevance.

The history of the papacy from the turn of the fifth century to the accession of the Emperor Justin I in 518 is dominated by its relations with Constantinople, both with the imperial court and with the patriarch. During the schism Roman clergy and aristocracy were divided in their attitudes. For some, reconciliation with the patriarch and the government were high priorities; others were suspicious, fearing that any such rapprochement risked compromising the integrity of the western Churches' fidelity to the doctrinal settlement reached at Chalcedon. Pope Anastasius II (496–8), for instance, incurred the wrath of many of his more intransigent clergy when he received a Greek deacon, Photinus, into communion. This division in Roman circles was further complicated by other matters, including questions – always apt to become quarrels – over church property, and allegations of financial irregularity. Not least important was the matter of papal policy towards the Germanic rulers, especially of Italy.

By the end of the fifth century much of the territory of the western empire was ruled by Germanic barbarians. Most of Gaul was under the control of Frankish kings, who from Clovis (d. 511) onwards were Catholics. The Burgundian kingdom was soon absorbed into the Frankish one. In Britain, English settlements had brought about the isolation of the Christian Churches that survived from the days of Roman rule. Though Christian communities undoubtedly existed in pockets in the conquered areas, organized Churches survived only in the north and the west. Pope Celestine had sent a bishop to the Christians established in Ireland around 430, but since then the papacy had had no contact with them, and now knew little even of their existence and character. In the Iberian peninsula a variety of Germanic tribes had settled in the course of the fifth century; by around AD 500 Sueves and Visigoths shared rule over it. Christianity was established in both nations in its Arian form, and coexisted in sometimes uneasy symbiosis with the Catholicism of the native populations. In the last decades of the sixth century the Gothic kings consolidated control over most of the peninsula, and from 589 united the

Interior of San Lorenzo fuori le Mura, Rome.

Interior of the Pantheon, Rome (118–28). Became the church of Sta Maria ad Martyres, consecrated by Pope Boniface IV, 609.

population under Catholic orthodoxy. The Arian Vandals, who had crossed into North Africa and settled in its most romanized and wealthiest regions, were least well disposed towards their Roman and Catholic subjects. Both areas were effectively outside the papal orbit, and had little contact with the bishops of Rome. It was naturally otherwise in Italy, where Germanic rulers had also succeeded imperial rule since the deposition of Romulus Augustulus, a Roman usurper of the imperial office in the west, in 476. From the 490s the Ostrogoths were in control, under their great king Theodoric.

Gothic rule was an additional bone of contention in Rome, giving rise to conflicting attitudes towards the barbarians. Pro- and anti-Gothic feelings complicated other disagreements, such as those concerning doctrinal rapprochement with Constantinople and quarrels over financial matters. To some extent the divisions ran along class lines: a large part of the aristocracy was most favourably disposed to reunion with the empire and the eastern Church, and least favourably towards barbarian rule.

While the ruling emperors were seen in the west as heretical, such divisions could easily flare into conflict. In 498 they led to a contested papal election. Two factions, one leaning towards Constantinople and reconciliation, the other opposed to these aims and more pro-Gothic in its sympathies, each elected their own popes: Laurence and Symmachus respectively. The double election resulted in a papal schism not resolved until 507. The schism divided not only the Roman clergy, but also the people and the senate. Bitter dispute, charges and counter-charges, and street fighting in Rome ended with the recognition of Symmachus as pope. The schism brought to light myths of papal history, in particular picturesque legends about the Emperor Constantine and Pope Sylvester. The collection of papal biographies now known as the *Liber pontificalis* was born from the polemics engendered by the schism, and has been transmitted in two alternative versions, rooted in the propaganda of the rival factions.

The schism was resolved with the help of the scrupulous correctness and adroit diplomacy of the Gothic king. Theodoric prided himself on the Roman legality – *civilitas* – of his regime, and he continued using the Roman civil administrative system, adhering to its traditions and keeping its Roman personnel. In the last years before he died in 526 the latent tensions inherent in Germanic domination manifested themselves sharply. On the Gothic side there was division between supporters and opponents of Theodoric's pro-Roman regime; on the Roman side between supporters and opponents of Germanic rule. The accession of the Latin, western-oriented Justin in 518, followed by his nephew Justinian in 527, gave encouragement to Italians with little sympathy for their Germanic rulers, and turned many western eyes towards Constantinople. In pro-imperial circles hopes for an initiative from Constantinople for reconquest and resumption of direct imperial rule over Italy had not died out. These tensions disturbed the last years of Theodoric's remarkable peaceful reign. The learned and distinguished aristocrat Boethius and his father-in-law Symmachus were accused of treason and executed under the Gothic regime. Pope John I (523–6), though old and ill, was forced to lead an embassy to Constantinople to obtain relaxation of the imperial persecution of Arians. He was received with great honour in Constantinople, but his embassy had little success. The pope was imprisoned on his return to Ravenna and died a few days later, to be venerated as a martyr.

After Theodoric's death in 526 the tensions eased. But from 533 the reconquest launched by Justinian changed everything. The grand plan to reunite the empire under one government, one law, and one faith transformed the papacy's position in the imperial scheme, while creating new problems both for the papacy and for the government. The imperial plan of restoration required doctrinal unification, which was to prove elusive. The settlement reached at Chalcedon was far from universally accepted. 'Monophysite' groups, who believed in the single nature of Christ, were strong in the eastern Churches, especially in Egypt and Syria. As through most of the century since Chalcedon, the government's problem was to reconcile adherents of the Alexandrian theology of the Cyrillian tradition, the monophysite movement, with westerners insistent on absolute fidelity to Chalcedon. The compromise devised by Justinian, the condemnation of the 'Three Chapters' (some writings that Chalcedon had admitted as orthodox) alienated most of the western Church. Pope Vigilius (537–55) was abducted from Rome and subjected to intense pressure at Constantinople. Imperial intervention was abhorred, and papal compliance with it seen as treachery to Chalcedonian orthodoxy. Resistance was widespread in the west, especially in North Africa. In 550 the pope was excommunicated by an African council. After much indecision and several changes of mind Vigilius succumbed to imperial pressure, and finally endorsed the second Council of Constantinople (553) which had followed Justinian in condemning the *Three Chapters*.

One of Vigilius' deacons, Pelagius, had been with him at Constantinople. He was one of the western churchmen who tried to strengthen the pope's steadfastness in the face of imperial bullying. After the council, however, Pelagius changed his mind and rallied to the emperor's cause. On Vigilius' death on his way back to Rome he succeeded him as Pelagius I (556–61). In the eyes of most western churchmen the papacy was now fatally compromised. For the next forty years and more Pelagius, and after him his successors, had to devote all their powers of persuasion and diplomacy to the attempt to convince western bishops of their steadfast fidelity to Chalcedon. Even so, the northern part of the Italian Church remained in schism until the end of the seventh century.

The schism in Italy was accentuated by a new wave of Germanic invasion: within a few years of

Justinian's death in 565, the Lombard invaders conquered most of the north Italian plain and, by the end of the sixth century, large areas in central Italy around Spoleto and Benevento. These were the circumstances in which Gregory I ('the Great', 590–604) succeeded to the see of Rome. He belonged to an old Roman family, some of whose members had held ecclesiastical and secular office. Pope Felix III (483–92) and perhaps Agapetus I (535–6) had been among his ancestors, and his father had been a lay official of the Roman Church. The family had a tradition of public service and of Christian piety. Gregory himself had served as prefect of the city of Rome before assisting his predecessor Pelagius II (579–90) as a trusted official, first in Rome, and for several years as papal representative at the imperial court in Constantinople.

Members of such families were in demand in these troubled times. Italy had never recovered from the wars launched by Justinian in the 530s to free the land from Gothic occupation. Plague followed shortly after, and recurred several times from the 540s to the end of the century. The social fabric was tattered; education, the economy and administration were impaired by the collapse of the classes on whom their working depended; and now Lombard invaders were at large. In the summer of 590 the plague struck again and carried away Pelagius II. There were floods and famine. Gregory, long inclined towards the contemplative life, was now living as a monk in a family house in Rome which he had turned into a monastery; but he gave way to popular demand, and, more important, to what he saw as God's will, and succeeded Pelagius II as Bishop of Rome.

By inclination Gregory was contemplative. Much of his thought circled around the tension he had experienced, and would never cease to experience, between the demands of the contemplative and the active lives. He began his episcopal career by taking stock of his spiritual dilemma: how could contemplation of divine truth be integrated with the busy life of ministry and secular responsibilities? The result was a little book, *On the Pastoral Care: a clarification of his own vocation*, destined to become a classic of pastoral,

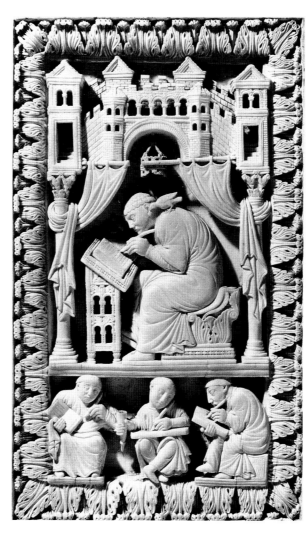

Pope Gregory I, 'the Great' (590–604), at his writing desk. Late tenth-century ivory panel from Reichenau.

political and spiritual literature. It delineated the image of the 'servant of God's servants' which he bequeathed to his successors. This stemmed, like so much in Gregory's thought, from what he had found in Augustine of Hippo and made his own, often in his highly personal way.

The most distinctive feature of his complex personality is this tension between the would-be monk and the energetic and highly effective organizer and administrator. He undertook a thorough reorganization of the papal household and of the administration of the Roman Church. The ascetic style of government Gregory adopted offended some of the more conservative clergy in Rome; and the new staff appointed to carry on the Church's varied tasks – monks in the papal household, professional officials in the various administrative offices – alienated sections of clerical opinion in Rome. Gregory's trusted aides were despatched to take charge of the many possessions of the Roman Church, scattered over Italy, Sicily, North Africa, Gaul and elsewhere. Revenue from these lands was crucial for the vast programme of charitable work undertaken by the Church in the city, its population now swollen by refugees, its traditional administration under severe strain, its urban fabric crumbling. Large resources were needed even to feed the people; the universal Church, it was said in Rome, had become the universal larder. Gregory was a conscientious landlord. He took close and serious interest in the running of the estates, even down to small details such as the most profitable way to sell unwanted farm implements. He was especially concerned to check any oppression by his agents, and was constantly writing to them with orders to protect people exposed to injustice, poverty or brutality.

His pontificate is better documented than that

Pope Gregory I writing his 'Dialogues' or 'Lives'. Musée Conde, Chantilly. Manuscript from a collection of Writings (1432–7) on St Benedict.

of any pope before the eleventh century; what survives of his correspondence (more than 850 letters) and his preaching provides an insight into the routine working of the papacy as well as a portrait of one of its greatest holders. Although Gregory's greatness rests on his personal qualities, his pontificate shows us the nature of the office as that had become shaped by the reforms of Justinian. Justinian's legislation had incorporated the Church into the structure of the empire to an unprecedented degree. The Church had become a public institution of the first importance, its law a part of the imperial law, its affairs a matter of public policy. Bishops and clergy had very wide public responsibilities, a duty to supervise state functionaries and an important role in the running of their local communities. Conversely, they were exposed to the government's supervision and control in a multitude of ways. The conditions of a province in the course of conquest and settlement by invaders, by no means fully pacified, as was Italy in Gregory's time, also combined to give bishops, and especially the Bishop of Rome, an unprecedented role in society.

Gregory belonged to two worlds: to the Roman world, now confined to its eastern ('Byzantine', as we may call it now) part, and the Germanic world in western Europe which had taken its place in the course of more than a century of settlement and state building. All his instincts made Gregory a deeply loyal subject of the empire. As a deacon he had spent several years in its capital Constantinople, and he retained lifelong friendships and contacts there. His pontificate was a blend of unquestioning acceptance of the established legal and institutional arrangements of the empire, and of free pastoral improvisation outside those institutional structures. He never questioned the emperor's right to intervene in the affairs of the Church. Even when the Emperor Maurice laid down rules which restricted freedom of entry into the monastic profession, restrictions which Gregory found abominable, he remonstrated with the emperor 'in my private capacity', without questioning his right to legislate; and he duly forwarded the legislation to the bishops of the ecclesiastical provinces subject to Roman authority.

Pope Gregory I in the church of San Francesco in Assisi, by Giotto (1266–1336).

He always addressed the emperor as 'his most serene' or 'most Christian lord'. The empire he saw as 'the Christian commonwealth'. This loyalty and obedience was unshaken by a conflict with the patriarch of Constantinople over the title 'ecumenical patriarch' (equivalent to 'universal bishop'), an honorific which the patriarchs had been using for almost a century, but which seemed to Gregory to undermine the legitimate standing of all other bishops. Though the title was no more than a formality, he denounced it as a sinful and godless 'word of pride'. His own title, 'servant of God's servants', may have been adopted in response, and was to become a standard part of papal protocol.

Gregory came into the most serious conflict with imperial authority over the policies adopted by the emperor and his representatives in Italy towards the Lombards. Gregory in effect conducted his own independent policies, which he saw frustrated by imperial intransigence. In Gregory's Italy the two worlds of the empire and the Germanic kingdoms overlapped and coexisted in uneasy equilibrium. Here Gregory's cares embraced not only the normal detailed oversight of the Churches of central and southern Italy, but the delicate relations with the north Italian Churches, now divided between Lombard and imperial control. The Lombard court sided with the schismatic Churches which had not accepted the condemnation of the *Three Chapters*, and denounced the papacy's compliance with the imperial orthodoxy. In the areas under imperial control the effectiveness of papal influence was limited by the strength of the links between local Churches and the civil administration, and of local or regional traditions (particularly strong in North Africa) with sometimes strong aspirations to independence.

A Roman, with the heritage of the Roman achievement behind him, long since appropriated by the Christian Church, Gregory was also deeply

The portico of San Lorenzo fuori le Mura, Rome, built by Pope Honorius III.

concerned with the Christianity of the new, Germanic kingdoms established in the western territories of the empire. The kings of Visigothic Spain had just been converted to Catholicism when Gregory took office. In 589 the first of the great councils of Church and kingdom was held in Toledo to proclaim the fact, and to inaugurate the close alliance between the two which distinguished Catholic Spain until its conquest by Muslim forces early in the eighth century. The papacy had little influence in this unitary, centralized Church. Rather more open to Roman influence was the Frankish kingdom, divided into part-kingdoms under Clovis' heirs. Here the papacy had long sought to exert influence, mainly through the bishops of Arles who were made the pope's vicars, following earlier precedents. Gregory continued this policy, while relying also on the administrator of the Roman Church's lands in Provence, and on the royal courts. A programme of reform, mainly intended to eliminate what he considered simony – the

appointment of bishops in return not only for payment, but for loyal service and support – stood little chance of success without royal backing, and in the event had little success until later, when taken up independently by the kings themselves.

The culmination of Gregory's concern for Christianity in western Europe was his sending of a mission to convert the heathen English conquerors of lowland Britain. In 596 he despatched Augustine, a monk of his own community on the Coelian hill in Rome, with a party of monks to convert the English. After a false start, the mission arrived in Kent in 597. Christianity was familiar here through the presence of Bertha, a Christian Frankish princess married to King Æthelbert, and a Frankish bishop who acted as her chaplain, but paganism had deep roots. The missionaries were received with caution but were soon given support, living quarters, a church and permission to preach, and established themselves at Canterbury. Before long the king was reported to have become a Christian, and a large body of his followers to have been baptized with him. On hearing of their success, in 601 Gregory sent reinforcements to the missionaries and laid plans for the organization of the new English Church. These were politically unrealistic, and came to nothing in the short run, when pagan reaction after Æthelbert's death (616) forced the bishops to flee. The mission had depended from the start on the collaboration of the Frankish Church, and Gregory had always intended to associate the new English Church with its Frankish neighbour to promote reforms within it.

Gregory's initiative in sending a mission beyond the frontiers of the empire, from pastoral concern for the good of heathen English souls and in obedience to the command 'Go ye and teach all nations' (Matthew 28:19), was to be a model for missionaries in the following generations on and beyond the boundaries of the Frankish kingdom. The strategy that he came to adopt in the English mission was also a turning point in papal history. In all his previous efforts to bring about the conversion of pagans – principally in the Italian islands – Gregory had acted on the established model of Roman imperial Christianity: preaching backed by the coercive power of the ruling authorities. This was the approach he had also initially adopted for the English mission. But he was quick to abandon it when it became apparent that it was unrealistic in the circumstances of Britain. The reports from the missionaries made him realize that a gradual approach to the conversion of English pagans, making use of their pagan cult sites and shrines and adapting them for Christian use, would have more success. This revolutionary change in strategy would have significant consequences in the long run.

Less revolutionary, but no less characteristic of Gregory's flexibility of mind and of the supreme importance he attached to pastoral considerations, are his instructions to his missionaries on liturgical and moral norms. They were not to impose Roman usages merely because they were Roman, but to choose what seemed best from whatever source, Roman or non-Roman. Here, and elsewhere,

Gregory always valued diversity in such matters and thought that it contributed to the richness of the Church without harming its unity in charity. In this respect he presents a sharp contrast with some of his papal predecessors, notably Innocent I, and some of his successors, for instance Gregory VII; though he could claim the authority, among others, of his master Augustine of Hippo. His advice to Augustine of Canterbury on questions concerning ritual purity, and the rules he laid down concerning prohibited degrees of relationship in marriage, were notably liberal-minded, even to the extent of incurring suspicion as to their authenticity and opposition to their mildness in the seventh century.

The Baptism of Christ by St John the Baptist. Sixth-century mosaic on the dome of the Baptistry of Ravenna Cathedral.

The death of Pope Gregory I, 'the Great' (590–604).

The mission to the English was Gregory's most personal and most characteristic act. Among the English he was particularly venerated as their special apostle and father. But for the papacy, the new English Church remained on the margin of its interests. These remained concentrated within the imperial boundaries for another hundred years or more. The papacy was involved in a series of struggles with the Greek Church and the imperial government, both in Italy and in Constantinople. Hostility towards 'Greeks' was growing in Italy. Fiscal pressures led to resentment of the government in Italy; repeated rebellions in parts of the army opened the way for struggles between usurpers and the recognized imperial forces and officials. The popes were inevitably drawn into these conflicts in Italy. In 640, under Severinus (28 May–2 August 640) the Lateran treasury was attacked by Italian troops, and in a punitive expedition the exarch confiscated much of its treasure.

More significant than such conflicts was the renewed doctrinal strife which began under the Emperor Heraclius (610–41). The legacy of the christological debates which Chalcedon failed finally to lay to rest resurfaced in controversy over the 'monothelite' doctrine – that Christ had a single will. Military conditions on the empire's eastern borders made the reconciliation of monophysite dissent imperative. In an attempt to find a formula to which eastern monophysites would assent without alienating western Chalcedonians, the emperor and Sergius, patriarch of Constantinople, put forward a formula which referred to one *energeia* (action, operation, energy) in Christ. This, it was hoped, would achieve the desired result. Pope Honorius I (625–38), misled by ambiguous communications he had received, was drawn into giving his approval, using the phrase 'one will'. Subsequent debates focused on this ill-advised phrase and the papacy found itself repeatedly embarrassed by imputations of heresy – in fact unjustified – to Pope Honorius. As opinions hardened and the phrase became seen as objectionable, the emperor made an attempt to close the debate with a formula, the *Ekthesis*, in 638. The lead in the opposition was taken by the Greek abbot Maximus ('the Confessor'), a distinguished theologian who had fled to North Africa, where he rallied impressive support against the imperial theology. The papacy and the North African Church under Maximus' leadership were now united in their opposition to monothelitism. Greek monks and clergy who had settled in Rome as refugees from the east alerted Rome to the dangers of the new doctrines being advocated in Constantinople. Pope Theodore (642–9), a Greek theologian from Jerusalem, took a firm stand, and the emperor, now Constans II, sought once again to end debate, by suppressing discussion with his *Typos* (648) in a manner reminiscent of Zeno's *Henotikon*. Theodore died at a crucial moment in this clash. The decisive confrontation took place under his successor, Martin I (649–53, d. 655).

Martin had been papal representative in Constantinople before succeeding Theodore as pope, and was learned and well informed on the theological issues. In 649 he called a synod at the Lateran in Rome to deal with the matter. The synod was in effect bilingual, using Greek as well as Latin documentation. Greek refugee monks acted as translators; both versions of the proceedings survive. Theologically the synod was dominated by Maximus. Although canonically an Italian provincial synod, in its intellectual horizons and procedure the Lateran synod resembled a universal council. It condemned the monothelite christology, but refrained from attacking the emperor. The emperor tried to impose the *Typos* by military power, but the attempt was frustrated by solid support for the pope. A second military action, however, led by the exarch Theodore Calliopas, carried out the imperial order. Martin was taken captive to Constantinople, maltreated, tried in 653, and sent into exile on the Black Sea, where he died in 655. He was revered as a martyr by both Greek and Latin Christians. Maximus and one of his leading associates were also tried, severely punished and deported.

The Roman clergy, cowed into submission by imperial violence, elected a more compliant successor. But conflict continued during the reign of Constans. In 666 he granted the see of Ravenna

independence of Roman jurisdiction, an act greatly resented in Rome. Tension between pope and emperor came to an end only with the murder of Constans in 668. His successor, Constantine IV, wishing to end a conflict he saw to be increasingly harmful, took a more conciliatory line. Under Pope Agatho (678–81) the Roman see forcefully revived its tradition of independence and primacy. A Roman synod held in 680 made its position clear, and upheld the orthodoxy defended by Martin. A council called by the emperor in Constantinople, held in the imperial palace in 680–81, endorsed the western stand and re-established orthodoxy. It was recognized as the sixth ecumenical council. Its aftermath was a period of apparent peace in Rome. Under a series of popes of Greek origin from 685 to the election of Gregory II in 715 the papacy again made a stand against imperial interference, and recovered something of its prestige. The autonomy of Ravenna was surrendered in 677. The *Three Chapters* schism was finally brought to a close by Pope Sergius I (687–701), who also successfully resisted the emperor's attempt to obtain by force his

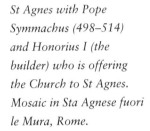

St Agnes with Pope Symmachus (498–514) and Honorius I (the builder) who is offering the Church to St Agnes. Mosaic in Sta Agnese fuori le Mura, Rome.

Christ blessing with saints.
Mosaic from the triumphal
arch in San Lorenzo fuori
le Mura, Rome.

consent to the decrees of a council he had held in Constantinople in 691–2; the 'Quini-Sext' (so called because it was meant to tidy up the loose ends left by the fifth and sixth councils). It was a period of church-building and renovation in Rome.

During much the same period, the local Roman aristocracy and the Roman military class and its leaders were gaining strength and independence. The militia was increasingly identified with local interests. While this meant that its detachments could not be relied on to carry out imperial orders, and in time of conflict tended to rally to the pope's side, it also led to its being drawn into the divisions within the ranks of Roman clergy and local power élites; this brought contested papal elections. The last decades of the seventh century also saw the development of a more complex and more sophisticated papal bureaucracy, and papal ceremonial not unlike that of a court. The lineaments of a 'papal state' were beginning to become visible, even while the papacy remained either in forced subjection or in willing and generally unquestioning loyalty to the empire.

These developments invitably strengthened the papacy's links with local Roman and wider Italian interests, at the expense of the interests of central government in Constantinople. In 715–16 the

military pressures on the empire reached crisis and led the Emperor Leo III to take desperate financial measures. The papacy's resources came under serious threat from his harsh fiscal regime. General discontent in Italy flared into rebellion against the imperial agents, and Pope Gregory II (715–31) was drawn into it. His own position in the rebellion is not clear; he has been seen both as one of its leaders, and as a loyal supporter of the emperor. At a later stage of the rebellion he certainly urged loyalty to the empire. The momentum of events, however, swept the papacy into alliance with Italian officials and military personnel against the emperor.

At this crucial point in the relations between the government in Constantinople and Italy the new religious policy adopted by the court was the occasion of the most decisive breach between them. Controversy over the use of images in worship had recently arisen in the eastern Churches. Imperial edicts against the veneration of icons met with fierce resistance, especially, though by no means only, in the west. Gregory II was now in the forefront of the fight for orthodoxy and for the Church's freedom from imperial tyranny. The iconoclastic controversy was not a debate confined to theologians; popular piety and long established habits were offended, and violent feelings were raised. In accents reminiscent of the stark denunciation of imperial interference by Pope Gelasius I, Gregory II championed the cause of orthodoxy. The Italian rebellion was at a stroke transformed into a struggle for the defence of the faith; and the Lombards exploited the situation to further their plans for domination in Italy. Imperial rule over Italy was saved for the time being; but the episode had irretrievably loosened Italian loyalties to the empire. Leo III's attempts to consolidate the empire, under dire military threat, ended in drastically changing the papacy's world. The iconoclastic crisis cut the papacy off from its imperial setting and turned it into a western European institution.

A devotion to the Roman saints Peter and Paul was general among the Germanic nations of western Europe, and could easily coexist with a strong sense of independence in their Churches, often amounting to resistance to Roman rulings. A sense of belonging

XYSTVS EPISCOPVS PLEBI DEI

*Triumphal arch depicting (top) the Presentation of Jesus
in the Temple transformed into a celebration of Roma
renovata:* priests of Dea Roma replace the Apostles, in
front of the templum Urbis *of Rome. Mosaic c. 430 Sta
Maria Maggiore, Rome*

*Justinian handing the
Pandects to Trebonianus;
the judicial virtues; Pope
Gregory IX approving the
Vatical Decretals. Fresco
by Raphael Sanzio
d'Urbino (1483–1520) in
the Vatican.*

together as Germanic nations, united by a shared Latin ecclesiastical culture and obedience to the Roman see, was slow to develop in western Europe. A crucial stage in its emergence was the work of St Boniface (680–754), begun under the pontificate of Gregory II and continued under his successors. A product of the vigorous English Church which had developed in the century since the Gregorian mission, Boniface – following a precedent set by Willibrord – took the initiative to begin preaching the gospel in Frisia in 716. In 719, before setting out on another mission in the eastern territories of the Frankish kingdom and in neighbouring Bavaria, Boniface visited Rome to obtain papal blessing for his enterprise from Gregory II. His missionary work was later to expand into extensive reforming activity within the Frankish Church under Charles Martel.

These missionary and reforming labours, which were to be rounded off with the alliance of the papacy and the Carolingian kings (see the next chapter) were the decisive stage in the creation of western Christendom. This had been neither intended nor foreseen by Gregory I when he sent his missionaries to England. They were sent to bring English souls to Christ, not to create a western Church outside the orbit of the Byzantine imperial Church, a sphere for the exercise of the papal primacy so often frustrated by Byzantine power. Gregory the Great's own interests and activities remained centred within the imperial orbit, and his successors' even more so. Gregory II was credited by the papal biographer writing in the *Liber pontificalis* with 'preaching the message of salvation in Germany through St Boniface'; but in fact the initiative had come from Boniface, and Gregory's primary concerns were within the imperial realm. The work of conversion, christianization and reform was indigenous; but it prepared the ground for the papacy to assume ecclesiastical leadership in alliance with Frankish political power.

The iconoclastic controversy destroyed what was left of the world the popes had taken for granted. The slow alienation from the empire suddenly escalated into crisis. The Byzantine empire had shrunk through Arab conquest, and the horizons of the Greek Church

narrowed correspondingly. The Christian west, centred on Rome, one of the five patriarchates, was marginalized, while the unification of the rump of the imperial Church became the overriding imperative. Eastern Christendom was closing in on itself. The papacy's redirection of interest towards the west completed this rupture. The destruction of the Mediterranean orbit which had formed the context of its life and action for centuries was even more drastic, however, than the papacy's isolation from Constantinople and from the eastern Mediterranean. Before the end of the seventh century most of North Africa, including Carthage, was in Muslim hands. Latin Christendom was thus deprived of what had been intellectually and spiritually one of its most vigorous constituents. Worse still, Rome was deprived of Carthage, its historic sparring partner in the Latin west. The tensions between the two great ancient sees were cut off; and with that loss Rome lost the one focus of a creative tension, the one Latin Church it had always needed to reckon with. Henceforth Rome, in its isolated grandeur, was condemned to have its own way in western Europe. It became the mistress of barbarian peoples; and they were only too willing to learn.

FURTHER READING
Caspar, E., *Geschichte des Papsttums*, 2 vols, Tübingen, 1930, 1933
Davis, R., ed., *The Book of the Pontiffs* (Liber pontificalis), ed. R. Davis, Translated Texts for Historians, Latin series, vol. V, Liverpool 1989
Jalland, T. G., *The Church and the Papacy*, London 1944; *The Life and Times of St Leo the Great*, London 1941
McShane, P. A., 'La Romanitas et le pape Léon le Grand', Recherches, no. 24, Paris–Tournai 1979
Markus, R. A., *Gregory the Great and his World*, Cambridge 1997
Noble, T. F. X., *The Origins of the Papal States*
Richards, J., *The Popes and the Papacy in the early Middle Ages, 476–752*, London 1979
Ullmann, W., *Gelasius I (492–496)*, Päpste und Papsttum, Bd. 18. Stuttgart, 1981; *The Growth of Papal Government in the Middle Ages*, 2nd edn, London 1962

CHAPTER THREE

REFORM AND THE PAPACY

715–1085

PROFESSOR UTA-RENATE BLUMENTHAL

FOR ALMOST TWO CENTURIES after the death of Gregory I in 604 the papacy was struggling to maintain its position in the face of Lombard wars, Byzantine exactions and theological quarrels with the emperors at Constantinople. At the time Byzantium was engaged in a desperate struggle with Bulgars and Muslims, the latter not defeated until 718 under the very walls of Constantinople by Emperor Leo III the Syrian (717–41).

Leo's policies were not always so successful, in particular his approach to the question of images. The Church had largely dropped its old hostility to images and the cult of icons had grown, with attendant stories of miracles. Some regions, in particular Armenia, continued to reject this new trend that seemed to them idolatrous. In the early 720s several iconoclastic bishops of Asia Minor attempted, unsuccessfully, to gain the support of Patriarch Germanus I (715–30). Leo, however, shared these sentiments and, probably in 726, exhorted the populace no longer to honour icons. To set an example he ordered the removal of an icon of Christ from his palace in Constantinople. A riot ensued, but the emperor was not dissuaded and eventually, in January 730, issued an edict prohibiting the cult of images, thus initiating what mistakenly has become known as iconoclasm – according to the decree the icons were not to be destroyed, but only to be placed above the reach of the faithful who longed to touch them. Those who resisted were persecuted; Patriarch Germanus I of Constantinople had to abdicate. But contemporary accounts of martyrs are an exaggeration.

In Italy, the prohibition of the cult of images was to have political consequences, in that it further strengthened regionalism. This tendency had found already one focus in opposition to Byzantine financial exactions. The most prominent leader of this opposition was Pope Gregory II (715–31). He had been educated in the Patriarchium Lateranense and had served as treasurer and librarian before his election to the papacy. Gregory resisted, and encouraged general resistance to, the collection of taxes by Byzantine officials in Italy. Three times the

Tomb of Charlemagne, King of the Franks and Holy Roman Emperor (742–814) in gold, precious stone and enamel. German school (1165–1215).

Romans frustrated attempts by the emperor to arrest the pope and have him brought to Constantinople.

It was in the midst of these upheavals that the prohibition against the cult of images arrived from Constantinople. Ravenna, Venice and the Pentapolis rose up against the imperial policy, and Gregory became the leader of a bitter civil war, backed by the magnates and people in Rome and northern Italy. It looked as if the feeble hold of Byzantium on the entire Italian peninsula might be broken; but in the end it was Gregory who called a halt. He refused to support a pretender set up by the troops of Byzantine Italy, and had the Romans arrest and execute him, sending his head to Constantinople. Moreover, he urged his supporters to remain loyal to the Roman Empire.

Byzantine sovereignty in Italy was nominal at best when Gregory II died in February 731. But his successor, a Syrian who took the name Gregory III (731–41), was at pains to show that the end of the war did not mean a pliant papacy that would unquestioningly accept imperial mandates. A Roman synod in 731 excommunicated 'the despisers of ecclesiastical custom, who refused to honour sacred images and profaned them'. Two years later Emperor Leo, unable to make any headway in Italy, decided to cut his losses and condemn Rome to insignificance. He confiscated the papal patrimonies in southern Italy and Sicily and attached Sicily, Calabria and the prefecture of Illyricum in the Balkans to the patriarchate of Constantinople.

During these years it seemed possible that Byzantine dominance in Italy would be replaced by that of the Lombards. But Lombard power and authority was divided, chiefly between the Lombard kingdom of Pavia and the great duchies of Spoleto and Benevento. The popes, by constantly shifting alliances, bribery, and moral authority, managed to hold their own, supported only by the Roman militia. Gregory III could even intercede with the Venetians and procure the return of Ravenna to the exarch by King Luitprand

(712–44), who had occupied the city in 732–33.

During his campaign to enforce his suzerainty over Lombard Spoleto, Luitprand besieged Rome in 739. Although the king lifted the siege, the danger to Roman independence remained. Gregory twice sought the aid of the Frankish leader Charles Martel. The Franks, however, were allied with the Lombards; Luitprand had just come to the Charles' assistance against the Muslims in Provence. Charles did, nevertheless, send an emissary who helped to negotiate a peace between Luitprand and the pope that was to last almost to the end of the reign of Gregory's successor, the Greek Pope Zacharias (741–52). Luitprand's successor Ratchis (744–9) was overthrown by his brother Aistulf (749–56), who occupied Ravenna in 750–51, and in 752 began to threaten Rome. He demanded that the Romans should recognize Lombard sovereignty and pay tribute to Pavia. No military help came from Constantinople. In despair Pope Stephen turned to Pepin, son of Charles Martel and now king of the Franks.

In response to Stephen's appeal Pepin sent emissaries to invite the pontiff to the Frankish kingdom. At the same time a Byzantine envoy arrived, asking the pope to try once again to negotiate with Aistulf in the emperor's name. Stephen and both the Frankish and the Byzantine envoys left Rome in October 753 for Pavia. But Aistulf remained inflexible. Stephen and the Franks then continued their journey to Ponthion, where the pope was solemnly received by King Pepin on 6 January 754. The king dismounted and ceremonially led the papal horse to the palace. During the negotiations the pope appeared in sackcloth and with ashes on his head, falling before the king and imploring him to 'support the suit of St Peter and of the republic of the Romans'. The king swore that he would come to the pope's assistance.

Further negotiations between Pepin and Aistulf led nowhere, and the Lombard king tried to use Pepin's brother, Carloman, to sow dissension among the Franks. Pepin unenthusiastically prepared for war, and at a general assembly at Quierzy near Laon gained the agreement of his Franks for an Italian campaign. He promised the pope that he would restore the rights and territories of the republic. At Quierzy pope and king formally became allies through a mutual sworn friendship.

The Lombard army was defeated in the spring of 755 at Susa. Aistulf fled to Pavia, where he was forced to agree to restore Ravenna and other cities. In the treaty signed between 'Romans, Franks and Lombards', the Byzantines are not mentioned. In January 756 Aistulf broke the treaty and besieged Rome; once again he was defeated by the Franks. This time the terms were much more severe. The Lombards had to surrender a third of their treasure, resume the payment of annual tributes, and restore to the pope Ravenna, most of the exarchate towns in the Pentapolis, some towns in Emilia, and Comacchio and Narni. These regions were later to be known as the papal states.

Formally the republic of St Peter still belonged to the empire; records were dated by imperial years, and imperial gold coins were minted at least into the reign of Stephen II. But power had shifted now that papacy had the Franks as protectors. This is evident in a famous forgery, the 'Donation of Constantine'. Linguistic evidence dates the Donation to the third quarter of the eighth century, and suggests that it was written at the papal court; but there is no evidence that Stephen used it during his negotiations with Pepin. The document pretends to have been issued by the Emperor Constantine. The fifth-century legend of the baptism of Constantine in Rome by Pope Silvester precedes a deed in which Constantine confers on Silvester the Lateran palace, the city of Rome 'and all provinces of Italy and the western regions', and his crown. Silvester rejects the crown, but does not demur when Constantine declares himself unworthy to rule beside Silvester and withdraws to the east to found Constantinople.

The exercise of temporal authority by the popes on behalf of the emperors, occasional at first, was routine by the eighth century. The Lateran Patriarchium became the Lateran – in analogy to royal centres of administration. Pope Zacharias probably constructed the colonnaded porch below the great staircase leading up to the papal living

quarters, where the popes exercised many of their public functions. In the square in front of the colonnades processions assembled on feast days, and each new pontiff accepted the acclamations chanted by the clergy and people of Rome during the accession and consecration ceremonies.

Rome's gradual political separation from Constantinople, due largely to Lombard military pressure and the judicial needs of the pope, was recognized with the coronation of Charles the Great (768–814), son and heir of Pepin, as Roman emperor. Tensions between Rome and both Charlemagne and the Lombards increased again when Lombard expansion resumed under King Desiderius. Probably in 771, Charles repudiated his wife, a daughter of Desiderius, possibly to satisfy the pope, who disliked the alliance implied by the marriage. Desiderius had intervened in Frankish

Coronation of Charlemagne by Pope Leo III at St Peter's, Rome in 800, from the Grandes Chroniques de France, *late-fourteenth-century French manuscript.*

Charlemagne, King of the Franks and Holy Roman Emperor (742–814). Carolingian bronze equestrian statue, c.870.

affairs too, by trying to force the pope to consecrate Charles' nephews as Frankish kings and thus as opponents. Hadrian I (772–95), elected pope to reconcile internal Roman factions, therefore had an easier task than his predecessors when he sought Charles' help against Lombard advances in 773. After a long siege to conquer Pavia, in June 774 Charles declared himself king of the Lombards. He had visited Rome earlier at Easter, evidently causing Hadrian some apprehension. Much as he needed a Frankish victory over the Lombards, it would be imprudent to permit Charles to exercise his sovereignty in Rome.

Charles was received with all due honour and entered the city on Holy Saturday – after swearing an oath pledging the security of the papacy. He renewed the promise his father had given twenty years earlier at Quierzy. Hadrian did not succeed in taking possession of all the territories and towns promised him, but it may be noted that from 781/82 the Byzantine imperial regnal years on Hadrian's documents were replaced by the years of the pontificate and the papal name. His coinage, too, publicly proclaimed independence from Byzantium. Politically the pope was now a sovereign.

Hadrian's successor, Leo III (795–816), not born of a Roman noble family, had to rely far more on Frankish support. Leo's concept of collaboration with Charlemagne is perhaps best expressed in the famous mosaics and frescoes decorating one of the banquet halls he constructed at the Lateran, familiar from seventeenth-century drawings. One fresco shows the apostle Peter, who on his right invests Pope Leo III with the pallium and on his left Charlemagne with a banner. Spiritual and secular power stand side by side, both subject to the Prince of the apostle.

Opposition to the pope in Rome came to a head in an attack on Leo in April 799. He was stripped of his vestments and perhaps formally deposed in the monastery of San Silvestro in Capite. Later he managed to escape from the monastery of San Erasmo near the Lateran and meet Frankish emissaries at St Peter's. Under their protection, eventually he was solemnly received by Charles at

Perspective drawing of the temple of Septimus Severus, Rome. The Carolingian
Renaissance saw increased interest in such magnificent monuments of the classical past.

Paderborn in Saxony. Leo's opponents also arrived and formally charged the pope with adultery and perjury.

The canonical principle that 'the Apostolic See is not to be judged by anyone' played a prominent part in the case. A decision was postponed, and Charles' legates accompanied the pope back to Rome to gather information. This was eventually presented at a council called by Charlemagne in Rome, which met on 1 and 23 December 800. The ecclesiastics and magnates, both Franks and Romans, refused to sit in judgement on the pope. Leo declared himself willing 'to purge himself of the false charges in the presence of the assembly'. According to Roman judicial principles only the emperor was legally entitled to judge rebels against the pope. Judicial needs, therefore, as well as the political situation in Rome, impelled the pope two days later to place a crown on Charles' head with a brief blessing during Christmas

mass in St Peter's basilica. The congregation immediately acclaimed Charles as Roman emperor. Leo made obeisance to the new emperor according to Byzantine ceremonial.

The imperial coronation of Charlemagne, the Frankish ruler, was a momentous event in the history of the papacy, assuring its safety and the possession of its territories. However, the ties to the Franks set limits to papal sovereignty. The inhabitants of the Republic of St Peter were obliged to swear loyalty to the Frankish rulers, who also secured rights to prevent serious abuse of power in papal elections. It might seem as if secular rulers had appropriated ecclesiastical functions, but during the entire period ecclesiastical and secular affairs were closely intertwined. The Frankish scholar-bishop Jonas of Orléans described the king and the priest as the two pre-eminent persons of equal rank within the one Church whose head is Christ. The Carolingian ideological inheritance was taken up eventually by the Ottonian and Salian rulers of the East Frankish (German) half of the former Frankish Empire. From the imperial coronation of Otto I in 962 by Pope John XII (955–63) in Rome, these emperors once again asserted leadership in the Church, and also, in the Salian period under Emperor Henry III (1039–56), a leading role in the growing ecclesiastical reform movement.

The valuable patronage that could be dispensed by the pontiffs, and the great wealth of the Apostolic See, led influential Roman and Tuscan clans to try to bring the papacy under their own control. The break-up of the Carolingian kingdom after 843 weakened the ties between the papacy and the Franks, and popes came to depend increasingly on Roman and Italian factions. Without the aid of some outstanding popes such as Pope Nicholas I (858–67) and John VIII (872–82), the proud papal traditions might have been forgotten. Nicholas maintained the right of all to appeal to the Holy See, claimed that only conciliar canons approved by the pope were valid, and held that because of their sin the laity, including kings, were subject to papal judgement. He proved his point by refusing to approve conciliar decisions that would have freed King Lothar II (855–69) to divorce his childless queen and marry his concubine.

But in general, the popes' sphere of action was restricted. Not even the revival of the western imperial tradition by the Ottonians in 962 could avert the threatened decline of the the papacy to a merely local force. The affair of Pope Formosus (891–6) shows how much licence this allowed to the Church. Formosus had been a bishop before his election. Canon law forbade the translation of bishops to other sees, since they were considered married to their Churches of ordination. Opponents of Formosus used this rule as an excuse to depose him posthumously. At the infamous synod of 896/97 Pope Stephen VII had the decaying corpse of Formosus dressed in papal regalia, deprived of his rank and thrown in the River Tiber.

The accession of Sergius III (904–11) brought comparative stability. Sergius had the support of Theophylact, whose family dominated Rome until 963, when another noble family, the Crescentians, succeeded them as chief support of the papacy, eventually replaced in their turn by the Tusculani. Under Alberic II (932–55), grandson of Theophylact, Rome enjoyed the greatest degree of tranquillity it had known during the tenth century. Alberic completely dominated the papacy, but also brought monastic reform to Rome, inspired by Abbot Odo of Cluny. Benedict VIII (1012–24) was the first pope of the Tusculan family. In contrast to the Crescentians, who had largely followed the interests of their own dynasty, the Tusculans used their power to improve the standing of the papacy. Benedict began by restoring to the Roman Church some properties that had been on long leases to lay magnates. In this he was strongly supported by Emperor Henry II (1002–24), with whom he celebrated a synod at Pavia in 1022. The concluding resolution focused on the restitution of ecclesiastical property and the moral reform of the clergy. Clerics were to lead celibate lives as canonically required, and to give up wives and children. Success seems to have been ephemeral, judging by the abject poverty of the papacy and the violent objections to celibacy among Italian clergy by mid-century.

Among the reforms of the Tusculan popes were changes in the organization of the Lateran palace. Best known among early papal officials are the seven deacons of Rome, an influential oligarchy from whose ranks many of the early popes, including Gregory I, were elected. By the mid-tenth century the leading officials were the 'judges', a term then meaning dignitary rather than judge. The offices of the 'judges' are described in two documents of 1002–4 and before 1032. The latter shows that the still predominantly liturgical links between the popes and cardinal-priests and cardinal-bishops were re-emphasized. A new office of 'Chancellor of the sacred Lateran Palace' was introduced. The renewal of the imperial dignity in 962 and new links with the imperial Ottonian/Saxon court influenced these developments and recalled past greatness. It was also a reminder that since the coronations of Louis II (844, 859, 872) the imperial coronation had become a papal prerogative. No king who hoped to be

*Coronation of Emperor
Louis I, 'the Pious'
(778–840), by Pope
Stephen IV at Reims in
816, from the* Grandes
Chroniques de France, *late-fourteenth-century
French manuscript.*

practical terms the successes of a great pontiff like Nicholas I were ephemeral, but legally and doctrinally they were invaluable. The increasing separation between the eastern and the western Churches contributed to the decisive strengthening of Roman primacy in the second half of the eleventh century. Without obligatory contacts with the patriarchate of Constantinople as a constant reminder of the division of authority, the Roman patriarchal role changed to one of primacy in the Church at large.

Invasions by Vikings, Saracens and Magyars had threatened Europe during the ninth and tenth centuries. Especially endangered by piratical raids were monasteries and cathedrals, because of their wealth and lack of defences. The monastic reforms envisioned by the Councils of Aachen of 816/817, issued by Emperor Louis the Pious under the guidance of Abbot Benedict of Aniane, were therefore limited in effect. But they formed the background for a spontaneous wave of spiritual renewal among laity and clergy throughout Europe in the tenth and early eleventh century, fusing monastic and eremitical traditions.

The latter originated mainly in Italy, where Greek traditions remained alive in the monastic communities of Calabria and Apulia. The most famous representative of Italo-Byzantine monasticism was Nilus, who died in 1004 at Grottaferrata, which he had founded. The third-century traditions of the desert fathers were also represented by the recluse Romuald, a son of the duke of Ravenna. He entered San Apollinare in Classe at Ravenna as a young man in 972, but sought a more ascetic life first in the marshes of Venice as a hermit and eventually in the Catalonian monastery of Cuxa. Returning to Italy around 988, he founded several monasteries and hermitages, among them Valdicastro and Camaldoli (*c.* 1010). The continued existence of Romuald's institutions was mainly due to the efforts of the learned Peter Damian (d. 1072), later Cardinal of Ostia, who had experienced a

emperor, or needed the title to maintain his sovereignty, could forget his dependence on papal support.

The aristocratic popes and their entourage in the Lateran remained largely preoccupied with local concerns. Bishoprics and monasteries north of the Alps rarely came to their attention. Yet the special veneration accorded to St Peter throughout the Latin west was kept alive by countless pilgrims, not to mention the export of Italian relics. Until the end of the tenth century, the cult of saints evolved spontaneously and locally, but in 993 John XV (985–96) became the first pope to officially proclaim a saint at the request of the German ruler. It was the first step in a process that under Pope Innocent III (1198–1216) was to lead to the exclusive papal prerogative of canonization.

Whatever the strengths and weaknesses of individual popes, therefore, the papacy was well prepared for the universal role it was to assume. In

Fresco of Pope Nicholas II (1058–61) from San Clemente, Rome.

View of the Castel Sant'Angelo across the Tiber, Rome.

conversion and in 1034 entered Fonte Avellana, one of Romuald's foundations. Camaldoli provided a refuge for another Italian hermit-monk, John Gualberti, who in 1036 founded Vallombrosa, a cenobitical community strongly influenced by Camaldoli.

Farther to the west these powerful religious sentiments had stirred even earlier, at the dawn of the tenth century. Brogne near Namur, Gorze in Lorraine and Cluny in Burgundy led the movement for the reform of monastic life. There was also a renewal of houses of canons, initiated by the bishops of France and Italy. The most famous new foundations, Saint-Ruf at Avignon, San Frediano at Lucca and San Lorenzo at Oulx, date to the first half of the eleventh century. Their influential preachers contributed to a renewal of Christian life in general. Monastic reforms prepared the way for the reform of the Church at large. Reform connotes both renewal and return to an earlier, more perfect condition. In a monastic context, the ideal was represented by the desert fathers and the Aachen rules; in an ecclesiastical one, by a return to the primitive Church – a term that was never precisely defined. The reformers looked to a way of life that seemed to be reflected in the correspondence of Pope Gregory the Great and the ancient canonical collections. Both branches of the reform, ecclesiastical and monastic, were expressions of the contemporary spirituality, whereby Church and world were different aspects of a single Christian entity.

The reforms had made great strides by the mid-eleventh century, even in Rome. Pope Benedict IX, elected in 1032, expelled from the city in the autumn of 1044 and replaced briefly in January/February 1045 by a member of a rival family, Sylvester III, no longer felt safe in Rome. In return for the payment of an indemnity, he agreed to resign in favour of his godfather, John Gratian, who assumed the papal name Gregory VI.

But the papacy was not to be reformed so easily. It required the intervention of Emperor Henry

III (1039–56) in 1046 at the two councils which were convoked at his behest at Sutri and Rome shortly before his imperial coronation on Christmas Day 1046. Peter Damian tells us that Gregory VI was deposed by the synod assembled at Sutri 'because venality occurred', in other words, because of simony – evidently the payment to Benedict IX. On December 24 the Roman synod elected and consecrated a new pope, Bishop Suidger of Bamberg, formerly court chaplain to Henry III. He assumed the papal name Clement II and on Christmas Day celebrated the imperial coronation of Henry and his queen, Agnes, of the family of the dukes of Aquitaine, the founders of Cluny. Henry's actions were widely welcomed, though a few critics complained that he had no right to interfere in ecclesiastical affairs. Gregory VI went into exile in Cologne accompanied by his chaplain Hildebrand, later Gregory VII.

The papacy was no longer in the pocket of the nobility of Rome. Although the reigns of Clement II and Damasus II, his German successor, were too brief to allow for much activity, the election of Bishop Bruno of Toul, a cousin of Henry III, brought further ecclesiastical renewal. Bruno was nominated by Emperor Henry III at an imperial assembly in December 1048. He entered Rome in pilgrim's dress, for he had insisted on election by the clergy and people of Rome in accordance with canon law as a condition for acceptance of the nomination. The Romans acclaimed him joyously. He was consecrated pope under the name Leo IX (1049–54). With him arrived men who were to be among the foremost reformers of the Church: Humbert from the monastery of Moyenmoutier in Leo's diocese of Toul; Archdeacon Frederick of Liège, brother of Duke Godfrey the Bearded of Lorraine and later to become Abbot of Monte Cassino and Pope Stephen IX (1057–8); and Hildebrand, who returned after the death of Gregory VI.

Leo was confronted with three main problems: eliminating simony and nicolaitism (marriage or concubinage of clergy) in the Church; protecting the papal states from Norman attacks; and resolving disputes with Constantinople. Gregory I had inter-

preted simony widely as the purchase of ecclesiastical offices, estates, and sacraments for cash – even disguised as fees or gifts – or in return for services or favours, or by calling on personal influence. This definition was revived and expanded. Since the Council of Nicaea (325) the higher clergy had been required to live chaste lives, something now all but forgotten, although married bishops were rare. Leo's decrees of 1049 against marriage

Pope Gregory VII, from a fresco by Raphael Sanzio d'Urbino (1483–1520), in the Vatican.

and fornication met furious opposition, but priestly celibacy became generally accepted in the course of the twelfth century.

The failure of Leo's embassy of 1054 to Patriarch Kerullarios (1043–58) of Constantinople, led by Cardinal Humbert, probably Leo's closest collaborator, has to be seen in the context of Leo's Norman policies. The Normans, first welcomed in southern Italy as defenders against Saracen attacks, were, by the second decade of the eleventh century, seen as a danger by Lombard principalities, the papal states and Byzantine interests alike. The first

HELL
Canto 19

official recognition of Norman conquests had come from Emperor Henry III. In the course of his Italian expedition, probably in 1047, Henry had brought some peace to southern Italy by granting Drogo, one of the sons of Tancred of Hauteville, the region of Melfi. Leo could therefore reasonably expect support when he travelled south in April 1049 to enforce both imperial and papal claims.

In 1051 the citizens of Benevento appealed for papal aid against a Norman siege. Leo IX took over the city on behalf of the empire and the papacy, and concluded an alliance with the *dux et princeps* of Italy who had been appointed by the Byzantine Emperor Constantine IX Monomachos. The pontiff also visited Henry III a year later, looking for German imperial troops as well. However, he had to settle for hiring mercenaries. In June 1053 at Civitate a united Norman force slaughtered Leo's army and captured him. The pontiff was treated honourably and released six months later. But Leo died within a year, on 19 April 1054, long before Humbert, sent to Constantinople to revive the anti-Norman alliance and to assert papal primacy, deposited a bull of excommunication of the Byzantine patriarch Kerullarios on the altar of Hagia Sophia.

Kerullarios had long stirred anti-Latin sentiments in Constantinople, and Emperor Constantine IX could not make him recognize the primacy of the Roman Church. The demands were couched in terms taken from the 'Pseudo-Isidorian Decretals', a ninth-century Frankish forgery claimed to be the correspondence of the popes from Clement to Gregory II, which mingled authentic material with invention. It provided the papacy with much of the juridical terminology in support of the new hierarchical vision of the Church, and was much cited later.

In 1059 at Melfi Pope Nicholas II (1058–61) legitimized Norman conquests in southern Italy. Nicholas invested the Norman leaders Robert Guiscard and Richard of Capua with the territories they had conquered and received them as vassals of the Roman Church. Robert Guiscard was also granted future possessions: Bari, still in the hands of the Byzantines, and Sicily, under Muslim rule. Robert promised to protect and aid the pope, to transfer all churches to him, to pay feudal dues, and never to swear fealty to anyone except with a provision in favour of the Roman Church. Should Pope Nicholas or his successor die, Robert promised to support and aid the 'better' cardinals and the Roman clergy and laity in the choice of a new pontiff. Melfi transformed the papacy into a feudal suzerain.

The balance of power in southern Italy had significantly shifted from the emperor to the pope – although when Gregory VII acccepted the oath of fealty of Richard of Capua, he did not object to a second oath to the German king, provided that it contained a clause of exception in favour of the papacy. The Normans did not keep their promise not to attack territories under papal dominion, but they paid their dues and gave military assistance elsewhere. In 1059 they provided troops when Nicholas II attacked the Count of Galeria who supported the antipope Benedict X; in 1061 Norman troops made possible the enthronement of Alexander II; and Robert Guiscard, excommunicated by Gregory from 1073 to 1079, still came to his rescue in 1084 when his troops accompanied the defeated pope to Salerno.

At the earlier Lateran Council in April 1059 a decree regulating papal elections had been passed. It stipulated that the election was to be in the hands of the cardinal-bishops, who would subsequently consult with the other cardinal clergy. The remaining clergy and the people were then to give their consent to the election. The future pope was to be selected from the Roman clergy if a suitable candidate could be found; if not, he could come from another Church. If conditions in Rome did not permit a free election, it could be held elsewhere. The royal 'honour and reverence due to our beloved son Henry, now king and future emperor' were to be preserved in every respect – a clause much debated among historians, because it left the rights of Henry IV vague. There was a clear shift in attitude away from reliance on imperial intervention.

Nicholas' decree of 1059 brought drastic changes. The papal election was removed entirely from the influence of noble Roman families, who were merely invited to consent. The papal office was no longer theirs to use as a route to success and riches. Their place was taken by a new group of papal advisors, the cardinal-bishops. The beginnings of the future college of cardinals lie in the pontificate of Leo IX. For centuries, the cardinal-bishops of the sees around Rome and the cardinal-priests and cardinal-deacons of the title churches in Rome had had mainly liturgical functions. Under Leo and his successors these were exchanged for a role in papal government. Some of the foremost collaborators with the popes were cardinal-bishops, including Peter Damian, who became cardinal-bishop of Ostia; and Humbert of Moyenmoutier, cardinal-bishop of Silva Candida.

The council of 1059 for the first time officially recognized the political pre-eminence of the

Early ninth-century mosaic of Christ and Sts Peter, Pudenziana and Zeno, in the church of S Prasede, Rome.

cardinals, a declaration repeated by Pope Alexander II (1061–73) in 1063. Nicholas sent out letters informing bishops of the most important decisions, usually including an abbreviated version of the election decree. The emphasis, however, lay on generally applicable decisions regarding the moral life of clergy and laity. Just as the clergy were to live chastely and to avoid simony, so laymen were forbidden under pain of excommunication to marry within the prohibited degrees of consanguinity or to have a concubine. They were to return tithes to bishops and were not to give churches which they owned to clerics, either for a fee or free of charge. Nobody was to enter a monastery hoping to become abbot there, and laymen could be promoted to the clergy only after a trial period.

Hildebrand became one of the truly great popes

as Gregory VII (1073–85), a name he adopted probably to express his reverence for Gregory I. He was born around 1020–25 in southern Tuscany, perhaps at Soana, into a family with good connections in Rome. His letters survive in his official papal register in the Archivio Segreto of the Vatican. Gregory speaks of having spent his youth in the bosom of the Roman Church, and refers to a Roman palace, very likely the Lateran, where he attended school with noble Romans. January 1047 is the first secure date in his biography, when he accompanied Pope Gregory VI into exile. He returned to Rome in February 1049 in the entourage of Leo IX. It is generally assumed that he had become a monk by this time. Leo promoted him to subdeacon and made him rector – or manager – of the Abbey of San Paolo fuori le Mura. As a papal legate Hildebrand held councils in France at Tours and Châlon-sur-Saône and visited the German imperial court, where he was much honoured. His successful presentation of the case for a 'monasticization' of the cathedral canons at the Lateran synod of 1059 rejected the permissiveness of the Aachen rule. His drive to renew the Church in accordance with ancient prescription, as interpreted by the reformers, typified his asceticism and austerity.

Around this time Hildebrand rose to become archdeacon of the Roman Church. The office included financial, judicial and military tasks: he acted as vicar during the pope's absence from Rome, and oversaw the administration of the papal states. Yet despite his many responsibilities he, and others, were startled when the Romans spontaneously proclaimed him pope during the very funeral of his predecessor Alexander II, on 22 April 1073. He understood his election as a personal call by God to continue the renewal of the Church. He emphasized papal primacy and continued the battle against simony and clerical unchastity. In Gregory's opinion all Christians, including kings and emperors, owed the pope unquestioning obedience, for only the pope would always be a true follower of Christ, thanks to his mystical connection with St Peter. Obedience towards God, therefore, became obedience to the papacy. At the same time he knew very well how to

make use of a political situation that served his purposes. His policy of declaring rulers vassals of the papacy in order to further papal territorial claims is one example.

Gregory did not intervene in England after William the Conqueror rejected the papal request of 1080 to become a vassal of St Peter. The pope thought highly of William's government and was content with the continuation of the payment of the Anglo-Saxon Peter's Pence. In Spain, gradually being reconquered from the Muslims, papal claims to superiority were usually well received. In France and Germany, however, serious tensions arose. In December 1073 Gregory described King Philip I of France as the worst oppressor of the Church because the king refused investiture to a canonically elected bishop – that is, refused to allow him to administer the secular components of the bishopric. Gregory threatened the king with excommunication and, a year later, with deposition. Despite harsh words – Gregory's language is justly famous – the quarrel remained intermittent and his threats were never carried out. The situation improved especially after 1075, when the pope had named Bishop Hugh of Die, his fiery follower, and the more diplomatic Bishop Amat of Oloron, as legates for France. Gregory could now withdraw and allow his legates to administer the papal programme in all its severity. In 1078, for instance, at the Council of Poitiers, Hugh deposed almost the entire French episcopate. The pope could respond to their appeals by emphasizing pardon and forgiveness, and reinstate them or allow them to keep their offices.

Germany was less malleable. At the last synod of Alexander II, in March 1073, several of Henry IV's advisors had been excommunicated, perhaps because of simony or over the nomination of the next Archbishop of Milan, a city rent by civil factions. The excommunication affected Henry as well, for anyone who had dealings with an excommunicated person might suffer the same penalty himself. This may be why Gregory did not inform Henry IV of his election, as was customary. However, a year later Henry was reconciled with the Church. The major stumbling block to reform of the German Church seemed to be the episcopate. Gregory counted on

Henry's help when he tried to uphold the rules for canonical elections and to eliminate simony and clerical marriage. At the same time, however, he also addressed his requests for assistance to dukes, counts, and the laity in general, as he had done in France. The population was to rise up against disobedient ecclesiastics and chase them from their sees or Churches. Such appeals to the laity contravened canon law as well as tradition, since they often caused lower-ranking persons to accuse their superiors. The bishops saw themselves deprived of their ancient prerogatives and independence.

Like his Ottonian and Salian ancestors, Henry IV relied greatly on ecclesiastics in his administration. The close ties between the crown and the Church served to hold the secular nobles in check. The ruler nominated candidates to bishoprics and abbacies, ideally in agreement with the clergy and people. In return, the ecclesiastics promised him loyalty, sometimes with an oath. The ruler could call upon the Church for services in support of his government, including military support and exaction of taxes, in return for royal protection of the Church. Gregory's pursuit of change disrupted the delicately balanced relationship; but first it resulted in an alliance between king and bishops.

In December 1075 the pope severely reproved Henry for disobedience in a letter delivered by papal envoys, who may have threatened the king with deposition. At issue were Henry's nominations to Italian bishoprics (parts of Italy as well as Burgundy were part of the Roman empire) and his contact with excommunicated advisors. From Worms in January 1076, Henry and nearly all the German bishops sent an even harsher response to Gregory's threats. In a letter addressed to 'Brother Hildebrand' the bishops withdrew their obedience from Gregory. Henry requested the 'false monk' to renounce the papacy, and called on the Romans to elect a new pope. North Italian bishops joined their German colleagues. Gregory's response was immediate. In a solemn prayer to Peter he declared Henry deposed, anathematized him and absolved his subjects from their oath of loyalty. Never before had a ruler been deposed by a pope.

Gregory's deposition of Henry IV remains to this day the most controversial action taken during his reign. Henry's challenge to his legitimacy as pope had provoked Gregory so severely that he put into practice his conviction that the papal primacy applied not only to affairs within' the Church but even more so to the monarchies. The Gelasian/ Carolingian theory of a duality of spiritual and secular power was now replaced by a hierarchical view. One result was the prohibition of the investiture of ecclesiastics by secular persons, including kings and emperors. This was to cause severe problems for Gregory's immediate successors.

The bishops quickly deserted the king, who was faced by general opposition, especially in Saxony. To save his crown, Henry submitted to Gregory in January 1077 by an act of public penance at the castle of Canossa. Gregory, urged by Matilda of Tuscany and Abbot Hugh of Cluny, Henry's godfather, eventually and reluctantly absolved Henry in a pastoral act. The encounter of king and pope at Matilda's castle had interrupted a papal journey to Augsburg, where the German princes had intended to elect a new king in Gregory's presence, an example of the dramatic change in the position of the papacy caused by the reforms.

Despite Henry's absolution, in March the princes elected Rudolf of Swabia as anti-king in the presence of papal legates. Gregory hesitated, but at the Lenten synod of 1080 he renewed Henry's excommunication and deposition and pronounced in favour of Rudolf. However, the second excommunication was hardly noticed except by Henry's enemies. A synod held at Brixen in June 1080 in the presence of Henry IV formally deposed Gregory VII and nominated Archbishop Wibert of Ravenna as pope. Henry now undertook an Italian campaign with considerable military support, especially from northern Italy, but only in March 1084 could he enter Rome, after Gregory VII had been deserted by most of the Roman clergy because of his inflexibility and refusal to negotiate with Henry. On 24 March Wibert was elected and consecrated as Clement III in St Peter's basilica, on 31 March he crowned Henry emperor. Gregory had

Fresco of the Donation of Constantine, in the church of Santi Quattro Coronati, Rome.

fled to the Castell Sant'Angelo. His Norman vassal Robert Guiscard came to his rescue, but the Norman troops provoked the Romans with their plundering and destruction. After only three days they had to leave the city. Gregory left Rome with the Normans and withdrew to Salerno, where he died under their protection on 25 May 1085. His death transformed him into a martyr in the eyes of his few remaining supporters.

Whether seen as a religious genius, a revolutionary, or both, Gregory irrevocably changed the history of the papacy, translating his personal religious experience into political reality. His intuitive perception of the Church under papal direction was to be elaborated by the popes of the twelfth and especially the thirteenth century. Pope Paul V canonized Gregory in 1606, and in 1728 Benedict XIII prescribed his feast day of 25 May not only for Salerno but for the whole Church.

FURTHER READING

Barraclough, Geoffrey, *The Medieval Papacy*, New York 1968

Blumenthal, Uta-Renate, *The Investiture Controversy: Church and Monarchy from the Ninth to the Twelfth Century*, Philadelphia 1988

The Church in the Age of Feudalism, ed. F. Kempf, H.-G. Beck, E. Ewig, J.A. Jungmann, transl. Anselm Biggs (Handbook of Church History, ed. H. Jedin and J. Dolan, vol. 3), New York and London 1969

Noble, Thomas F.X., *The Republic of St Peter: The Birth of the Papal State, 680–825*, Philadelphia 1984

Partner, Peter, *The Lands of St Peter: The Papal State in the Middle Ages and the Early Renaissance*, Berkeley and Los Angeles 1972

Robinson, I.S., *Authority and Resistance in the Investiture Contest: The Polemical Literature of the Late Eleventh Century*, Manchester/New York 1978

Tellenbach, Gerd, *The Church in Western Europe from the Tenth to the Early Twelfth Century*, transl. T. Reuter, Cambridge 1993

PAPAL MONARCHY

1085–1431

DR ROBERT SWANSON

GREGORY VII'S FORLORN death in exile, with Rome held by the antipope Clement III, marked the nadir of the reforming papacy. However, his successors continued the struggle to make the world and the Church conform to the papalist ideology. The following century saw the emergence of the so-called 'papal monarchy', with the papacy established as the leading force in the Church, and the Church becoming an increasingly legalistic and bureaucratic institution, in many ways a 'state'.

This was a fundamental transition, even if undramatic and drawn out. It contrasts with the attention-catching appeal of the crusades. Gregory had proposed an expedition to the east, but it was Urban II who proclaimed the 'armed pilgrimage' at the Council of Clermont in November 1095. Whatever Urban's own aims and intentions, the name Jerusalem caught the popular imagination. After prolonged hardship, and against the odds, Jerusalem was captured on 15 July 1099; Urban died a fortnight later, unaware of the success. A kingdom of Jerusalem was established, which lasted until the

fall of Acre in 1291. The retention of a Latin Christian hold in Palestine became a constant of papal policy; yet the second papally authorized crusade was not proclaimed until 1145, after Edessa was captured by the Turks. Further papal summonses followed: in 1189 after the Battle of Hattin and the loss of Jerusalem; in 1198 for the fourth crusade, which brought the destruction of the Byzantine empire and the rape of Constantinople; and others in the thirteenth century, increasingly desperate and decreasingly under papal control.

Meanwhile, in the west, the struggle against the German kings continued after Gregory's death. Urban II was more pragmatic and realistic than Gregory, but the basic issues were unresolved. An attempted settlement in 1106 failed, but Pope Paschal II persevered. In 1111 he suggested that clerics abandon their holding of 'regalia' from the crown in Germany and Italy. When the proposals were revealed at Henry V's imperial coronation, uproar ensued, during which the pope was abducted by imperial forces. Although the dispute was

Pope Urban II (1088–99) initiates the crusading movement with his speech at the Council of Clermont, 1095, from a fifteenth-century manuscript illustrated by Jean Fouquet.

Portrait of Pope Hadrian IV (1154–9).

increasingly concerned with matters of practice rather than principle, neither side would back down. Only in 1122 did Henry make peace, by now with Pope Callistus II, in the concordat of Worms. This ambiguous agreement still did not properly define the relationship between the German king and his major prelates, although it provided a better solution in Italy, where the popes were perhaps most interested in gaining a settlement. While the question of royal control over the Church rumbled throughout Europe during succeeding centuries, the concordat traditionally marks the end of the investiture contest.

Yet there was no peace for the papacy. Italy was in political turmoil, as the decline of royal power allowed the cities to assume self-government. In Germany Henry V's death in 1125 ended the Salian dynasty, leading to a disputed succession. In 1124 tensions around the papacy erupted with the rivalry of the Pierleone and Frangipani families at the papal election itself. Their mutual hostility proved uncontrollable in 1130. Anacletus II, a Pierleone, was elected by a minority, against Innocent II, the Frangipani candidate who had been elected in hurried secrecy. Anacletus remained in Italy and sought aid from the Normans, making Sicily into a kingdom in repayment. Innocent fled to France, where he gained the support of Bernard of Clairvaux, whose talent as a publicist counted for more than armies. Bernard brought Louis VI and Lothar III to the cause, and procured an imperial invasion of Italy. Most of Europe supported Innocent, yet only the death of Anacletus in 1138 brought an end to the division, with Innocent's acceptance as unquestioned pontiff when the successor antipope, Victor IV, resigned.

The schism of 1130–38 offers something of a distraction from the more significant but less dramatic growth in papal powers and status. The new papal supremacy found expression in the calling of general councils. The first three were held, appropriately, at the Lateran, in 1123, 1139 and 1179. The papal summons, and the use of the councils to define ecclesiastical legislation, were a precedent for the future.

The developments in law and legislation probably gave the papacy its most powerful weapons during this century. Arguably, however, the key event occurred without papal participation: the production at Bologna around 1140 of a massive summary of canon law, Gratian's *Concordance of Discordant Canons* (usually called the Decretum). This comprehensive but accessible overview of canon law supposedly resolved the contradictions within the existing body of law. More importantly, it did so from a highly papalist standpoint. Its immediate utility may explain why it rapidly became the universal textbook of canon law – even though not officially sanctioned – which meant that future interpretations of the law would tend to follow its papalist lead. The Decretum also gave the popes legislative authority. Such control of the law and its procedures was a significant weapon. Henceforth papal determinations – decretals – were considered binding throughout the Church, and universally applicable. Both the Decretum and the decretals attracted interpretations and glosses, producing a whole new profession of canon lawyers.

Nevertheless, the papacy's newly claimed status had to be recognized by those over whom the popes claimed authority. Achieving that was the great success of the twelfth century. There was ready acceptance of the emergence of a body of law which offered solutions to tricky ecclesiastical questions (including social and moral issues which were generally left to the Church to deal with, such as marriage and contracts), and with a court structure which allowed appeals but might provide a definitive judgement. Those who turned to the papacy for help necessarily limited their own freedom of action by accepting its jurisdiction: in a short time they would find themselves subject to regulations imposed on them rather than voluntarily submitted to.

Despite the benefits of creating an ecclesiastical legal system focused on the papacy, it was not faultless. Like all legal systems, it became a vehicle for exploitation; it could be frustrated by delays in communications, ignorance of local conditions, and

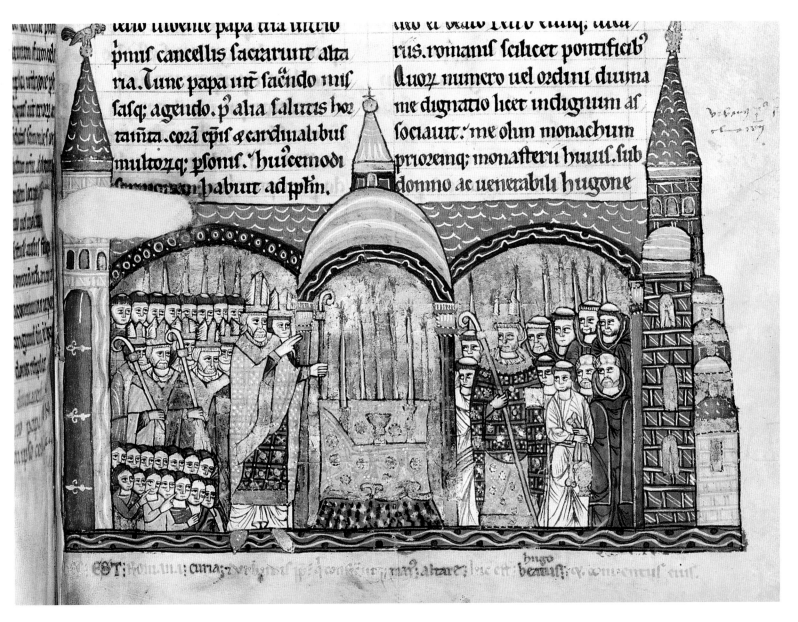

ceio uioenie papa tia uitcio
pmuf cancelluf faccrarunt alta
ria. Tunc papa ntr fackndo muf
safq; agendo. p alia falutis ho
tamita. cozd epif g cardinalibuf
multozq; pfonif. huicemodi
... pabuit ad ipfin.

rus. romanif fcilicec pontificab?
Quoz numero uel ordini diuina
me dignatio licet indignum af
fociauit. me olim monachum
prioremq; monaftern huuif. fub
domno ac uenerabili hugone

EST: ... cuma ... mari. altare; ... hugo bezauff... conuentuf enuf.

biased information; it was soon overburdened as cases from throughout western Europe flooded to the Curia. That also bolstered the system, providing further material for appeals and counter-actions, at the cost of increased cynicism. However, the papacy lacked an adequate administration to complement the legal system: although a papal bureaucracy was emerging in the twelfth century, it remained fairly rudimentary. The fiscal system was certainly primitive: the popes lacked financial resources and the rest of the Church was unwilling to provide them; only in 1192 were its revenues catalogued. Papal government over the western Church was built on

insecure foundations; it was considered that dealing with law and government distracted the pope from his primary role as a spiritual leader. St Bernard castigated Eugenius III, the first Cistercian pope, for turning himself into a Justinian and abandoning his role as a fisher of souls.

The weakness of those foundations was shown later in the twelfth century. Rome itself was attracted by the communal movement which was affecting northern Italy: from 1143 to 1155 the city was in revolt against the papacy, until quelled by an alliance of pope and emperor. Papal-imperial relations were not always so co-operative. The (perhaps deliberate) mistranslation of a letter to Frederick I in 1157 suggested that the empire was held in fief from the papacy. If that was what Hadrian IV did mean, the resulting furore caused a rapid retraction. Further problems came in 1159 with another confrontation, between Pope Alexander III and the antipope Victor IV (a different man from the Victor IV who resigned in 1138). Alexander's legitimacy was almost unchallengeable; but Frederick I intervened, arguing that as emperor he would decide between the claimants. Alexander rejected this claim; Victor accepted it. Alexander did not attend the imperial

synod at Pavia; Victor did. Frederick, unsurprisingly, declared Victor the lawful pope – acquiring an obligation to him and his successors which was to complicate relations between Frederick and Alexander, and indeed between Frederick and most of western Europe (including the Italians whom he was trying to beat into submission) until 1178.

Frederick had the initial advantage. In 1162 Alexander fled Italy to the relative safety of northern France, where he stayed for three years. He was rarely to reside in Rome before 1177, the city being frequently held by antipopes while Alexander wandered around central Italy. Despite the uncertainties of his existence, Alexander made his mark on the papacy. His chancery produced a steady flow of propaganda and decretals. A lawyer by training, Alexander used his theoretical legal powers to extend the web of practical authority over the Church. The bitter conflict with Frederick, in which the pope allied himself with Italian communes that were resisting attempts to impose imperial rule, continued until 1177. Finally, by the Peace of Venice, Frederick recognized Alexander as pope.

Alexander's death in 1181 apparently left the papacy secure. His successors to 1198 were little more than caretakers, keeping the machinery ticking over. However, things were not completely static: new procedures for papal elections introduced in 1179 set a two-thirds majority of the electing cardinals to determine the successful candidate. In 1179 Lucius III issued the decree *Ad abolendam*, to counter the growing threat of heresy. Movements in southern France and northern Italy were challenging the Church's authority. The Waldensians and Humiliati demanded scriptures in the vernacular, and claimed for the laity the right to preach doctrine – something which threatened the pre-eminence of the priesthood. Although their claims were rejected, a loophole was left open (at least for the Waldensians) to avoid charges of heresy; but they refused to exploit it and accordingly were condemned. In contrast the Cathars posed a major doctrinal threat, made more potent as they established a separate ministerial system, episcopal hierarchy and diocesan structure. Their dualistic doctrines, proclaiming a fundamental

opposition of good and evil principles, challenged monotheism; their hostility to created matter denied Christ's humanity and the Church's legitimation of sexual activity in marriage; their denial of the sacraments and their separatism undermined the pastoral and social control exercised through priesthood, especially through confession and penance. Initially the Church sought to convert the Cathars back through debate, but that would prove ineffective and force would have to be used.

That crusade was one of many important events in one of the most significant pontificates in papal history. Only thirty-seven when elected in January 1198, Pope Innocent III proved a dynamic personality at the centre of the European stage. Until his death in July 1216, he appears as the dominant individual in Europe – although that may be because enough sources survive to analyse his actions, and because a personality cult has developed around him among ecclesiastical historians.

In dealing with the Church, Innocent aimed to establish the papacy on the firmest of intellectual foundations. Building on and co-ordinating ideas derived from his predecessors, by careful and deliberate exploitation of language and images he created an ideal status for the papacy which made it supreme above everyone else. The pope was vicar of Christ, exercising Christ's powers as lord of the world; he was the sun to the imperial moon, the priest-king Melchisedek whose person combined spiritual and temporal functions, the embodiment of the Church as successor and heir to Peter. Innocent insisted on the papacy's elevation above any collegiality with bishops or cardinals. His successor Honorius III used the analogy of the pope as emperor, while the cardinals were the equivalent of the senate; Innocent would not have disagreed. The status of lesser ecclesiastics – bishops and arch-bishops – was even lower; they were mere minions. They shared in the duty of care attached to their pastoral functions, but any power they exercised came ultimately from the successor of St Peter.

Innocent sought to realize this ideal of his authority. His letters are full of instructions, of attempts to interfere which reflect his urge to action. Yet, despite his dynamism, he faced major problems – not of his making, but often compounded by his actions. In 1198 the death of Emperor Henry VI left Innocent as guardian to his infant successor – by birth king of southern Italy, by expectation emperor and ruler of Germany and northern Italy, and in consequence a threat to papal territorial security in central Italy. Innocent was an ineffective guardian: his role as feudal overlord was more threatening than

Pope Innocent III (1198–1216), who took the papacy to new heights of political involvement across Europe. In this thirteenth-century fresco from the cloister of San Benedetto, Subiaco, he holds a deed of gift to the monastery.

St Francis of Assisi (1181–1226). Painting (1235) by Bonaventura Berlinghieri from San Francesco, Pescia. The stigmata (the reproduction of the wounds of Christ on his body), was a sign of his especial favour with God and contributed to his identification as a Christ-figure in later spirituality.

and may be regarded as their real founder. In complex negotiations with successive imperial claimants, he sought territorial concessions in exchange for approval of candidacy. These concessions were usually short-lived: would-be emperors habitually passed through and took over supposedly papal territory. Yet by astute use of his limited real powers, and by balancing his relations with neighbouring towns, he secured formal recognition of papal lordship in these territories. That lordship was acknowledged at the parliament of subject towns which Innocent assembled at Viterbo in 1207.

Other dramas and embarrassments crowded in. In 1202 the fourth crusade sacked the Christian city of Zara in Dalmatia, and later diverted to sack Constantinople. Innocent desired neither event, and excommunicated those who had attacked Zara; but he could not ignore the outcome. Constantinople's capture promised an end to the schism of 1054, as the patriarch could now be a Catholic. But the Greeks refused to give in. A Latin empire established at Constantinople proved ephemeral, falling in 1261 despite strong support from later popes, including crusades called to defend it against the Greeks.

In the west there were other disputes and crises: in France with Philip II over his marriage; in England with King John over Stephen Langton's appointment as Archbishop of Canterbury, and later an entanglement in the Magna Carta crisis. The complexity of such cases made a mockery of papal consistency, and made the papacy seem like just another secular power – especially when it collected kingdoms as fiefs. By 1216 Aragon, England, Bulgaria and several other realms were nominally papal vassals.

Spiritual threats also had to be confronted. The expanding Cathar heresy was increasingly self-confident: much of Languedoc had effectively seceded from the Catholic Church. Conversion by preaching failed. Then, in 1208, Cathars assassinated the papal legate, Peter of Castelnau. The following year Innocent III proclaimed an anti-Cathar crusade. Real papal involvement was limited – this became a war of conquest by northern France against the south

protective, and southern Italy sank into chaos. Germany also collapsed into civil war between Otto of Brunswick and Henry VI's brother, Philip of Swabia. Innocent intervened, his 1201 declaration (which found for Otto IV) establishing the pope's determinative function in imperial succession disputes. It settled nothing: Germans still threatened the papal territories; the imperial claimants continued their rivalry and refused to be puppets; Innocent vacillated. He turned to Frederick II, Henry VI's son, as a last resort. The trap he had sought to eliminate at the start of his reign was re-created at its end; all safeguards were to prove valueless.

Innocent had greater success in the papal states,

⊞ ⊞ ⊞

– but the proclamation of the crusade, and the resulting atrocities, have ever since blotted Innocent III's memory. Whether Catharism could have been countered otherwise than by force is questionable. Innocent certainly considered his actions justified, and for him that was enough.

Other reformist forces were increasingly threatening the established Church. Often trapped by events, reacting rather than controlling, Innocent nevertheless remained a visionary. His greatest service to the Church was his recognition that nonconformity was not necessarily deviance, that different approaches to Christianity might be equally valid. While anxious to quell heresy, he legitimated the apostolic poverty movement which some of his predecessors had feared and condemned. His efforts at compromise and reconciliation saw some Waldensians return to the Catholic fold, while the *Humiliati* were established on a formal basis within the Church. Most significant was his acceptance of the poverty movement represented (in markedly different ways) by St Francis and St Dominic. The latter was not particularly threatening, but the first Franciscans could easily have been condemned as heretics. Innocent saw their potential, their concern to be Catholics, and by confirming Francis' place within the Church ensured that a vibrant spirituality was harnessed to Catholic purposes. Admittedly it became a problem within a few decades; but those problems were nothing to the challenge which would have resulted if Franciscan spirituality had been forced underground.

The zenith of Innocent III's pontificate came at its end. The fourth Lateran council in 1215 was the largest council so far, attended by Latins from recently conquered Constantinople, and even eastern-rite Maronites. A wide range of doctrinal decrees, including that on which the doctrine of transubstantiation is based, provided definitions that could be used against heresy. Numerous reform decrees established the programme for a pastoral revolution, whose implementation would demand the attention of prelates for the remainder of the middle ages.

Innocent III's early death left a complex inheritance. For the rest of the thirteenth century, the development of the 'papal monarchy' proceeded apace, as papal influence over the lower layers of the Church expanded, and papal headship was energetically enforced. Episcopal and archiepiscopal autonomy was reduced as popes claimed increasing authority over the localities. A succession of 'lawyer popes' – Honorius III, Gregory IX, and Innocent IV – provided a dynamic headship which increasingly made the Church like a state. In 1234 Gregory IX issued the Decretals as an official supplement to Gratian's Decretum. By 1300 the papacy had

The acceptance of St Francis and his mission by Pope Innocent III (1198–1216) was among the most significant events of a dynamic pontificate. The tradition that the pope dreamt of a young man (Francis) supporting the tottering church is reflected in this fresco by Giotto (1266–1336), in the basilica of St Francis at Assisi.

*Pope Honorius III (1216–27) confirms the Rule of the
Dominican Order, 1216. Founded to help the fight against
heresy, the Dominicans provided some of the leading
intellectual figures of the thirteenth century, including St
Thomas Aquinas. Painting by Leandro Bassano
(1557–1622) in the sacristy of the church of SS Giovanni*

established its claim to make 'provisions' (appointments) to most benefices within the western Church, and had created a fiscal structure which included powers to tax the Church, though not always efficiently or profitably. The subjects of the papal monarchy were learning what that subjection actually meant.

More arresting was the Wagnerian drama of the papacy's battle against the Hohenstaufen dynasty in Italy and Germany, which lasted until 1268. Frederick II had promised Innocent III in 1216 that he would resign his hereditary realm of Sicily to his son, retaining only Germany. He broke his promise: holding on to both the imperial title and southern Italy, he had his son crowned king of Germany as Henry VII. The dynasty's hold on both northern and southern Italy threatened to persist, encircling the papal territories. Civil unrest further increased the Hohenstaufen threat. Frederick's inability to meet a papal deadline for departure on crusade in 1227 gave a pretext for his excommunication. Gregory IX was not mollified when Frederick, having reached the Holy Land in 1228, made a treaty with the Saracens which temporarily returned Jerusalem to Christian control, with access through a land corridor; or when Frederick proceeded (despite excommunication and interdict on the Holy City) to crown himself King of Jerusalem – a title he claimed by his marriage to the child-queen Isabella II.

Tensions between Frederick and Gregory (now in alliance with the Italian cities against imperial powers) in due course led to outright war; but the papacy lacked the strength to drive Frederick from Italy, while the emperor refrained from direct attack on the pope. The stalemate continued until Gregory's death in 1241. The harsh conditions then imposed on the cardinals to procure an election – incarcerated in an old Roman prison, with the threat that Gregory IX's corpse would be sent to join them – proved counterproductive. Celestine IV died seventeen days after his election. The liberated cardinals fled. Two years passed before his successor was chosen.

Frederick seemingly expected relations with the papacy to improve with the election of Innocent IV; he was soon disabused. Innocent was an experienced

lawyer, a relative of Innocent III, and a convinced papalist. His outlook is exemplified in his contacts with the Mongols, whose irruptions into Europe and the middle east presented unanticipated problems and opportunities. Innocent sent emissaries to the Great Khan demanding peace, conversion to Catholicism, and recognition of the pope's status as vicar of Christ. For Innocent, that vicariate did make the pope 'Lord of the World' – if only in theory.

Nearer home, Innocent supported opposition to Frederick in Italy and Germany, and claimed the possession of the southern Italian kingdom as a papal fief. In 1245, in exile, he summoned another general council, at Lyons. Frederick II was declared deposed, being replaced by the first of a series of anti-kings to wage civil war on the pope's behalf. Innocent also began to tout the Sicilian crown around Europe. Frederick's deposition marked a major escalation in papal claims: henceforth popes would often claim that they were the true emperors, with the secular bearers of the imperial title merely acting as their minions.

While this first Council of Lyons gave the appearance of papal hegemony, it also revealed the

Marble tombstone of Pope Urban V (1362–70), originally from the Benedictine church of St Martial, Avignon; now in the Musée du Petit Palais, Avignon. Urban had journeyed to Italy in 1367, but returned to Avignon to die.

*Opposite:
Dante Alighieri (1265–1321) inspires the city of Florence with his book* The Divine Comedy. *Detail of a painting (1465) by Domenico di Michelino (1417–91).*

Pope Boniface VIII (1294–1303). Despite the aura of majesty conveyed by many surviving statues of him (this, attributed to Arnolfo di Cambio, is now in the Museo dell'Opere del Duomo, Florence), his reign ended in disaster and the Outrage of Anagni.

Part of the Palais des Papes, Avignon, Papal Residence, 1309–76. Begun under Pope Benedict XII (1334–42), the papal palace at Avignon became a focal point for Europe, the centre of an extensive bureaucracy and the main base for a papal court until the early fifteenth century.

first cracks in the edifice, with growing resistance to papal intrusion into the affairs of local churches and the exploitation of local resources for non-local concerns. Robert Grosseteste, Bishop of Lincoln, delivered a resounding critique of papal interference, and of the undermining of episcopal authority which accompanied it – not just directly, but through papal support for exempt orders, a complaint which would shortly focus on the papal privileges granted to the friars. Potentially more threatening, Louis IX of France also protested against abuses, subtly claiming for secular rulers the authority, right, and duty to defend their local churches against excessive papal interference. This was a foretaste of the frequent later struggles between local rulers and the papacy – often resolved by compromises in which the supposed opponents collaborated to crush and exploit the Church over which they were supposedly arguing.

Under Gregory IX and Innocent IV, hostility to Frederick II became an obsessive determination to eliminate not only him, but his whole dynasty. After 1245, thanks in part to the popes' efforts, the empire went into marked decline. The great interregnum from 1250 to 1273 saw no emperor in office, and

The restoration of papal power in central Italy in the mid fourteenth century was primarily the work of Cardinal Gil Albornoz (d. 1367). This manuscript illustration shows him receiving the keys of the cities of the Patrimony of St Peter. Archivio Segreto Vaticano, Arm. XXXV, cod.20.f.1.

The coronation of Pope Boniface IX (1389–1404), the second pope of the Roman line during the Great Schism. From a fifteenth-century manuscript of Froissart's Chronicle *(London, British Library, MS Harl. 4379, f.34).*

papal resistance to any appointment not on papal terms. Meanwhile, in southern Italy, the machinations to remove the dynasty bore bitter fruit.

Frederick II died in 1250, and his son Conrad represented the dynasty in Germany until his own death in 1254, remaining nominally ruler of Sicily. His son Conradin was displaced there by Frederick's bastard Manfred, who sought to restore his dynasty's power in Italy, against unrelenting papal hostility. Successive popes sought a replacement ruler for southern Italy. Henry III of England accepted the Sicilian crown for his son Edmund, but proved unreliable. Charles of Anjou then took the poisoned chalice, and duly invaded. In 1266 he defeated Manfred and took the throne. In 1268 at Tagliacozzo he faced an attempt by the teenage Conradin to

The pope orders the building of a monastery. Romanesque altarpiece, c. 1240.

reclaim his inheritance; this last Hohenstaufen was summarily executed after his defeat in battle.

The demise of the Hohenstaufen exchanged Scylla for Charybdis: the popes had merely exchanged would-be masters, and the Angevins proved more adept at imposing their will on the papacy. Successive pro- and anti-Angevin pontiffs now alternated on St Peter's throne, as Frenchman succeeded Italian and Italian succeeded Frenchman. The situation was further complicated after 1282 when in Sicily the massacre of the French known as the 'Sicilian Vespers' gave the popes leverage to exploit the resulting political rivalries between Aragon (whose Peter III had seized Sicily) and Naples. After 1282 southern Italian history is an unwholesome tale of civil wars and bloody coups, ended only when Alfonso V of Aragon reimposed order in the mid-fifteenth century.

The mendicant experiment which Innocent III had ratified also turned sour. The new orders made an important contribution to the Church; friars soon became prominent in many spheres. The first mendicant pope was Innocent V, a Dominican, in 1276; the first Franciscan pope was Nicholas IV, elected in 1288. Despite their vitality and usefulness, the friars' ecclesiastical status caused problems, as their extensive privileges undermined the jurisdiction and pastoral authority of bishops and parish priests. Additionally, the Franciscans suffered tensions caused by their attitude to poverty. The 'conventual' party among them accepted the changes brought by time, which eased Francis' harsh asceticism. They still considered themselves absolutely poor: the popes technically owned all their property. The 'spiritual' faction maintained the original ideal, rejecting all forms and claims of ownership. The outcome was an ideological struggle within the order, lasting to the 1320s. Both factions raised the stakes by arguing that as friars they were not just following Francis, but perfectly imitating Christ. This made the absolute poverty of Jesus and the apostles a matter of faith, explicitly challenging the credentials of the institutional Church. A war of attrition broke out between secular and mendicant clergy, which lasted throughout the medieval centuries. In the 1250s, matters boiled over in Paris when one over-

enthusiastic Franciscan exploited prophecies to declare his order the herald of a new age in which the established Church would be superseded. Yet the Franciscans, paradoxically, depended on papal authority: their very existence and privileges derived from papal bulls, which could only be upheld by asserting a form of papal infallibility. Nicholas III confirmed the absolute poverty of Christ, but his successors were less sound: to prevent a change of heart, the Franciscans argued that popes were bound by the pronouncements of their predecessors, who were in effect infallible.

Meanwhile, pope still succeeded pope – too quickly. Between 1254 and 1300 there were several short pontificates, making stability of purpose a rarity. Rome constantly threatened to revolt. In November 1268, Clement IV's death was followed

by a long vacancy, resolved in 1270 with what is usually considered the first papal conclave. The citizens of Viterbo, exasperated by the cardinals' failure to elect a pontiff, imprisoned them, offering release only after an election. When the cardinals still delayed, they withheld food, and let rain in by removing the tiles from the building. On 1 September 1271, Gregory X was chosen. New arrangements for election in conclave were formally decreed at the second Council of Lyons in 1274. More significant in that council's business were the ban on further foundations of mendicant orders, and the negotiations which produced a formal reunification of the Greek and Latin Churches. That, however, remained a formality: although the Emperor Michael VIII of Constantinople sought to enforce it, the decree soon became a dead letter.

Ideally pope and cardinals would work together in the government of the church. Here Pope Boniface VIII (1294–1303) is shown with his cardinals in an illustration to a copy of his own contribution to the canon law, the Liber sextus *(promulgated in 1298). London, British Library, MS Add 23923, f. 2, a Bolognese manuscript of the fourteenth century.*

The pope receives a delegation at the Council of Constance, 1415. From the Chronicle of the Council of Constance *of Ulrich of Richental, printed in Augsburg in 1483.*

The death of the scheme for reunion, the chaos in southern Italy and Germany, the sack of Constantinople in 1261, growing resentment at papal interference in the local churches, the problem of the spiritual Franciscans, and the final loss of a Latin base in Palestine with the conquest of Acre in 1291 made the high hopes at the apotheosis of Innocent III at the fourth Lateran council in 1215

seem hollow. The full extent of the changes was bluntly revealed as the thirteenth century reached its end.

When Nicholas IV died in April 1292 the cardinals could not agree on a successor. The vacancy lasted over two years, ending with the election of Peter of Morone as Celestine V. For once the cardinals chose a holy man, indeed a hermit, who seemed to embody the century's spiritual aspirations. That made him singularly unfit to be pope. Elected in July 1294, he resigned in December – allegedly at the prompting of his successor. The abdication shocked many: did a pope actually have the power to resign? To avert his restoration, Celestine was kept in custody, dying in prison in 1296. His only legacy was another religious order, the Celestines, whose asceticism was akin to that of the spiritual Franciscans.

Boniface VIII, Celestine's successor, was a very different person; in other circumstances he might have been a great pope. Instead, he appears as a counterfeit Innocent III, despite the success of the first jubilee, which he proclaimed for 1300. He battled to control the papal states, struggling against the rival Colonna family. He confronted kings and defended Church liberties, notably in the bull 'Clericis laicos' of 1296 which sought exemption from state-imposed taxes, and in successive battles with Philip IV of France. He summoned bishops to Rome, and made sonorously hierocratic pronouncements: his 'Unam sanctam' of 1302 offers perhaps the pithiest summary of papal claims ever issued. But Boniface could not be another Innocent III. That was dramatically demonstrated on 7 September 1303, when French and Colonna troops invaded the papal palace at Anagni and threatened the pope's life, demanding his resignation. Boniface was speedily liberated by popular action but died a month later, a broken man.

The outrage at Anagni set off a chain of events of momentous import for the papacy. In the short run, the death of Boniface VIII and reign of Benedict XI suggested that nothing much would result: despite

Philip IV's determination to gain revenge on Boniface in a posthumous trial, all might be swept under the carpet. The election of Clement V in 1305 radically altered the situation.

A Gascon with connections with both the French and English courts, Bertrand de Got seemed an ideal compromise candidate. Already infirm, he posed no threat of over-activity, and seemed unlikely to interfere in matters which others did not consider his business. Bowing to pressure, he summoned another western general council, to meet at Vienne. Lasting from 1310 to 1312, it suppressed the Knights Templar as an independent order, largely in response to the demands of Philip IV of France. The council also condemned recent outbreaks of heresy, and sought to establish a network of language schools across Europe, teaching Arabic, Hebrew, Greek, and 'Chaldee', to aid missionary work in infidel

territories. That ambition soon foundered without trace. There was also talk of reform, including debates about the power and status of the council itself; such debates became increasingly widespread in the next couple of centuries.

Clement V, still on his way to Rome but held up by infirmity, died in 1314 at Roquemaure in southern France. In 1309 his court had stopped at Avignon. Technically in the empire but at the other end of a bridge from France, a royal fortress owned by the Angevin ruler of Naples, the city was surrounded on three sides by papal lands, the Comtat Venaissin, spoils of the Albigensian crusade. The sojourn was meant to be temporary; but for most of the fourteenth century this remained the site of a papal court. The 'Babylonian captivity' of the papacy had begun.

Petrarch's vituperations have given the Avignon papacy a poor reputation. A sink of iniquity, a

The twelfth century saw architectural revival in Rome, under papal auspices. Here Pope Innocent II (1130–43) is depicted alongside SS Lawrence and Callistus in the mosaics of the church of S Maria in Trastevere, Rome, which he rebuilt.

virtually monopolized the cardinalate; but the emergence of a Limousin clique belies the homogeneity implied by calling it a 'French' college. Particular dynasties were prominent among the cardinals, none more than the Roger family, which produced Popes Clement VI and Gregory XI.

Yet the Avignon popes were neither mere cyphers for faction, nor inactive, nor individually reprehensible. John XXII developed a highly efficient administrative system, which in some ways makes the Avignon period the high point of the papal monarchy. Avignon had logistic advantages over Rome – more centrally located, with easier communications, fewer health hazards, and in a zone of relative peace, it could be much more a European capital than Rome. While successive popes proclaimed their intention to return to Rome, obstacles prevented this, and stability had attractions. Benedict XII started work on a vast new papal palace. Until 1348 the popes were nevertheless only guests of the Angevins of Naples; then Clement VI bought the city from Queen Joanna I. Avignon and the Comtat remained papal territory until the French Revolution.

John XXII, despite his administrative activity, poured a fortune down the black hole of a prospective return to Italy. The papal states were distant and ungovernable; only force could restore papal authority there, which required mercenaries, and money to pay them. While the papal fiscal system and revenues expanded, the costs of war left little to show for the sums spent. Meanwhile, disputes over the empire, continuing Franciscan insistence on apostolic poverty, and the disturbing political theories advanced by Marsilius of Padua and William of Ockham, two of the period's leading

second Babylon, the seat of corrupt and corrupting popes who lay prey to international rivalries and petty faction among cardinals who feathered their nests and ignored the decay around them, the Avignon papacy seems to offer a foretaste of Borgia decadence. But impartiality was not Petrarch's best quality. There was certainly faction and bias, and the papacy was effectively Gallicized. The French

intellectuals, threatened papal serenity. The Franciscan issue peaked in 1323, when John XXII rejected their notion of Christ's poverty so forcefully that it could never be revived. The ideas of Marsilius and Ockham on the invalidity of the pope's temporal power provided ammunition for Louis IV of Bavaria, the would-be emperor whom John was desperately determined to keep out of Italy. He failed: Louis invaded in 1327, and marched on Rome. The last imperial puppet-pope was appointed when Louis declared John deposed in 1328 and replaced him by an obscure Franciscan as 'Nicholas V', who crowned Louis emperor, and then left Rome in the imperial baggage train. His ignominious reign ended in capture and imprisonment in 1330.

Unfortunately for John XXII, the capture of Nicholas V neither destroyed Louis nor ended the Franciscan challenge. In 1332 the pope even faced charges of heresy. In his private capacity as a theologian, rather than as pontiff, he had preached on the Beatific Vision – on whether the justified see God immediately after death, or only at the last judgement. To some his views seemed unorthodox, incurring condemnation not only from extremist Franciscans (who argued that he had thereby forfeited the papacy), but from Parisian theologians, and King Robert of Naples. The pope partially retracted his views on his deathbed.

John's labours were continued by his successors. Benedict XII, who as Jacques Fournier, Bishop of Pamiers, had overseen the famed heresy trials at Montaillou, was something of a reformer, especially of the religious orders. Even Clement VI had redeeming features. Although his claim that 'My predecessors did not know how to be popes' set the tone for a pontificate which lived down to some of Petrarch's slanders, he endeavoured to maintain the status of his office. He confronted the Black Death with some dignity, and sought to balance French and English pressures during the Hundred Years' war – despite English charges of favouritism. At his death the cardinals tried to secure their oligarchic position by establishing an 'electoral capitulation', which would be binding on whoever among them was elected pope. Innocent VI was chosen, but

immediately annulled the compact. However, the possibility of binding a future pope would re-emerge in the fourteenth and fifteenth centuries.

⬚ ⬚ ⬚

Avignon's relative peace and stability provided the calm which allowed increasing consolidation and sophistication in papal administration; but the continued absence from Rome caused misgivings. According to the tag, 'Where the pope is, there is Rome'; but Avignon was not Rome. Clement V and his successors had proclaimed a determination to return; yet while Italy remained in chaos, that would be too dangerous. Clement VI compensated by reforming the papal liturgy to make Avignon more a reflection – a pale reflection – of Rome, but that was not enough. Money, mercenaries and the military proficiency of Cardinal Albornoz did eventually restore a semblance of peace to central Italy. In 1367 Urban V did his duty and left Avignon, entering Rome on 16 October. In 1370 he changed his mind, returning to Avignon, where he soon died. His successor Gregory XI likewise set off in 1376, entering Rome on 17 January the following year. Unfortunately for himself – and, as it turned out, for the Church – he did not return to Avignon quickly enough. He died at Rome on 27 March 1378.

⬚ ⬚ ⬚

Gregory's death precipitated immediate crisis. The Curia was divided, with several cardinals and much of the administration still at Avignon. Faction reigned among those cardinals actually at Rome, who would now choose a pope. The Italians wished to stay in Rome, the French to go back – but they were themselves split, between the Limousins and the others. And, of course, the Roman people wanted a say: having just regained the golden goose of a papal presence, they would not readily relinquish it. On 8 April the conclave began, while outside a mob bayed for a Roman, or at least Italian, pope. The choice fell on Bartholomew Prignano, vice-chancellor of the Roman Church and Archbishop of Bari – but not a

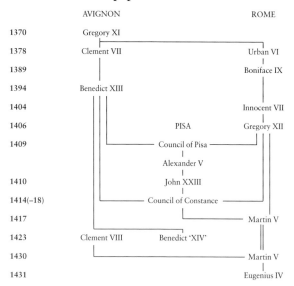

Tomb of antipope John XXIII, by Donatello, in the Baptistry in Florence.

he had no intention of returning to Avignon. By June the antagonism was such that a group of cardinals quit the Curia, renounced their obedience, declared Urban's election invalid because performed under duress, and on 20 September elected in his stead Cardinal Robert of Geneva, who took the name of Clement VII. So began the Great Schism. Until the election of Martin V at the Council of Constance in November 1417, the papacy was to be disputed. Even Martin's election did not formally end matters: final reunification came only with the resignation of the antipope Clement VIII in July 1429.

Had the initial warfare between the rivals in Italy produced a clear winner, the dispute might have ended quickly. It did not. By 1380 Clement VII had returned to Avignon, taking up the reins of an administration which had not been seriously disrupted. In Italy Urban VI created an essentially Italian papacy, effectively from scratch. The division gave Europe's princes the opportunity to confirm their political rivalries by adopting rival popes, but it was some time before decisions were taken everywhere. France supported Clement. Against the background of the Hundred Years' War, the English supported Urban ... so the Scots adhered to Clement. Most of Italy and Germany were for Urban. The Spanish kingdoms, after considerable dithering, eventually chose Clement – but dynastic upheaval in Portugal in 1385, rejecting Castilian claims to the throne, produced a sudden switch to Urban.

Although a division existed, it was not fully entrenched: that required a death and a succession. In 1389, Urban died; his cardinals elected Boniface IX to follow him. That made settlement a more distant prospect; even more remote when in Avignon in 1394 Clement VII died and Benedict XIII succeeded him. Benedict reigned until 1422, while in the Roman line Boniface IX gave way to Innocent VII in 1404, in turn succeeded by Gregory XII in 1406. Each election unavoidably made compromise more unlikely, as new colleges of cardinals were created, as obediences became entrenched, as separate (sometimes duplicate) hierarchies evolved, as interests became increasingly irreconcilable. Europe learned to live with the division: rival popes granted

cardinal. As the mob broke in the cardinals fled, fearing for their lives if they announced the election, leaving the aged Cardinal-Archbishop of Florence as a decoy to stem pursuit. Despite the chaos Prignano's election was confirmed the next day, as Pope Urban VI.

The Great Schism: papal successions 1378–1430

	AVIGNON	PISA	ROME
1370	Gregory XI		
1378	Clement VII		Urban VI
1389			Boniface IX
1394	Benedict XIII		
1404			Innocent VII
1406			Gregory XII
1409		Council of Pisa	
		Alexander V	
1410		John XXIII	
1414(–18)		Council of Constance	
1417			Martin V
1423	Clement VIII	Benedict 'XIV'	
1430			Martin V
1431			Eugenius IV

At first all seemed well; but Prignano proved a singularly poor choice. Crass snubs to powerful local princes and undiplomatic attempts to impose reform on the cardinals eroded loyalty. It became clear that

dispensations for marriages across the frontiers, as in 1396, when England's Richard II married Isabella of France; they co-operated in offering crusade privileges, as in 1395–6, for the expedition which ended in disaster in Nicopolis. Tolerance and co-operation were not universal; the division was conveniently exploitable for political ends. Urban VI supported the future Charles III of Naples against Joanna I. John of Gaunt's military expedition for the Castilian throne was disguised as an Urbanist crusade. In 1406 Owain Glyndwr cemented his revolt in Wales by a French alliance which foresaw Wales adhering to Benedict XIII, and the abolition of ecclesiastical ties with England.

Exasperation with the schism developed slowly. Benedict XIII's election in 1394 followed a promise to negotiate and if necessary resign. His failure to do so led to French pressure to force negotiation, and in 1398 a formal withdrawal of obedience. Benedict was effectively imprisoned in the palace at Avignon

until a dramatic escape in 1403, which coincided with a palace revolution in France, and the restoration of recognition. Among the Romanists a policy of withdrawal had little support, despite French encouragement. Only Liège followed the French lead, in 1399. It remained outside any papal obedience until 1405.

Innocent VII was the first Romanist pope to make a promise of negotiation similar to that imposed on Benedict. In fact, he did nothing. In 1406 Gregory XII also took an oath which might incur his resignation. Both claimants now seemingly accepted that movement was needed, that the threat of permanent division in the Church was real, that they had to act. Tentative steps towards negotiation produced a stately movement towards Savona, the designated meeting place. But neither side would make the decisive move. Meanwhile Gregory appointed new cardinals. This allegedly broke a pre-election commitment, and the old senior cardinals

The return of Pope Gregory XI (1370–78) to Rome from Avignon in 1377. His death in the city in March 1378 was followed by the election of Urban VI, and the outbreak of the Great Schism. Fresco by Giorgio Vasari and others in the Sala Regia, Vatican.

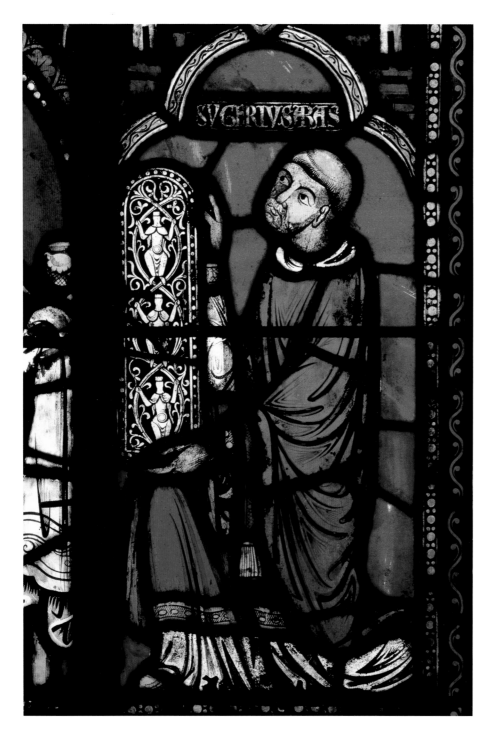

The twelfth century saw widespread artistic revival across Europe.
Here Abbot Suger, the leading adviser to King Louis VI of France,
is shown in twelfth-century glass from the Tree of Jesse window in the
Lady Chapel of the abbey church of St Denis, outside Paris,
which he had rebuilt in the novel Gothic style.

revolted. Using arguments developed since 1378, they claimed the authority to call a general council, invited Benedict's cardinals to join them, and summoned representatives to meet at Pisa.

The Council of Pisa of 1409 was a revolutionary movement. Yet, despite the hopes for reform and reunion, it achieved little – save the creation of a third papacy, established by the election of Alexander V. Meanwhile Gregory XII and Benedict XIII declared their own conciliarist credentials by holding assemblies respectively at Cividale in Italy and Perpignan in Catalonia. Needless to say, these reaffirmed the legitimacy of their respective pontiffs. Europe now had three popes, although much of it accepted Alexander V. He was soon succeeded by John XXIII, amid rumours of death by poisoning. John's dubious reputation before his election was further blackened by charges levelled at the Council of Constance to justify his deposition; but he faced no immediate opposition within his obedience. The outcome of Pisa threatened to be another stalemate, perhaps worse than before. The position suddenly changed in 1414. Under pressure from Sigismund of Hungary, emperor-elect since 1410, John XXIII called another council. This would meet at Constance, in Germany, partly to counteract the feared numerical swamping by Italians at any such gathering, partly to ensure that Sigismund could supervise proceedings. John wanted the meeting to confirm his own status, and act against Benedict XIII and Gregory XII (both of whom retained supporters). Those at the council – and perhaps Sigismund himself – saw it as an opportunity for major ecclesiastical reform, and action to end the schism. Within weeks of its opening in November 1414, tensions were developing. In March 1415 John fled – hoping thereby to throw the council into confusion, even dissolution. The ploy failed. Instead, the council began to act unilaterally, its decree 'Haec sancta' asserting that it held authority directly from Christ (rather than from the pope), and that everyone – even a pope – was subject to its authority in matters of faith. John was captured and imprisoned, and moves began for his deposition. Sordid dealings with Gregory XII procured his resignation; Benedict XIII

was again declared deposed. As in 1409, he did not accept the judgement. This time, however, his adherents drifted away. Scotland, the last realm in his obedience, remained loyal until late 1418; the Counts of Armagnac in France never abandoned him.

Having to its own satisfaction removed the rival popes, the council's next steps were uncertain. Disputes over the priority of reform or a papal election, and national and other rivalries, slowed progress. Only in June 1417 did the atmosphere change. Arrangements were swiftly made to hold an election; and on 11 November 1417 Oddone Colonna emerged as Pope Martin V. He presided over the council's last sessions (it dispersed in April 1418), and slowly began the progress back to Rome. Martin V's restoration of papal authority will be considered in the next chapter, but the schism's ending can be disposed of here. Although Martin's election usually identifies the end of the split, Benedict XIII stubbornly held out until his death in 1422. Even then his rump papacy continued under Clement VIII. Clement lasted until 1429, when he abdicated. Martin V was then elected his successor, thus not

denying the legitimacy of the Avignonese line. History, however, has passed judgement: another Clement VII was elected in 1523. The next Alexander was in fact numbered VI, but otherwise the Pisan line's claims have now been rejected.

In 1429 a united legitimate papacy was re-established. For Eugenius IV, elected Martin's successor in 1431, that was not the most immediate concern: before dying Martin had summoned another council, at Basle, which offered a much more challenging legacy.

FURTHER READING

G. Mollat, *The Popes at Avignon, 1305–1378,* London etc. 1963.

C. Morris, *The Papal Monarchy: the western church from 1050 to 1250,* Oxford 1989

F. Oakley, *The Western Church in the Later Middle Ages,* Ithaca and London 1979

I. S. Robinson, *The Papacy 1073–1198: continuity and innovation,* Cambridge 1990

W. Ullmann, *A Short History of the Papacy in the Middle Ages,* London 1972

The struggle for power in northern Italy during the twelfth and thirteenth centuries frequently became a battle between popes and emperors. Here the Emperor Frederick I (Barbarossa) offers his submission to Pope Alexander III (1159–81), ending a conflict originating in the emperor's support for the antipope Victor IV in 1159. From a fresco by Spinello Aretino (1346–1410) in the Palazzo Pubblico of Siena.

CHAPTER FIVE

THE RENAISSANCE PAPACY

1420–1565

THE REVD DR JOHN W. O'MALLEY SJ

THE NINETEEN POPES who reigned in the century and a half between Martin V's return to Rome in 1420, after the cataclysm of the Great Schism, and the conclusion of the Council of Trent in 1563 under Pius IV, faced daunting challenges to their security and prestige. Some of their attempted solutions to the challenges won scathing denunciation from their contemporaries and later historians for perversion of their sacred office. Luther called the papal court a Babylon, Erasmus wrote a satirical dialogue in which St Peter refused Pope Julius II admission into heaven, and in the nineteenth century John Addington Symonds, the English littérateur and historian, waxed eloquent against them all from a high moral platform. 'The contrast between the sacerdotal pretensions and the personal immorality of the popes was glaring', he wrote with barely concealed delight. They 'cavorted on the bed of harlots ... with hypocrisy and cruelty studied as fine arts, with theft and perjury reduced to system.' Even today the words 'Renaissance popes' evoke winks and sly smiles.

But these same popes have been lauded as the patrons responsible for some of the greatest artistic monuments of western civilization, who employed in their projects for the city of Rome the most towering geniuses of an epoch of great artists, culminating in Bramante, Raphael and Michelangelo – the Sistine chapel, the papal *stanze*, the new Saint Peter's basilica. Their cultural legacy defies exaggeration. Moreover, these popes, whose predecessors had been chased from the city of Rome innumerable times in earlier centuries, finally achieved a territorial security and stability for themselves and their successors that would last, in the main, up to the present. They convoked the Council of Trent and thus finally marshalled a Catholic response to the Reformation.

Our positive assessment of the brilliant role the Renaissance popes played as patrons of learning and the arts seems utterly secure, not subject to substantial revision. In recent decades, however, historians have qualified earlier criticism of individual popes, and to some extent of all of them, for their worldliness and their political policies.

Cesare Borgia (1475–1507). Painting on panel (1520) by Altobello Melone. Cesare Borgia was the son of Pope Alexander VI, and through Machiavelli's writings his name came to be synonymous with political cunning and ruthlessness.

Left:
*Pope Martin V. Tomb
effigy in bronze, c. 1443, in
the church of St John
Lateran in Rome.*

Eugenius IV, Nicholas V, Pius II and especially, sad to say, the shorter-lived popes – Pius III, Hadrian VI, Marcellus II – were churchmen of unquestionably upright character and dedication. Paul IV was a religious zealot. Though some, such as Leo X and Paul III, let their concern for their families and, in Paul's case, for children and grandchildren, influence their policies to the detriment of the Church, in other respects they sincerely strove to fulfil the obligations of their office. The wild orgies in the papal palaces supposedly sponsored by Pope Alexander VI, one of the 'Borgia popes', we now see to have been figments of his enemies' heated imagination.

Yet it is inconceivable that the Renaissance popes will ever be fully rehabilitated as religious leaders. We understand more clearly today, however, that many aspects of their behaviour and policies that we find reprehensible, or at least baffling, were due not to moral degeneracy but to fiscal and ecclesiastical systems that almost required them to act as they did, to politico-ecclesiastical situations where no alternative seemed to them viable or even conceivable, and to certain assumptions about their responsibilities that were as self-evident and correct to them as they are opaque and alien to us.

Of the nineteen popes sixteen were Italians, which marked a definite break with the unbroken series of French popes during the Avignon residency and of foreign rivals during the schism. After 1523 there would not be another non-Italian pope until John Paul II in 1978. Among the nineteen there are no canonized saints. A few came from great families like the Colonna or, more parvenu, the Medici. Most of the others came from well-established families of lesser rank, for whom the papacy meant new wealth and social standing. Practically all of them had relatives in the College of Cardinals before their election, and while pope most of them appointed further relatives to the college. Family ties and connections counted. It comes as no surprise, therefore, that Paul II was the nephew of Eugenius IV, just as Pius III was of Pius II, Julius II of Sixtus IV and Alexander VI of Callistus III (the two Spanish, or rather Catalan, popes of the period); Clement VII was Leo X's first cousin.

Right:
*Pope Alexander VI
(1492–1503). Detail from
fresco of the Resurrection
(1492–5) by Bernardino di
Betto, known as
Pinturicchio (1454–1513)
in the Vatican. Intelligent
and enigmatic, Pope
Alexander VI helped bring
the papacy into disrepute
by his political
machinations and by
flaunting his children.*

*The School of Athens. Fresco by Raphael Sanzio d'Urbino
(1483–1520), painted for the papal apartments in the
Vatican for Julius II (1503–13), with Plato and Aristotle as
central figures.*

Although all of them were cardinals when they were elected, some had not yet been ordained to the priesthood; after Leo X was elected Bishop of Rome while still a cardinal-deacon, for instance, he was ordained a priest and then a bishop and then, finally, took possession of his see. Innocent VIII was the first to acknowledge that as a cardinal he had fathered children, but Alexander VI and Paul III later did the same. Julius II donned armour and led his troops into battle against the enemies of Italy and the Holy See.

The central problem the popes faced, beginning with Martin V but extending throughout the Renaissance, was how to establish and maintain the authority of the apostolic see, catastrophically diminished by the scandal of the schism. The Council of Constance had ended the scandal, but it did so by asserting the council's authority to depose bad popes, thus opening an era when councils would sometimes defiantly challenge papal authority. Moreover, when Constance called for 'reform in head and members', by head it meant the papacy. The cry for reform of the financial and administrative practices of the papal Curia – for the elimination or curtailment of nepotism, of bribes, of unwarranted fees for dispensations and reservations, and of other 'abuses' that made the papacy seem to some nothing more than a big business intent only on profit – would resound as a bill of indictment against the popes for the next century until the Reformation exploded.

But the popes needed the money the system provided. Their city had fallen to pieces during the schism and their long absence in Avignon. The papal state, without whose buffer the city was defenceless, was in an even more desperate situation. It had degenerated into political chaos, and now had to be brought to order – which could not be done without money and troops. In this volatile situation, the popes needed to appoint family members to key positions, for it was not always clear who else they could rely on, since treachery seemed to lurk around every corner. Leo X, to secure his position after an abortive attempt to poison him, on 1 July 1517

packed the College with thirty-one new appointments.

The schism had taught the popes they could trust no foreign power to protect them – not the emperor, not the king of France – so they had to rely on whatever financial, political, diplomatic and military force they could muster themselves. This self-reliance became their fundamental axiom, which led during this period to the full development of the 'papal prince' as a new kind of player in Italian and

Pope Leo X. Marble statue (1514) by Dom. Aimo (d. 1539) in Sta Maria in Aracoeli, Rome. This unflattering statue of Leo X is a contrast with the more idealized portrait by Raphael on p. 112, painted a few years later.

Pope Julius II (1503–13). Portrait (1511) by Raphael Sanzio d'Urbino (1483–1520), oil on panel. Raphael captures the strength of character of Julius II as well as his declining energies during the last years of his life.

even international politics. To the ordinary observer, the pope looked like any other temporal ruler.

Although many of the popes seemed to pursue worldly security and prestige with more zeal than religion, they were not pagans or religious sceptics, as the nineteenth century sometimes considered them. No matter how they may occasionally or habitually have behaved, they were believing Christians, who, while labouring sometimes under curious (at least for us) assumptions about what duties their office entailed, took those duties seriously.

How can we begin to understand these popes? The word 'office' is a good place to begin – not 'vocation', because the popes almost certainly did not look upon their careers as a manifestation of some inner call from God. The clerical state for both the high-born and the low-born was what we today would call a career opportunity, respectable and socially useful, entailing a conventionally upright life but nothing more. A good way to grasp this mentality is to pay attention in nineteenth-century novels to younger sons in good Anglican families seeking a 'living'; that is, an endowed position, off whose revenues they could live as clergy. That is how the popes, like other bishops, looked upon their state in life. Underneath the pastoral imagery they sometimes used to describe themselves they had a basically juridical understanding of their office.

Foremost among the duties of that office was defending and building the prerogatives of 'the apostolic see', the only bishopric in the west that guarded the tombs of two apostles, Peter and Paul. The popes' bishopric was no ordinary one. They had to defend the 'lands of Peter', those vast territories in central Italy that over the course of the centuries had been given not to themselves or even to the Church, but to St Peter himself. Safeguarding these lands was a sacred trust. The political ambitions and manoeuvres of the popes can by no means be reduced to this simple formula, nor can many of their actions be justified on account of it, especially when they themselves coolly subverted it by parcelling out Peter's lands to relatives. Invoking the trust was sometimes only a pious excuse for perfidy, or an excuse to secure the revenues these lands provided,

which were ever more desperately needed as the administrative machinery of the Roman Curia expanded and its style of living became ever more princely. Nevertheless, the sacred character of the lands figured large in the papal ideology.

Julius II was 'the warrior pope'. He took up arms for those lands to drive out usurpers and robbers. He seems to have identified himself with the angry Jesus driving the moneychangers from the Temple, and had no inkling of Jesus as the sentimentalized 'good shepherd' of recent centuries. Even more pertinent, Julius, like all his

Tomb of Pope Julius II (1503–13) by Michelangelo Buonarroti (1475–1564), now in the church of San Pietro in Vincoli, Rome.

Pope Leo X (1513–21) with Cardinals Luigi de' Rosso and Giulio de' Medici. Portrait (1517–18) by Raphael Sanzio d'Urbino (1483–1520), oil on panel. Leo X was the first Medici pope, and he is shown here with his cousin Giulio de' Medici (the future Pope Clement VII).

contemporaries, believed that the Old Testament contained the New in veiled form, thus blurring the distinction between the saints of the two testaments. He could therefore in perfectly good conscience model himself on ancient biblical heroes to lead his troops in the battles of the Lord.

There was yet another deadly threat. Since the late eleventh century the popes had assumed leadership in crusades against 'the infidel', that is, the Muslims. That responsibility took on a new urgency after 1453 when the unthinkable happened: the Turks captured Constantinople, which gave them a gateway into western Christendom. From that day forward rallying princes and gathering military forces in a defensive crusade became an even higher papal priority.

Besides defending the papal state from enemies and defending the west from the Turk, the popes in other ways felt responsible for defending, adorning and exalting the apostolic see. One such way was the princely one of patronage of scholarship, of literature, of works of art. They desired to restore the city of Peter to a condition where it would impress diplomats and rulers with Peter's (or their) authority. Rome was, moreover, a place of pilgrimage, containing innumerable sites precious to Christian memory. Guarding these sites and making them attractive to pilgrims was a clear papal duty – and

The pope returning the consecrated host to the altar, from the Predella of the Profanation of the Host. *Panel, c. 1468. Paolo Uccello (1397–1475) in Palazzo Ducale, Urbino.*

pilgrims also brought revenue.

Martin V began the work of restoration almost as soon as he entered the crumbling city, pitifully neglected for a century. The process picked up momentum under Sixtus IV some fifty years later, as symbolized especially in the construction of the Sistine chapel and its decoration by the most celebrated artists of the day. In the early sixteenth century it reached a great climax under Sixtus' nephew Julius II, the first great papal patron of Michelangelo and Raphael. The enterprise would continue, however, well into the seventeenth century, making Rome an incomparable treasure of Renaissance and baroque art.

Among these great monuments the Sistine chapel and St Peter's basilica deserve special mention, for they point to another aspect of how the Renaissance popes understood their office. The papal

liturgies celebrated in these sites were another 'ornament' of the apostolic see, but their significance is far deeper than that. These services were at the centre of the religious obligations of the papal office. If by tradition the pope had any clear-cut religious duties, his fostering of this worship and his presence at masses, lauds and vespers was the most important. Especially when this worship was done in its full solemnity, with the papal choir and all the Roman dignitaries, it was seen not so much as 'a gathering of the Christian community', as theologians would describe it today, but as a replication on earth of the worship of the heavenly court – where all the saints and angels bowed down in reverence and unceasingly sang their hymns of love and praise. This earthly worship required the best in music, architecture and the other arts that human genius could provide.

Unlike the popes of our day, those of the

FIORENZA

Renaissance did not look upon themselves as theologians, if we understand 'theology' properly not as dogmas or doctrines but as disciplined reflection upon them. They never dreamed that making theological statements or writing encyclicals was part of their task. Theologians were to be found in universities, and they could be called on when their services were needed. Nevertheless, the popes recognized that they had a responsibility for right doctrine in the Church, for orthodoxy. They also knew that on rare occasions they had to pass judgement on theologians, when these theologians' speculations or rantings seemed to deny or endanger some central Christian belief. They recognized they had a responsibility to condemn heresy, and their contemporaries concurred. During the Renaissance

they found little occasion to exercise this responsibility until the Reformation erupted. Then they responded, and eventually convoked the Council of Trent.

In Florence in 1419, a year before Martin V was able to enter the papal city, he invited the celebrated painter Gentile da Fabriano to come to Rome. This invitation presaged Martin's many initiatives to repair the damage Rome's churches and other buildings had suffered, and to enhance them with the best his age could offer. Martin's biographer Platina, the papal librarian of Sixtus IV, states that the pontiff's first concern after bringing peace and

View of Florence, c. 1490. Watercolour after an engraving by Francesco Rosselli (1445–before 1513). Florence produced most of the great artists whom the popes employed during the Renaissance to enhance Rome and the Vatican.

security to Rome and the papal state was 'to make the city and its churches beautiful'. Martin's policy of urban and artistic renewal, followed by his successors until 1506 when Julius II replaced it with a more comprehensive strategy, was to concentrate on those holy sites and antique monuments that attracted the most pilgrims. On 9 February 1427 Martin issued a bull ordering the restoration and redecoration of the papal residence at the cathedral of Rome, the church of St John Lateran, and of the portico of the old basilica of St Peter. He also ordered restorations for the two most important early Christian basilicas after St Peter's – St John Lateran and San Paolo fuori le Mura. The cardinals, inspired and prodded by the pope, also began to repair their titular churches. Platina exaggerated when he said that 'it seemed the city had partly regained her ancient splendour', but a beginning had been made.

But Martin had other, more desperately urgent concerns. Besides worrying about the course the councils of Pavia–Siena and Basle might take, he needed to wrest most of the papal lands in central Italy from the powerful bandit Braccio da Montone. The contest between them did not end until May 1424, when Braccio was defeated by Martin's army and died on the battlefield. Then at last the pope could turn with some success to the recovery and reorganization of his state. The support of his ancient and powerful family, the Colonna, gave him the resources he needed to make Rome and the state more militarily secure than they had been for at least a century.

Even during the conclave that in 1431 elected his successor, Eugenius IV, stormclouds began to gather. The cardinals resented Martin's authoritarian style and were determined to exert pressure on the new pope to behave more in accordance with their wishes. Eugenius, a Venetian, had no strong Roman connections, and began in a considerably weaker condition than did Martin. He would prove himself as clumsy as a politician as Martin had been skilful. At the very beginning of his pontificate he offended the Colonnas, the baronial power base Martin had used to bring order to the papal state. Colonna reluctance to hand over their strongholds to

Pope and bishop. Printing and illumination from the Decretum Gratiani, Mainz, made by Peter Schöffer in 1473 (Corpus juris canonici Gregory IX). The twelfth-century compilation of canon law by Gratian was still the basic legal text governing the relationship between popes and bishops in the Renaissance.

Pope and cleric. Printing and illumination from the Decretum Gratiani, Mainz, made by Peter Schöffer in 1473 (Corpus juris canonici Gregory IX). This shows how a fifteenth-century German imagined a pope of his day.

Euerendo in Cristo patri suo duo Ge:

extraneu · Sz ex ipis scripturis debem2 sensu cap tatis · Jra tu or vbi quis vera didicerit · falsa et

Eugenius provoked war. Risings in the individual provinces and in Rome itself could be put down only with difficulty. In 1434, when Rome itself was menaced by armies at the gates, the people broke into open rebellion against Eugenius, forcing him to flee the city in a rowing boat, disguised as a monk. He spent most of the next decade in Florence and Bologna.

These troubles were minor compared with the challenge to papal authority Eugenius had to face from the Council of Basle, called by Martin shortly before his death. Eugenius, distrustful of the council from the beginning, managed to antagonize it by a premature attempt to dissolve it and, through other missteps, turned it into a nightmare that threatened

to create a new schism. The council reached its peak of defiance when in 1439, with ever more strident calls for 'reform of the head', it declared Eugenius deposed on a charge of heresy and elected a new pope, Felix V.

Eugenius was saved from an unexpected source. For years the Byzantine emperor, his capital threatened by the Turks, had sought better relations with the western Church in the hope of receiving aid against the infidel. He was even willing to heal the division between the Greek and Latin Churches dating back to 1054 by coming to a council in some western city, promising to bring along with him the Patriarch of Constantinople and Greek bishops. With uncharacteristic adroitness Eugenius seized the

Pope Nicholas V receives a book, from the Rosarium Decretorum codex by Pietro de Basiio Strasbourg (1452).

116

Pope Pius II (1458–64) convokes a meeting of Christian leaders at Mantua to launch a crusade against the Turks. From the series in Siena Cathedral, by Pinturicchio (1454–1513).

PIVS CVM ANCON·EXPEDITIONE IN TVRCOS ACCLER...

Pope Pius II (1458–64) set out to lead a crusade against the Turks but died at the port of
Ancona, shown here, before it could be begun. Fresco (1502–5) by Pinturrichio
(1454–1513).

opportunity and in 1438 opened a council at Ferrara, which he soon transferred to Florence. He thus struck a mortal blow at Basle, for the prospect of reunion of the Churches won support from rulers and bishops in the west.

The Council of Florence was superficially a success, for the participants reached agreement on the major doctrinal issues that divided them, including a somewhat vague recognition of papal primacy. A decree of union was signed on 5 July 1439. Unfortunately the decree could not win acceptance in the east when the imperial entourage returned, and any hope of reconciliation was dashed when Constantinople fell to Turkish forces.

But in 1439 Eugenius' prestige rode high on what he had seemingly accomplished, and in 1443 he was able to return to Rome and conclude his papacy in relative peace. The Council of Basle would drag on until 1449, with ever smaller numbers in attendance and with little impact on the life of the Church. The papacy had won. Nevertheless, memory of the dire threat this council posed would remain vividly alive for subsequent popes. The decree 'Frequens' of the Council of Constance, which obliged the popes to convoke a council periodically, was now a dead letter. At a crucial moment in history, 'reform of the head' was stalled.

❖　❖　❖

When Eugenius died in early 1447, he left a heavy legacy that required a diplomat, a lover of peace, and a person who could make rival groups work together for the good of the Church. With Tommaso Parentucelli, Bishop of Bologna and a compromise candidate, the cardinals found their man, who took the name Nicholas V. In Rome and the papal state the new pope began with pacification and in a short time succeeded through arms or money in calming the quarrelling factions and in winning back a number of cities. He had to put down a conspiracy against himself in Rome, but otherwise he ruled with a stability popes of the previous centuries could hardly have imagined. His last years were greatly saddened by the fall of Constantinople. His attempts

Adoration of the Magi. Stained-glass window (1516) by Gugliemo de Marcellai, originally given to Cortona cathedral by Pope Leo X, who patronized art and artists even outside Rome and Florence.

to rally western leaders to face the crisis failed, as would those of his successors.

Nicholas is best remembered for his patronage of arts and letters, and is deservedly called the first Renaissance pope. He seriously considered the extensive changes needed in the ancient and now dilapidated St Peter's basilica. This fitted with his decision to make the Vatican area of Rome the principal papal domicile in the city. He believed that the popes, as custodians of the keys given by Christ to Peter, should exercise that authority from the sacred precincts of the apostle's tomb. To enhance the dignity of the Petrine legacy, he planned to rebuild the Borgo Leonino, the area around the Vatican. He brought almost none of his plans into execution, but he set in motion an idea that his successors would take up enthusiastically. Nicholas' most lasting accomplishment in this regard are the exquisite frescoes by Fra Angelico in the small private chapel of Nicholas V in the Vatican.

He had more lasting success in his patronage of learning, and gathered many scholars at his court. He is rightly considered the originator of the Vatican library. The old papal library had been left behind at Avignon and, despite repeated demands for its return, it was not until the eighteenth century that

St Peter's, Rome. This new St Peter's, begun under Julius II and not completed for 150 years, replaced the original basilica built in the fourth century by the Emperor Constantine.

The future Pius II is here created a cardinal by Pope Callistus III. Painting by
Pinturicchio (1454–1513).

Pope Sixtus IV (1471–84) naming Platina Prefect of the Library; that is, naming Bartolomeo Sacchi as Custodian of the Papal Library in 1475. Fresco by Melozzo da Forlì (1438–94) originally in the old Vatican library but now in the Pinacoteca Vaticana. Sixtus IV contributed 3650 precious volumes to the Vatican library.

mouriesopra
detto Padre di
23 maggi

the final volumes found their way to the Vatican. Nicholas had an impressive personal library even before he became pope. Revenues from the successful jubilee he called in 1450 allowed him to make massive purchases. After the fall of Constantinople, Byzantine and Latin Christians fleeing the Turks brought priceless manuscripts with them, many of which became the property of the pope who gave their owners asylum. Nicholas provided impressive stipends for scholars to translate from Greek into Latin pagan classics and the works of the fathers of the Church. The inventory of the library made in 1455 just after the pope's death lists over 1,150 volumes, an incredible number for those times.

The next pope, Callistus III, showed little inclination to continue these initiatives. He devoted his short pontificate of three years to trying to raise a

The burning of Savonarola (1452–98). Seventeenth-century Italian painting.

Savonarola was a great preacher and political activist who criticized the papacy of Alexander VI. The pope subsequently did nothing to prevent Savonarola's execution by the government of Florence.

Portrait of a woman,
thought to be Lucrezia
Borgia (1480–1519),
daughter of Pope
Alexander VI. She married
Giovanni Sforza and, later,
Alfonso d'Este, and she
was more upright than
contemporaries or
subsequent generations
gave her credit for being.
Painting on panel by
Bartolomeo Veneto (active
1502–46).

crusade to push back the Turks. For the defence of Christendom he sent great sums of money to the Balkans, Hungary, and Albania to hire mercenaries, and thus many gold and silver objects from the papal treasury ended up in the furnace. His efforts achieved nothing.

He was succeeded in 1458 by Pius II, perhaps the most intriguing pope of the century, not least because, unlike the others, he was an accomplished writer, a humanist, and left behind a substantial body of works including autobiographical reflections and information. Until 1445 he had sided with the Council of Basle against Pope Eugenius, and he thus brought to the papacy a keen sense of the bitter complaints many sincere Christians throughout Europe levelled against the practices of the Roman Curia. Right after his election he began comprehensive preparation for a general reform of ecclesiastical procedures, including those of the Curia, but, sincere though he was in this regard, he was distracted by other concerns and never took action.

Despite himself he became embroiled in the usual disputes among the petty rulers still operating in the papal state, and in the greater intrigues in wider Italy. Once in office, like other popes he was affected by the fear of councils, and issued a decree, 'Execrabilis', forbidding appeal to a council over the head of a pope.

He became ever more single-minded about what he considered the most pressing issue of his day: rousing the leaders of Europe, and especially of Italy, to a crusade to rescue the Christians of the east from the Turks. Consistently frustrated by the vacillation and treachery of kings, princes and other magnates, he finally determined personally to lead the crusade, single-handed if necessary. Old and sick, he set out from Rome on 18 July 1464 with many cardinals and curialists, but died at Ancona a month later. His successor had no stomach for the enterprise. Paul II was in fact a man of mediocre talent, suspicious and authoritarian by temperament, whose pontificate of five years marked a general standstill.

Sixtus IV then thundered on to the scene for a pontificate of thirteen stormy years that seemed to betray everything his earlier life as Fra Francesco della Rovere stood for. Born poor, he entered the Franciscans at an early age and, thanks to his theological accomplishments and his skill as a preacher, rose to be minister general of the order. This would seem to indicate an unworldly pope of simple tastes. But within two weeks of his election he made two of his nephews cardinals, one of whom was patently unworthy – a harbinger of the flagrant nepotism still to come that led him into sordid political deals to advance his family and his designs for the papal state. Neither his contemporaries nor subsequent historians have been able to explain this man's soul; but he conducted himself, for the most part, like any other unscrupulous prince of his day.

He recklessly multiplied posts in the Curia and wittingly or unwittingly encouraged an ever more extravagant way of life among the cardinals, including his six nephews. The Curia's expenses mounted rapidly in this situation – payments for the still not altogether forgotten crusade against the Turks, for the papal armies in central Italy, for the papal nephews and other hangers-on, and for the elaborate works of art and architecture he commissioned. By his actions he thumbed his nose at the cries for reform becoming ever louder throughout Europe.

This is the pope, however, who with stunning vigour and intelligence transformed Rome into an incomparable centre of art and learning. He opened the Vatican library to the public, gave it an outstanding prefect in Bartolommeo Platina, and saw to its enrichment with hundreds of new books. He ordered the laying of new streets, the restoration of many churches such as Santa Maria del Popolo and Santa Maria della Pace, the opening of the new hospital of Santo Spirito, and numerous other projects. He is best remembered for the new chapel he constructed in the Vatican palace that bears his name. For its decoration he brought to Rome Botticelli, Perugino, Signorelli, Pinturicchio and others, the best talent of the day. Sixtus thus carried to a brilliant height the restoration of Rome inaugurated by Martin V and Nicholas V, which

*Marriage of King Frederick III, Holy Roman Emperor, and Eleonora d'Aragona. Painting
by Pinturrichio (1454–1513), in the Libreria Piccolomini, in the Duomo di Siena.*

would be surpassed even more brilliantly some decades later by his nephew Julius II.

Innocent VIII, pope for four short years until 1492, was as inconsequential as Sixtus was overpowering. Alexander VI, almost certainly elected with bribes, while not the moral monster of legend, was a man utterly worldly in outlook who became enormously rich at the expense of the Church. Already the father of several children, he possibly begot two more while pope. The influence on him of his favourite son, Cesare Borgia, only made a bad situation worse, further embroiling him in Italian politics and wars. His successor Pius III was godly and widely respected, but he lived only twenty-two days after being elected.

Cardinal Giuliano della Rovere, outwitting the crafty Cesare Borgia, managed to get himself elected pope on the very first day of voting, 1 November 1503 – one of the shortest conclaves in papal history. The election, not accomplished without cash and promises of favours, still produced a man widely admired for his integrity and his zeal for the prerogatives of the apostolic see. As a cardinal, Giuliano was implacably opposed to Alexander VI, and as Pope Julius II he refused to live in the rooms inhabited by his predecessor. Among the many cardinal-nephews of Sixtus IV, he was the dedicated churchman. He had had wonderfully wide experience in Church affairs for over thirty years and had learned well from it. As pope he struck those who met him with his *terribiltà*, the awe-inspiring fierceness of his personality.

Double portrait of Martin Luther (1483–1546) and Philipp Melanchthon (1497–1560). Panel by Lucas Cranach the Younger (1515–86). Luther and his pupil Melanchthon set off the Reformation, to which the popes responded with the Council of Trent.

127

Building on the political success of his despised predecessor in the papal state, he pursued consolidation, which could be achieved only by keeping the great powers, especially France, outside Italy. His policy comprised three stages: assuring papal rule in Rome and the papal state, winning back lost territories, and expelling foreigners, especially the French, from the Italian peninsula. He accomplished the first goal, which had eluded popes for centuries, so well that from this time forward papal sovereignty went without effective challenge until the nineteenth century. Through clever playing of international politics and shifting alliances, he also achieved the other two, but with only surface success and at the cost of bitter enmities.

In 1511 King Louis XII of France retaliated against Julius by persuading Francophile cardinals to convoke a council at Pisa with the intention of deposing the pope. The Holy Roman Emperor Maximilian I supported the council, for he hoped to become pope himself. Julius, acting with his usual force, saved this explosive situation by calling his own council in Rome the following year. In the face of a council convoked by the pope, Pisa lost support. Among the chief goals of this fifth Lateran council, which met over five years from 1512 to 1517, were organizing a crusade against the Turks and reform, especially of the Curia. The council in fact accomplished little. On his own, however, Julius from the beginning promoted the reform of the mendicant orders by trying to assure the election of worthy superiors general.

But Julius is immortal because of his patronage of Bramante, Raphael and Michelangelo, which brought the Renaissance in Rome to its culmination. He generated an electricity between himself and these artists that resulted in their surpassing anything they had created thus far. His genius as patron matched theirs as artists.

Three of Julius' decisions for the renovation of Rome outstrip all the others. First, as early as 1505 he decided on important repairs and changes in the old basilica of St Peter, which within a year resulted in a determination to tear it down and build a new one, with Bramante as architect. This project would not be completed for a century and a half and would engage the skills of Raphael, Michelangelo, Bernini and many others to produce the Church we know today.

In 1508 Julius singled out Raphael over more established artists to be in charge of the decoration of the rooms of the papal apartments (the stanze), which resulted in some of Raphael's greatest masterpieces, such as *The School of Athens* and *The Dispute on the Sacrament*. In that same year Michelangelo set to work on the ceiling in the Sistine chapel, chosen for the task by Julius, though Michelangelo considered himself a sculptor and up to that point had painted little. Julius, according to Michelangelo, gave him a free hand; but somehow Julius, ever larger than life, is present in those incomparable frescoes. Painting would never be the same.

When Julius died in 1513, the cardinals sought someone of milder disposition and elected Giovanni de' Medici, thirty-seven years old, the second son of the great Florentine statesman and politician Lorenzo the Magnificent. The contrast of Leo X with his predecessor could hardly have been greater. Mild of manner, learned, refined, devout yet a lover of the chase and other entertainments, he was even in his soft obesity different from Julius.

'Now that God has given us the papacy, let us enjoy it,' he is said to have remarked – though he never uttered those words. He was serious about his responsibilities and intelligent in dealing with them. But Leo lacked Julius' energy and vision, even in patronage of art and learning. He was also much distracted with promoting the interests of his family, the *de facto* rulers of Florence. To protect Florence and the papal state from the French army, in the Concordat of Bologna (1516) he conceded to King Francis I and his successors the right to nominate their own candidates for bishoprics and other important ecclesiastical offices in France, effectively nullifying canonical elections and giving the monarchy a control over the episcopacy that must have made Gregory VII turn in his grave. He dutifully saw the fifth Lateran council to its conclusion in 1517 but took no important measures

Opposite:
The mosaic ceiling of St Mark's, Venice. The figures in the cupola represent the apostles preaching the Gospel to the nations. The popes of the Renaissance tried to enhance their prestige by insisting they were successors of two apostles, Peter and Paul.

Overleaf:
The Creation of Adam. *Fresco (c. 1510) on the ceiling of the Sistine chapel, Vatican, by Michelangelo Buonarroti, the most famous of the series commissioned by Julius II (1503–13).*

Pope Clement VII. Portrait (1526) by Sebastiano del Piombo (1485–1547). Pope Clement VII, who excommunicated Henry VIII, was politically inept and more interested in advancing the Medici family than in dealing with the reform of the church.

to implement its decrees. He did continue work on the new basilica of St Peter, appointing Raphael architect in charge; and his deputies authorized the sale of indulgences to help pay for it that in 1517 resulted in Luther's ninety-five theses, the opening salvo of the Protestant Reformation.

Leo X issued a condemnation of Luther and bull of excommunication, but even by the time he died in 1521 he did not appreciate how serious the situation

had become. The difficult conclave for his successor resulted in the entirely unexpected election of the devout, austere and brusque Hadrian VI, Dutch and determined, who had a much better sense of the danger from Lutheranism and the urgency of reform of the Curia, which he actually undertook. But his impolitic ways lost him valuable allies on the Roman scene and, when he died after a pontificate of less than thirteen months, relief was general. From this time forward, though the pontiffs continued their usual activities, the Reformation created an entirely new situation that began to colour everything else.

St Ignatius of Loyola (1491–1556). Seventeenth-century French school. St Ignatius
founded the Jesuit order, approved by Pope Paul III in 1540.

Michelangelo's magnificent dome of St Peter's, Rome.

When Giulio de' Medici was elected in 1523, he seemed to astute observers the ideal choice, for he was intelligent, sober, well respected and experienced – and aristocratically handsome. But as Clement VII he was an almost unmitigated disaster. His situation was extraordinarily difficult, true; but his vacillation, indecision and half measures, as well as his gift for making bad political alliances, made it a hundred times worse. Like practically all his contemporaries, he feared that the new Holy Roman Emperor, Charles V, would make himself master of Europe, and in trying to frustrate him, even though Charles was a sworn enemy of Luther, he indirectly helped the Reformation spread and take root. To add to Clement's woes, his ill-fated political intrigues led to the brutal sack of Rome by imperial troops in 1527, with pillage, burnings, rape and murder, followed by a devastating plague – one of the worst disasters ever to hit the city.

Charles V had come to believe that a council was probably the only way the Lutheran situation could be effectively handled, and he began to demand that the pope convoke one. Even after the sack, Clement managed to avoid doing so, partly because he feared Charles might use it as an occasion to depose him or at least to impose draconian reforms on the papal court. His fear of the emperor probably played some role in his decision to uphold the validity of Henry VIII's marriage to Catherine of Aragon, Charles' aunt. When Clement died in 1534, almost a generation had passed without the papacy exerting any effective leadership in the religious crisis that by now had spread all over Europe. England was already in full schism.

Dissatisfaction with Clement and his ways resulted in a conclave of only two days to elect as pope the oldest, most intellectual of the cardinals, who promised political neutrality and openly professed the necessity of a council: Alessandro Farnese, the great Pope Paul III. Named a cardinal in 1493 at age twenty-four, educated in Florence at the court of Lorenzo the Magnificent, he performed his duties but led a worldly life until his ordination to the priesthood in 1519. Even after the significant change of heart that this brought in him, he still lived

in the style of a Renaissance prince, and allowed the advancement of his children and grandchildren to get in the way of the best interests of the Church, sometimes with dire results.

As pope he tried to repair the ravages in Rome and patronized great artists, especially Michelangelo. He put him in charge of construction of the new palace he built in Rome for his family, the Palazzo Farnese, commissioned him to fresco another chapel in the Vatican, the Cappella Paolina, and made him chief architect of St Peter's – a post Michelangelo held until his death in 1564, long enough for his great design for the dome to be on the way to accomplishment. Paul also saw to Michelangelo's undertaking in the Sistine chapel *The Last Judgement*, completed in 1541.

Despite opposition from some of the cardinals, in 1540 he officially approved the Society of Jesus and thereafter continued to help Ignatius Loyola and his order with support and benefits. He had already in 1536 confirmed Clement VII's approval of the Capuchin order, a reformed branch of the Franciscans, and 1546 he approved the Ursulines, recently founded and destined to become one of the first great orders of women dedicated to active ministry. He appointed a number of worthy men to the college of cardinals, including Reginald Pole and Giovanni Morone, and so began to change its character for the better.

He wanted to bring about peace between King Francis I and Emperor Charles V, partly so that a general crusade against the Turks could finally be organized. The situation had degenerated badly since 1520 when the extraordinarily talented young Suleiman became Sultan and launched a vigorous westward campaign that by 1529 brought his armies to the very gates of Vienna. Suleiman was eventually held at bay, but the pope played little part in that success. The Turkish problem would continue to bedevil the popes even after the important naval victory in 1571 at Lepanto.

Paul III's principal claim to greatness is his successful convocation of the Council of Trent, which after many frustrated attempts finally opened in December 1545. Though almost as distrustful of

*The concluding session of the Council of Trent in 1563. The council had been running for
eighteen years. Painting (1711) by Nicolo Dorigati (1692–1748).*

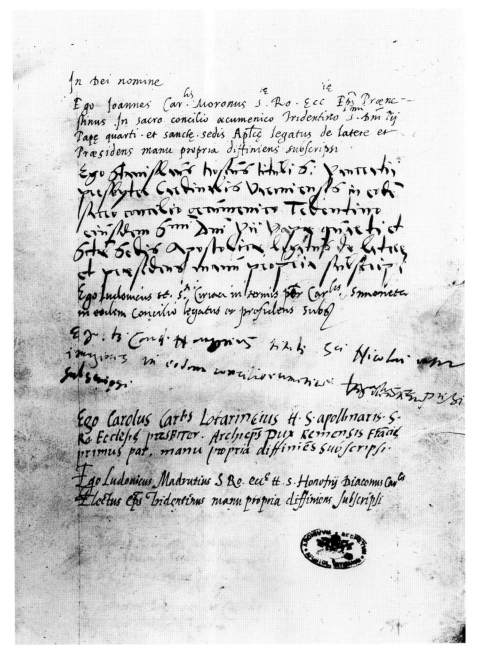

Signatures on the text of resolutions at the Council of Trent. Almost two hundred bishops were present at the close of the council on 4 December 1563, and they signed its decrees to show their assent.

period ended when Paul, forced to heed the emperor's protest after he transferred the council from Trent to Bologna, suspended the council. The council could not possibly go forward without the support of both the emperor and the pope. The resulting stalemate between them, made more problematic because Charles was aware of the political machinations against him of the pope's grandson, meant that Paul was unable to reconvene the council before his death in 1549.

After a difficult conclave of over two months, during which Reginald Pole failed by one vote to achieve the required two-thirds majority, Giammaria del Monte was elected and took the name Julius III. He had been one of his predecessor's three legates presiding at Trent and wanted to reactivate the council, even though he too feared Charles' might. By 1551 the council was again in session and made some progress, especially in affirming Catholic teaching on the sacraments. It had to be suspended again, however, when the next year Protestant armies had the emperor on the run and threatened the city of Trent itself.

Julius was lacklustre and easily swayed. He made some impressive gestures toward reform of Roman practices but did not follow through on them. He loved pomp, engaged Vignola as architect for an elaborate villa just outside the city walls, the Villa Giulia, and shamelessly promoted family members, including naming as cardinal an adopted nephew of questionable morals who was later imprisoned for homicide.

His successor, Marcellus II, promised to be a determined reformer of the Curia, but he died after only twenty days in office. Then, through a bizarre misfire of political intrigue within the college of cardinals, Gianpietro Carafa was elected as Paul IV, a man of irreproachable life but roundly resented for his autocratic manner and his narrow, uncompromising outlook. His hatred of all things Spanish and imperial boded ill for a resumption of the council, which he in fact had no intention of continuing; he could handle the situation very well by himself, he supposed. No one could have been more profoundly conscious of the majesty of his

the emperor as Clement had been, Paul was able to co-operate with him. Little did the pope dream that this council, which he hoped would end in a few months after an almost routine condemnation of Lutheran teaching and without touching reform of the Church, would continue for eighteen years until 1563. The first period of the council, 1545–7, during his pontificate, produced some of the most important decrees, including that on justification, in answer to Luther's teaching on justification by faith alone. This

Pope Paul III (1534–49). Portrait (1543) by Titian (1488–1576), oil on canvas. Pope Paul III was the first pope to respond effectively to the Reformation, and he was also a great patron of the arts. However, during his pontificate he was also dedicated to the advancement of his family.

The Mass at Bolsena. Fresco (1512) by Raphael Sanzio d'Urbino (1483–1520) in the Vatican. Raphael paints his patron Julius II assisting at mass and contemplating the miracle of the blood-stained eucharistic host in the town of Bolsena.

office or have held more extreme, or unrealistic, views on papal authority.

He earnestly undertook reform of the Curia, but inspired such resentment that whatever he accomplished was undone immediately upon his death. In 1559 he issued the first papal *Index of Forbidden Books*, a document so fanatically inclusive in its listings that it shocked even other ardent reformers. Convinced that Giovanni Morone and Reginald Pole, his fellow cardinals, were Lutherans, he had Morone thrown into prison and tried unsuccessfully to bring Pole back from England, where he was the papal legate appointed by Julius III,

to stand trial. He imposed severe restrictions on the Jews in Rome, forcing them for the first time into a ghetto and oppressing them with new taxation. When he died on 18 August 1559, the streets of Rome exploded with rejoicing crowds.

Pius IV immediately displayed his distance from his predecessor by sentencing to death for political crimes two of his nephews, Cardinal Carlo Carafa and Duke Giovanni. He would, however, pursue a more moderate course than this dramatic action suggests, and through careful and delicate negotiation with Europe's leaders he was able in 1562 to reconvene Trent, an action deemed

*Pope Paul IV (1555–9). Contemporary copper engraving
by Nicolas Beatrizet (active 1540–65). Paul IV published
the first* Index of Forbidden Books.

*Facing:
Marriage of Margarita of Austria (Queen of Spain) and
Alessandro di Medici (1536), with Pope Clement VIII.*

especially urgent because of the Calvinist threat to
Catholicism in France. When the council ground to a
halt over issues of Church reform, he dispatched a
new legate, Cardinal Giovanni Morone, who had
been released from prison immediately upon the
death of Paul IV. A perfect choice, Morone was able
to get the council moving again and push through the
programme of reform for bishops and parishes.
Morone also managed to remove reform of the Curia
from the council's agenda, leaving this great issue
still unresolved. He then succeeded in bringing the
council, finally, to conclusion on 4 December 1563.
Pius, disregarding the advice of many members of his
Curia to proceed slowly and selectively, courageously
and promptly confirmed all the decrees the council
had enacted over its long history. He thus took a
decisive step in asserting the papacy's prerogative to
interpret and implement the council. His young
nephew, Cardinal Carlo Borromeo, would within a
few years become as Archbishop of Milan the very
model of the reforming bishop designed at Trent.

When Pius died in 1565, an era was drawing to
a close. Calvin and Michelangelo had died the
previous year. Trent had articulated a Catholic self-
understanding that would prevail for the next four
centuries. Europe was religiously divided, and all
parties had dug in their heels.

FURTHER READING

Hallman, Barbara McClung, *Italian Cardinals,
Reform, and the Church as Property, 1492–1563,*
Los Angeles 1985

Hersey, George L. *High Renaissance Art in St Peter's
and the Vatican,* Chicago 1993

Jedin, Hubert, *A History of the Council of Trent,*
London 1957–61

Partner, Peter, *The Pope's Men: The Papal Civil
Service in the Renaissance,* Oxford 1990

Pietrangeli, Carlo *et al., The Sistine Chapel,* London
1986

Reynolds, Christopher, *Papal Patronage and the
Music of Saint Peter's, 1380–1513,* Los Angeles 1995

Stinger, Charles, *The Renaissance in Rome,*
Bloomington 1985

CHAPTER SIX

THE REFORMATION – AND THE COUNTER-REFORMATION

1565–1721

PROFESSOR A. H. T. LEVI

THE POPE CHOSEN on 7 January 1566 to succeed Pius IV immediately after the end of the Council of Trent was Michèle Ghislieri, a saintly Milanese Dominican who took the name Pius V and was to be canonized in 1712. He had been a notoriously severe inquisitor as well as a reforming bishop. He was also the only candidate to command the support of Philip II of Spain, who had lost influence to France under Pius IV. As pope, he curtailed venality by restricting dispensations, and nepotism by instituting his own commission to examine candidates for the episcopacy. He pledged to maintain peace in Christendom, to extirpate heresy, and to fight the Turks. Thinking in terms of an old-fashioned crusade, Pius organized the 'Holy League' against the Turks with Venice and Philip II, whose political and commercial interests were being threatened. When Turkish forces took Cyprus in 1571, a fleet with papal military support defeated them at the great naval battle of Lepanto on 7 October, which destroyed Ottoman power in the central and eastern Mediterranean.

The final profession of faith of the Council of Trent, included in the bull 'Iniunctum nobis' of 13 November 1564, affirmed belief in the sacramental system, the Eucharist, the sacrificial nature of the mass, the legitimacy of indulgences and prayers for the dead, the Church's teaching authority as exercised in the interpretation of scripture, and the authority of the pope himself. Taking up the formulation of Boniface VIII in his bull 'Unam sanctam' of 1302, it affirmed that the council's definitions were integral to the Catholic faith 'outside which no-one can be saved'. Faith was understood as a matter of belief – it was left to the theologians to work out how much it was necessary to believe. Heresy, because it led to the damnation of others, was the worst of all sins. For at least two centuries heresy had been regarded as excluding from salvation, and there had been popular lynchings for heterodoxy as early as the twelfth century. Trent was not saying anything new here, although the inclusion of Boniface's formula in the final conciliar document made it the most definite statement yet.

The Deposition of Christ. Painting (1602) by Caravaggio (1573–1610), oil on canvas.
The forceful dramatic unity of Caravaggio's painting inaugurates the specifically Roman
baroque which replaced the earlier ideal of a balanced composition.

The Battle of Lepanto, the last to be fought between galleys, 7 October 1751. Painting by Andrea Micheli, called Vincentino (1539–1614).

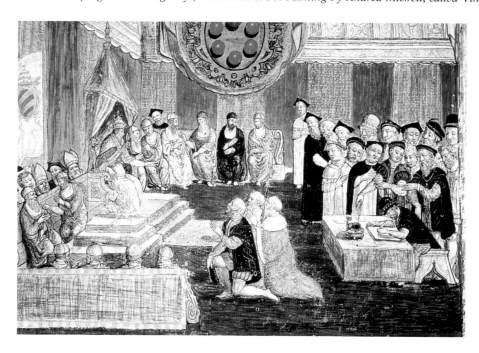

*Pope Pius V concluding the Holy Alliance against the Turks
in the Vatican, 1571. Sienese school, sixteenth century.*

Much of the activity of the Church in the late sixteenth and early seventeenth centuries reflects its urgent need to evangelize the infidel, especially in the newly discovered western hemisphere. Ignatius Loyola had missionary activity in mind when he included in the Jesuit constitutions, ratified in 1540, provision for the vow to obey the pope in all that concerned missions to preach the gospel. In their efforts to open the possibility of salvation to all, the Jesuits were to cause much controversy.

Other missionary orders such as the Theatines and the Barnabites were also active, but at first global evangelization took place under the auspices of colonizing nations, particularly of Spain and Portugal, and later also France. By 1568 Pius V had instituted a congregation of cardinals 'for the conversion of infidels', and in 1622 Gregory XV was to reorganize this into the Sacred Congregation for the Propagation of the Faith. The preaching of the gospel was now seen as central to the function of the Church, and required to be directed by the pope. For missionary purposes, the Curia divided the whole of the earth into twelve provinces, each of which had a hierarchical superior.

Most of Trent's concern had originally been with matters of discipline rather than doctrine, and the Tridentine doctrinal definitions, while defiantly anti-Protestant, were deliberately made open-ended. The council left it to subsequent theologians to explain how faith could be both an intellectual commitment and a virtue, and how each mass could be a new sacrifice identical to that offered on Calvary by Jesus without being a repetition of it. It also left unreconciled the two propositions that salvation was due to the grace of Jesus Christ, and that free decisions of the human will were necessary for salvation. This contradiction was to provoke severe doctrinal disputes.

It was difficult to find a middle course between the apparently heretical position that human nature could merit, accept, or require God's grace, and the orthodox (but religiously intolerable) view that human beings who had reached the age of reason could not in any way affect their fate after death. The dilemma would have been resolved by allowing that human nature itself was redeemed as well as fallen,

so that it was capable of meritorious acts, and faith could manifest itself in upright behaviour. That, however, would have entailed admitting that pagans could be saved, which would contradict the council's profession of faith.

The major doctrinal condemnations of the late seventeenth and early eighteenth centuries were to attempt to define the theological limits of a Christian spirituality consistent with God's apparently arbitrary distribution of predestination. The originators of two of the seventeenth century's most

The Spanish colonial kingdom in America: the Jesuit missionaries Martin, Horatio and Didacus went to the 'Indians' in Chile on 11 December 1612 and were slain. Seventeenth-century copperplate etching.

The Grand Inquisitor, Cardinal Ferdinando Niño de Guevara. Portrait (c. 1569/1600) by Domenikos Theotokopoulos, known as El Greco (1541–1614), oil on canvas.

powerful spiritualities, François de Sales and François de Salignac de la Mothe Fénelon, as young men both underwent panic-stricken crises during which they believed that they were damned and could do nothing at all about it. Both subsequently became strongly hostile to theologies which deprived the human will of self-determination.

The movement in the seventeenth century which came to be known as Jansenism was a reaction against this religious optimism, whereas the exuberantly confident Marian spirituality of early eighteenth-century Bavaria was in many ways its apotheosis. The sensually indulgent Bavarian rococo churches decorated during the period 1700–50, whether large monastic or rural pilgrimage, were informed by an intense spiritual euphoria, a smooth continuity between the sensual and the spiritual, the earthly and the heavenly. Already in the sixteenth century authors such as Erasmus and Rabelais had suggested that natural human instinct might be relied on as a guide to spiritually authentic virtue, a view developed into a philosophy by Descartes in the seventeenth century.

In his major work, the 1618 *Treatise on the Love of God*, François de Sales refers to 'the natural instinct to love God above all things'. As a spiritual doctrine it was revolutionary, and François' canonization in 1665 at the height of the Jansenist dispute was a theological statement by Alexander VII. It not only endorsed the saint's spiritual doctrine, but also his enthusiastic acceptance of the view – energetically propounded by the Jesuits – that whatever the theological explanation, human beings had to be endowed with the power of moral choice.

The Jansenist theology of grace, maintained principally by Antoine Arnauld in France and Pasquier Quesnel in the Low Countries, implied that Christ had not died for the whole human race. This in 1653 forced Innocent X into tacit acceptance of the availability of salvation to non-believers. The door at which Erasmus had timidly knocked early in the sixteenth century had apparently been closed by Trent, only to be reopened in the mid-seventeenth and exuberantly celebrated in the eighteenth

centuries. It called into doubt the nature of the Church's mission, if there could be salvation outside it. Trent had not envisaged any such question.

Pius V sternly implemented the Tridentine reforms. From the moment he took office he enforced a strict moral code, issuing edicts against the profanation of the sabbath, simony, blasphemy, sodomy and concubinage. Within months there were further measures against luxury of dress and lavishness of banquets. Inquisitorial trials multiplied. Clerical residence and the rules of monastic enclosure were enforced. Vagrants were banned in Rome, and Jews from all the papal states except Rome and Ancona. The *Index of Forbidden Books* instituted in 1564 was enforced. Death sentences were carried

Altar of St Ignatius of Loyola, designed by Andrea Pozzo; statue of St Ignatius, copy from the original by Pierre Legros (1666–1719), in the chapel of St Ignatius of Loyola in Il Gesù church, Rome.

The Descent from the Cross. Painting by Rembrandt van Rijn (1606–69), oil on canvas.

out. The city's pagan antiquities were simply returned to the people of Rome. A new catechism, missal, and breviary were published.

But alongside the theological debates and the disciplinary matters, the papacy had external problems to resolve. It needed to come to terms with the new nation states. Questions were increasingly raised as to whether secular sovereignties were in any sense subordinate to the spiritual sovereignty of the papacy. The responsibility for civil administration was being transferred from the Church and its great landowning ecclesiastical institutions to the chanceries of secular princes with empty treasuries. That inevitably meant diverting some ecclesiastical income to pay for secular administrators.

At first beneficed members of the higher clergy were appointed to the secular chancery posts, so the question of payment did not arise. But that also meant that the faithful were often left without pastoral care, and absenteeism and neglect by the principal benefice holders became a scandal. Yet the clergy was far the best source of literate administrators, and the system not unreasonably reflected the shift of administrative responsibility from Church to state. It also exposed the excessive size of many ecclesiastical endowments, and their exploitation for self-aggrandizement, artistic patronage, and luxurious living.

Even when Wolsey suppressed monastic foundations to found Cardinal College, now Christ Church, at Oxford, he could claim to be diverting misapplied endowments to education and the renewal of scriptural studies. As a legate with full powers, he was acting not anti-clerically, but with papal authority. As early as the fifteenth century the normal way of founding universities had been to endow a collegiate church and to make its canons the professors, so that their stipends could legitimately be drawn from ecclesiastical funds. In German-speaking Europe, and at times in England, France,

and Spain, a resident ecclesiastic normally did not have full delegated papal jurisdiction, so the annexation of pious bequests to found a university needed to be sanctioned by the pope himself.

At the beginning of the period papal sovereignty was still accorded a certain primacy even outside the areas of strictly spiritual jurisdiction, and ecclesiastical sanction was still considered necessary for some acts of civil administration. As national chancellors, Wolsey in England and Duprat in France were endowed with the highest secular jurisdiction, but they were also made full papal legates. The nation states were having to struggle for true independence, and this system of dual jurisdiction in

Pope Innocent X (1644–55). Portrait (1650) by Diego Velázquez (1599–1660), oil on canvas.

a single ecclesiastic served as a bridge. It also gave legitimacy to the use of ecclesiastical endowments for secular purposes. Both the English law of contempt of court, until recently still recognizably a secular form of excommunication, and the English coronation service contain traces of the need for secular authority to be given ecclesiastical jurisdiction.

In 1525 Clement VII readily acceded to the request of Louise de Savoie for ecclesiastical jurisdiction to be given to secular judges so that they had the power to prosecute a bishop for heresy. The distinction of jurisdictions was still carefully observed here; but the system evolved differently in different places. In Spain the inquisition was essentially a secular institution, inaugurated by the state with only an approval – which did not involve a sovereign act – from the pope. But it employed ecclesiastical officials and exercised a secular jurisdiction in matters of religious belief.

The exploitation of benefices by secular sovereigns inevitably, if erratically, came to depend on the recognition by popes and princes of each other's sovereignty. It was generally regulated by a

series of economic agreements between the nation states and the papacy, often pressed home by threats of schism on the English model by France and Spain, and threats of excommunication or interdict from the Curia. Lucrative rights to nominate to vacant benefices were traded off between the papacy and the national sovereigns, so putting ecclesiastical income at their free disposal. It became unnecessary for secular officials to hold benefices. In France, Richelieu died in 1642 as Louis XIII's chief minister with a huge income of which much was derived from ecclesiastical benefices, in spite of Rome's disapproval. Mazarin succeeded to the post but, although from 1641 he was a cardinal, he became rich through his association with Anne of Austria and with Fouquet, the principal tax officer, rather than from ecclesiastical sources. Colbert, his successor, was not a beneficed clergyman at all.

A further important element in the history of the papacy between 1565 and 1721 was the diminution of the political activity of the papacy as one national power among others. During the sixteenth century Islam had come to dominate Greece, the Balkans and Hungary, and had threatened Vienna before being temporarily repulsed by the coalition inspired by Pius V. Valois France and Habsburg Spain, still serious rivals for political hegemony in continental Europe, had momentarily allied to confront the threat, before the religious wars from 1563 to 1598 nearly split France in two, and the intense rivalry between France and Spain reopened.

Gregory XIII had publicly rejoiced at the St Bartholomew's day massacre of Huguenots on 24 August 1572 by attending a service of thanksgiving at the French church of San Luigi in Rome. In 1585 Sixtus V issued a bull declaring the future Henri IV and his ally the Prince de Condé, both Huguenots, incapable of succeeding to the throne. By releasing all vassals from allegiance to them the pope, under the guise of making a decision about moral obligations, was actually using his spiritual jurisdiction as a secular political instrument. In 1589 the Paris theology faculty, no doubt encouraged by a wave of anti-royal hysteria, pronounced all citizens released

Left:
Pope Alexander VII (b. 1599–d. 1667). Portrait by G. B. Gaulli.

Armand-Jean du Plessis, Duc de Richelieu (1585–1642). Portrait (1635) by Philippe de Champaigne (1602–74). Full-length standing portraits were considered the prerogative of royalty.

from allegiance to Henri III, again attempting to use spiritual jurisdiction as a secular weapon. Pius V had also recently attempted to exercise a secular as well as a spiritual primacy by not only excommunicating, but also formally deposing, Elizabeth I of England in February 1570. He achieved only increased harshness against recusants and further danger for the imprisoned Mary Queen of Scots. The situation in France was ultimately resolved by the conversion to Catholicism of Henri IV, king of France by right of conquest, but also with a marginally better claim to the succession than anyone else.

Clear separation between secular and ecclesiastical jurisdictions was to be established only in the seventeenth century, and only after bitter debate among political theorists defending existing political positions, and in the late sixteenth century promoting everything from the divine right of kings to the inalienable sovereignty of the people. The

Pope Gregory XIII. Portrait by Lavinia Fontana (1552–1614).

dispute between Cardinal Bellarmine and Paolo Sarpi over the immunity of the clergy from civil jurisdiction, resulting in an interdict imposed by Paul V on Venice in 1606–7, shows how a blurring of the boundaries between the two sovereignties was still necessary to justify on the one hand Roman claims to ecclesiastical exemption from civil taxation and judicial proceedings, and on the other the autonomy of nations, some of whose princes were in schism, to tax and legislate independently of ecclesiastical rights.

Doctrinal disputes were also swift to arise. The theologians of the high middle ages had sought to define what, in actual human experience, was due to God's gratuitous gifts, and what, like the power of rational thought, was implied by the creation of human nature itself. By the sixteenth century scholastic thinking had coarsened, and Renaissance theologians spoke as if Adam had been created with a purely human nature to which supernatural elevation had been added like a tier to a wedding cake.

But the Louvain theologian Baius (Michel du Bay) pointed out that human nature must itself have had an intrinsic aspiration to supernatural fulfilment, as it could not otherwise have sought or been satisfied by the Beatific Vision. For Baius, original sin must radically have affected the elevated nature with which Adam had been created. Human nature in its fallen state had become incapable of any act not dominated by concupiscence, and all acts of fallen human nature were necessarily sinful.

Louvain university censured twenty propositions of a Franciscan disciple of Baius called Sablons, who had reduced the will's liberty to a freedom from external compulsion – which had been Calvin's position. Baius agreed with the censure of eighteen of the propositions, and on 27 June 1560 the Paris theology faculty condemned eighteen of the propositions referred to it by Louvain's chancellor, Ruard Tapper. Pius IV issued two briefs in 1561 imposing silence on the issue, but Baius spelled out his teaching on man's original state, freedom, merit and justification in a series of treatises issued in 1563–4. At the request of Philip II many of Baius'

Adam and Eve under the tree of knowledge. Painting by Peter Paul Rubens (1577–1640), after an engraving by Raphael, oil on panel. Rubens was much favoured by the Jesuits for whom he executed important commissions.

propositions were censured at Alcalá on 31 March 1565, and then at Salamanca in August. In November 1566 Louvain asked Rome for a judgement. After a new version of Baius' treatises had been censured at Alcalá, Pius V condemned 79 out of 120 propositions on 1 October 1567. Baius submitted, but then defended his views again in 1569 before becoming dean of the faculty at Louvain in 1570. The condemnation of 75 propositions was promulgated in 1571, but Baius made the Tridentine profession of faith under oath in 1575. It seemed

briefly as if nothing too untoward had happened.

On the death of Pius V in 1572, Ugo Boncampagni was elected as Gregory XIII. He gave new vigour to the movement to preach the gospel in the new world, and in India, China and Japan, relying heavily on the Jesuits not only for missionaries, but particularly to carry through the Trent reforms in the education of the clergy. They opened the Roman college, provided the staffing for the united German and Hungarian colleges and for the English college, and commissioned Giacomo

E VINTO BVDA L TVO BEATO PIEDE
MANDA AVGV INSEGNE O SANTA FEDE.

BVDA VINTA LI 2. SETEMBRE 1686

Engraving celebrating the recapture of Buda from the Turks, 2 September 1686, by Giuseppe Mitelli (1634–1718).

reorganized the Church's internal administration, creating fifteen permanent commissions of cardinals, whose number he raised from twenty-four to seventy, and enforcing visits to Rome by bishops to report regularly on the state of their dioceses.

He was the last of the Renaissance popes, a person of astonishing energy, politically interventionist, although a dreamer with schemes for the conversion of England, the annihilation of the Turks, the conquest of Egypt and Palestine, and plans for ridding himself of his alliance with Spain and of securing France for Catholicism. It was he who declared both the future Henri IV and Condé incapable of succession. He also excommunicated Henri III for the murder of the Cardinal de Guise, but not for that of his brother, the duke. Absolution was withheld until the release of two senior ecclesiastics, the Archbishop of Lyons and Cardinal de Bourbon, arrested immediately after the murders.

Sixtus was also intent on making Rome Europe's finest city, and St Peter's its grandest basilica. He was responsible for redesigning the city's entire layout, chiefly by the construction of immense avenues which opened up a series of vistas anchored in obelisks radiating from the core of the built-up area immediately across the Tiber from the Vatican towards the hills to the east. The ostensible purpose was to open up the city to pilgrims, especially those visiting the seven penitential churches. But at the eastern edge of the scheme was Santa Maria Maggiore, next to the Villa Montalto, the pope's family property, which stood to gain immensely in value from the residential development the avenues encouraged. The large area between the hills to the east and the crook of the Tiber, once green and dotted with the villas of the aristocracy, had become deserted as the old Roman aqueducts fell into disrepair. Sixtus began to re-establish the ancient Roman water system and commissioned his engineer, Domenico Fontana, to produce a series of paintings for the Vatican library, grand perspectives of the developed city. He commissioned Fontana to design the summer palace on the Quirinal, to make major additions to the Vatican, and to produce plans to replace the ruined medieval residence at the Lateran.

della Porta, Michelangelo's pupil and the architect of St Peter's cupola, to erect the façade of their famous Roman church, Il Gesù, originally designed by Giacomo Barozzi da Vignola and completed in 1575. The interior was refurbished in the late seventeenth century. Gregory's best remembered achievement is the reform of the calendar, synchronizing it with the astronomical year by dropping ten days in October 1582. He also much enlarged the system of nunciatures to promote reform, changing the function of nuncios from being primarily diplomatic agents to filling a supervisory role over the local bishops, so creating an administrative hierarchy.

Gregory XIII also attempted by political means to win back into communion with Rome those parts of Europe which continued in schism, supporting Philip II in his wars in the Low Countries, and the French Catholic League which virtually sought Spanish dominion in France. He had a new corpus of canon law published, codifying thousands of decisions in a single volume which did much to unify the application of canonical legislation.

His successor Sixtus V, elected in 1585, ruthlessly restored order and rebuilt the papal finances, but only by taking so much money out of circulation that he caused a serious recession. He also

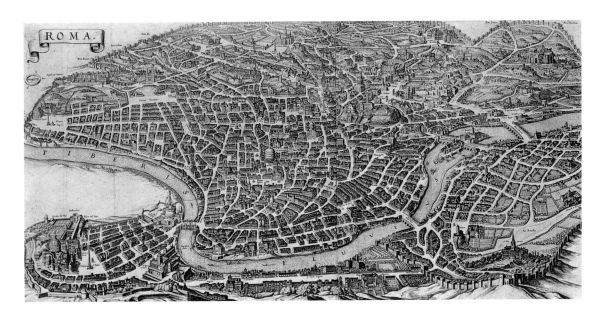

Plan of Rome looking northwards, c. 1600. Engraving by Merian. St Peter's is at the bottom left.
The proposed expansion was to the east of the built-up area.

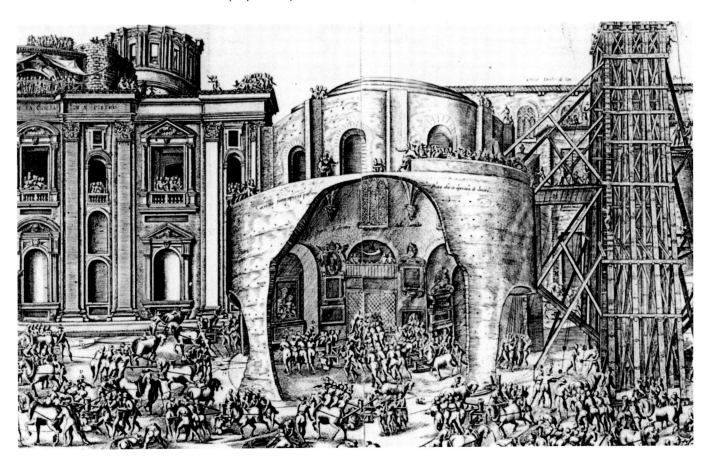

The erection of Domenico Fontana's obelisk in Piazza S. Pietro, 1589.
Engraving by Giovanni Guerra (1540–1618).

The façade of Sta Maria Maggiore, Rome, by Ferdinando Fuga (1699–1781).

Himself a scholar, Sixtus built the Vatican library and had the Vulgate Latin text of the Bible revised, although the new version contained so many errors that it had to be recalled and could be reissued only after further revision. He died in 1591.

There followed the three short and unremarkable reigns of Gregory XIV, Urban VII, and Innocent IX before the election of Clement VIII in 1592. While Spain continued to control Lombardy to the north and Naples to the south, Clement could at least play off France against the Habsburgs, and in fact mediated between them. He was also able to reincorporate Ferrara into the papal states on the failure of its ruling house of Este in 1598.

Clement has been seen as a nepotist, and he certainly raised three of his nephews to the purple, ruining the papal finances by excessive gifts to them.

But he was personally austere and assiduous in fulfilling his duties. He heard confessions for hours on end, ceremonially washed the feet of the poor, made a monthly pilgrimage on foot to the seven penitential churches, tightened the prohibition of books, and held a highly successful jubilee year in 1600, when over a million pilgrims were attracted to Rome by the indulgence offered. In 1600, however, Clement also allowed Giordano Bruno to be burnt as a relapsed heretic on the orders of the Roman inquisition. Bruno, a Dominican, was a mystically inclined syncretist philosopher who regarded the universe as infinite and God as the world soul. His view, in which individual things were manifestations of a single entity, appeared close to pantheism.

Controversies about the reconciliation of free will and grace resurfaced. In 1588 the Jesuit Luis de

Molina had attacked the views published in 1584 by the Dominican Dominicus Báñez, who held that grace determined the human will by a force he called 'physical premotion'. Molina defended the view that the will was endowed with a liberty 'of election'. Molina avoided the apparent Pelagianism of allowing to human nature the power of self-determination by affirming that God gave or witheld grace in the light of foreknowledge about whether the individual would have accepted or rejected it, if the choice had been given.

Not all Jesuits were so careful, and what became notorious as 'Molinism' was in fact the view of a professor at the Jesuit college of Louvain, known as Lessius, who said that the only difference between 'efficacious' grace and the 'sufficient' grace given to everyone was that the former was accepted. Báñez, Molina, and Lessius shared the assumption that justification, salvation, and the whole supernatural order were extrinsic to rational human nature, as if added on top. The Louvain university faculty, however, agreed with Baius that an aspiration to supernatural fulfilment had to be integral to human nature, and censured thirty-four theses of Lessius in 1587. Sixtus V enjoined silence at Louvain, but the following year Molina published his *Concordia* in Lisbon, reconciling free will and efficacious grace. It was at first suppressed by the Portuguese inquisition, but then released and reprinted at Lyons, Antwerp, and Venice.

The dispute between Dominican upholders of 'physical premotion' and Jesuit supporters of Molina became bitter. Clement VIII convoked the debate to Rome in 1594 and imposed silence in a decree, though the Roman inquisition withdrew this in 1598. In the ensuing dispute Molina, who died in 1600, came very near to condemnation. Clement VIII was not pleased when the Alcalá Jesuits held a disputation on whether it was a truth of faith that the reigning pope was the legitimate successor of St Peter, and was inclined to side against Molina. He did, however, allow the substantial questions to be debated before him in a series of sixty-eight disputations between 1602 and 1605. His successor, Paul V, reconvened the disputing parties but achieved

no progress. He dissolved the congregation and enjoined silence on all parties. The inquisition demanded on 11 December 1611 that in future all works on grace should be referred to it before publication. However, what was really at stake in the disputes involving Baius, Báñez, Molina, and Lessius was the whole nature of the Christian religion and its practice. The matter was far from ending.

Paul V, elected in 1605, was a strong upholder of papal prerogative, which Savoy, Genoa, Tuscany and Naples allowed to prevail. He forbade English Catholics to take the oath of allegiance, which denied the pope's right to depose the king, and in France provoked the 'Gallican' declaration of the Estates in 1614 that the king held his office directly by divine right, and therefore independently of papal jurisdiction. In Venice, however, an analogous resistance to the extension of papal rights led to an interdict in 1606. It was ignored by its government and most of the clergy.

The Venetian Servite theologian Paolo Sarpi accused Paul V of abuse of power and went as far as to declare obedience to him to be sinful. He enlisted the schismatic powers in Venice's support, and a European war was only narrowly averted. It would have occurred had Spain been willing to offer the pope military support. But no one else wanted war,

Self-portrait of Gian Lorenzo Bernini (1598–1680). Drawing (1624).

The Trevi fountain, Rome.

Tomb (1798–1805) of the Archduchess Maria Christine Habsburg-Lothringen (1742–98), favourite daughter of Empress Maria Theresa of Austria, by Antonio Canova (1757–1822), in the Augustinkirche, Vienna.

and a papal defeat disguised as a compromise was agreed in April 1607, when Cardinal Joyeuse absolved the Signoria on 21 April. In 1619 Sarpi issued his strongly anti-papal *History of the Council of Trent*. By that time the Bohemian revolution had sparked off the sectarian conflict which had long seemed inevitable, and the Thirty Years' War began. The Catholic alliance led by Maximilian I of Bavaria formed a league against the Protestant union led by the Calvinist elector Palatine, which had allied with England and Holland. War broke out when the Protestant nobles of Bohemia revolted against the future Emperor Ferdinand II, elected king of Bohemia in 1617 and king of Hungary in 1618. The popes contributed considerable sums from 1620 onwards.

Paul V's nepotism is estimated to have cost about 4 per cent of the papal income during his pontificate. He was succeeded in 1621 by Gregory XV, who canonized the founder of the Jesuits, Ignatius Loyola, together with Philip Neri, Teresa of Avila, and the most important of the early Jesuit missionaries, Francis Xavier. It was Gregory who in 1622 established the Congregation for the Propagation of the Faith. On Gregory's death in 1623, Urban VIII was elected. He was to reign until 1644, a competent diplomatist, a friend of France, and an ardent nepotist who prodigally enriched his family, making three relatives cardinals. He ended by doubling the papal debt; but at least he was the patron of Gian Lorenzo Bernini for twenty years. A few months after the death of Urban VIII in 1644 his family was exiled and their estates were confiscated. Most of the artists who had worked for him were summarily dismissed, and Bernini was obliged to

Facing:
Mother Marie-Angelique Arnauld (1591–1661), Abbess of Port-Royal, in 1648. Portrait by Philippe de Champaigne (1602–74),

Auto da Fé at the Plaza Mayor in Madrid, 30 June 1680. Painting (1683) by Francisco Rizi (1614–85), oil on canvas.

retire to mostly private practice from 1644 to 1655 during the pontificate of Innocent X.

Bernini was not just a sculptor and painter but an architect, celebrated for his brilliant solutions to the intricate problems of the construction and decoration of the interior of St Peter's and its piazza. He was the arbiter of artistic taste at the court of Urban VIII, and dominated decisions on everything from urban layout to the decoration of church interiors. It was Bernini's personal style that both unified the aesthetic values underlying Roman baroque and imposed them elsewhere on the Italian peninsula and even north of the Alps.

He was commissioned by Urban VIII in 1629 as architect to St Peter's, where Bramante's choir was ill juxtaposed with Maderno's nave. Michelangelo's mid-sixteenth-century project had derived its inspiration from Brunelleschi's cathedral in Florence, where the dome unifies the city as seen from the surrounding hills. He kept the basilica squat enough for the hemispherical dome to be seen over the low façade from the other side of the river. Following an architectural competition held in 1607, the basilica had been elongated by the addition of a nave in the direction of the concourse, not yet a piazza, with a full-height façade to conceal the nave roof. Bernini was commissioned to articulate the crossing under the dome, and designed the magnificent bronze *baldacchino*, complete with the mock tassels of processional canopies, as a means not only of fulfilling the liturgical requirement, but also of holding the visual balance between the high altar above the apostle's sunken tomb and Michelangelo's lofty dome. In 1657 Alexander VII commissioned Bernini to create the piazza, and Bernini designed his spectacular colonnade, two semicircles of four rows of columns, visually unifying the whole complex by aligning the top of the portico with the entablature of the façade. He also notably created the group of Church fathers supporting Peter's throne in the apse of St Peter's, and the great fountain in the piazza Navona.

Urban VIII had been no match for the skilful politics of Richelieu, perfectly prepared to ally with the Protestant powers in his battle with the Habsburgs. It is quite understandable that, to avoid a Habsburg hegemony, Urban VIII should have allowed Richelieu to occupy the Valtellina fortresses lining the alpine pass which provided the only overland route between the Habsburg lands of Lombardy and the Tyrol. But it is also clear that Urban could not afford to join the anti-Spanish alliance promoted by France in 1628. It is also unlikely that he seriously believed, as is sometimes asserted, that the Franco-Swedish alliance of 1631 would maintain Catholicism in the conquered territories or deflect Richelieu from a Protestant alliance in Germany. He fortified the surroundings of Rome, embellished the city, and wrote hymns for the new breviary, but his political stance was not motivated by religious considerations.

Innocent X, his successor, was again confronted with the problem of reconciling grace with the freedom of the will in the debates on Jansenism – a name used both of the rigorist spirituality associated chiefly with Saint-Cyran, and of the technical theology of nature and grace laid out in the monumental posthumously published volume of 1640 by Cornelius Jansen, Bishop of Ypres, entitled *Augustinus*. The spirituality pre-dated the theology and was independent of it until after the publication

of *Augustinus*, although that work presented a view of nature, grace, and redemption which supported the spiritual attitudes that Saint-Cyran had developed from the *Oratorian Condren*, who taught that for spiritual fulfilment human nature needed to be 'annihilated'.

There had been a close early association between Saint-Cyran and Jansen, and they had dreamt together of a plan to renew the Church as it had been in the fifth century; but the plan changed in 1621 when Jansen discovered the importance of the medieval assumption already attacked by Baius, that Adam's original state could be measured against a state of pure nature from which he had been elevated. Jansen, too, saw that the implication that supernature was a tier added to a pure nature complete in itself was a metaphysical impossibility. He went on to elaborate the theology of nature, sin and grace which he thought was that of Augustine, and which admirably suited the guilt-ridden spirituality of Saint-Cyran.

A draft of the first volume of *Augustinus* was sent to Saint-Cyran in 1630. The second was ready in 1634, and the final volume was completed before Jansen's death in 1638. Both Jansen, on account of his criticism of France's alliance with German Protestants, and Saint-Cyran, whose orthodoxy had been queried and whose gloomy spirituality was gaining too much influence, had irritated Richelieu, and Saint-Cyran was finally imprisoned in 1638 for criticizing the prayer to the Virgin for the protection of France published that year by the king. He was released on Richelieu's death, but died in 1643. The two strands of Jansenism, spiritual and theological, now came together in the single combative mind of Antoine Arnauld, a theologian and ex-lawyer closely associated with Saint-Cyran's spirituality and the monastery of Port-Royal, which had become its headquarters.

The Holy Office had tried again to impose silence in 1641, but the Louvain faculty had repudiated the decree. The injunction to silence was reiterated in the bull 'In eminenti', promulgated in 1643; but in December 1642, shortly before his death, Richelieu had arranged for Isaac Habert to preach against *Augustinus*. The sermons continued until Septuagesima 1643, when the Archbishop of Paris forbade their continuance. The situation flared up again when the preface by Saint-Cyran's nephew, Martin de Barcos, to Arnauld's 1643 work *De la fréquente communion* appeared to challenge papal supremacy in teaching and jurisdiction. Barcos defended himself in two further works which were themselves condemned on 25 January 1647. The pope considered that Barcos had created an association between Gallicanism and Jansenism. Successive popes now also had political reasons to suspect Arnauld.

Pope Clement X.
Marble tondo,
School of Algardi.

In 1649 the chairman of the theology faculty in Paris, Nicolas Cornet, put seven Jansenist propositions forward for condemnation, but the matter was delegated to a commission. Habert therefore wrote to Innocent X asking for a condemnation of five of the propositions in a petition signed by eighty-five bishops. Innocent X issued his bull of censure 'Cum occasione' on 31 May 1653. The letters patent required to authorize the bull's reception in France were not issued until 4 July 1654. Mazarin found it prudent to slip into the text the words 'taken from Jansen's book' to prevent Arnauld from using the defence that the propositions had never been held by Jansen. In the last proposition Innocent X effectively stated that Christ had died 'not just for the predestined', but for the whole human race.

A formulary was drawn up repudiating the condemned propositions, and its signature decreed by the assembly of the clergy in 1655; but it did not specify that the propositions were in *Augustinus*. Matters were allowed to rest until Alexander VII was elected successor to Innocent X on 7 April 1655. The new pope issued a constitution, 'Ad sacram beati Petri', in October 1656 which laid down that the propositions had been condemned 'in the sense in which Jansen had meant them'. Mazarin had Arnauld deprived of his doctorate but took no further action for several years. The formulary and signature were imposed from April 1661, just after Mazarin's death. But Arnauld rejected any compromise.

Relations between Alexander VII and France now deteriorated rapidly. Colbert was demanding large reparations following an incident in which the papal guard had fired on the carriage of the Maréchal de Créqui, the French ambassador publicly renowned for his stupidity. As a result the new Bishop of Paris, Hardouin de Beaumont de Péréfixe, was kept waiting nearly two years for bulls of appointment, which arrived only on 10 April 1664. On the 19th Colbert had the signature of the second formulary made obligatory. It was imposed by Archbishop Péréfixe on 8 June.

That pleased the pope, a friend of the Jesuits, not only because it crushed the Port-Royal faction in France, but also because it made the French administration realize that such measures required the exercise of papal jurisdiction. The bull 'Regiminis apostolici', issued on 15 February 1665, informed the French monarch that the pope would in future rely on his own jurisdiction. That was the year in which Alexander canonized François de Sales. Only the succession to the papacy of Clement IX in 1667 halted the humiliations being inflicted on France.

The next pope, Clement X, nearly eighty on his accession in 1670, reigned for just over six years, again aggravating relations between the papacy and France. In 1673 the French extended royal rights to the income and patronage of vacant episcopal sees and other benefices. Clement was succeeded by the reforming and saintly Innocent XI (1676–89), equally hostile to the French. There was a real threat of schism. Nicolas Pavillon, the Bishop of Alet, known for his Jansenist sympathies, excommunicated a royal nominee to a canonry and appealed to the pope.

It was now that Jacques-Bénigne Bossuet, the principal prelate at the court of Louis XIV, produced the political theory needed to support royal supremacy over the Church in France. He also inspired the assembly of the French clergy in 1682 which drew up four articles, maintaining the Gallican view that the pope had no jurisdiction over temporal sovereigns, and that the right to judge doctrine belonged jointly to bishops and pope. Innocent refused to grant bulls to appointees of Louis XIV. The formal revocation of the edict of Nantes in

1685, withdrawing toleration from the Huguenots, was the last in a series of measures inspired by Bossuet, who was personally committed to the conversion of the Huguenots.

Innocent XI took a distinctly political role in organizing support for Vienna when it was besieged by the Turks in 1683. His own dislike of the increasing French desire to dominate Europe led him even to support William of Orange against James II. On Innocent's death in 1689, his successor Alexander VIII was at first supported by the French, but still repudiated the four Gallican articles. He was succeeded in 1691 by the reforming Innocent XII who finally struck at the roots of nepotism, as practised even by his predecessor, by outlawing the grant of any estates, offices or revenues by any pope to a relative.

Innocent XII negotiated the virtual repudiation of the Gallican articles in France, with which he restored more harmonious relations; although his mild condemnation of Fénelon's *Explication des maximes des saints* was a snub to Louis XIV, who had wanted a more robust censure. Fénelon's twenty-three propositions on the disinterested love of God were condemned in the brief 'Cum alias' in general, not in detail; and as 'respectively' erroneous, not heretical. That meant only that some of them could lead the unwary into error; it was not said which. This diplomatic coup combined a gesture of calculatedly moderate friendship towards the king with a virtual vindication of Fénelon, whose adversary Bossuet died without receiving any further promotion from Rome.

Innocent XII was succeeded in 1700 by Clement XI, who reigned until 1721. In the war of the Spanish succession he first sided ineffectually with the French to recognize Philip V, and then with the emperor to support Archduke Charles. At the end of the war, the Treaty of Utrecht ignored the temporal interests of the papacy, a sign of its loss of real political power. Sardinia and Sicily, Parma and Piacenza were disposed of without reference to papal claims.

Clement XI took further measures against the Jansenism of Quesnel in the 1705 bull 'Vineam

Pope Paul V (1605–21). Bronze bust by by Gian Lorenzo Bernini (1598–1680).

domini' and the famous constitution 'Unigenitus' of 1713. Quesnel was in Amsterdam on the run from the French, who considered that his large network of religious associates made him dangerous. Clement, justifiably unwilling to compromise his political independence, kept the king waiting for several years for both bull and constitution.

The lack of enthusiasm in Rome over the revocation of the edict of Nantes, and the anti-Jansenist definition that Christ had died for the whole human race, reflected a lessened Roman confidence in the unique efficacy of correct beliefs as a means of acquiring grace. The Tridentine profession of faith had built on the immense importance of orthodoxy in late fifteenth-century

Spain; and this view persisted in the joyous Roman reaction to the 1572 St Bartholomew's Day killings in France. Like the tortures inflicted on condemned heretics to force recantation before death, ecclesiastical attitudes had been based on the urgency of mediating eternal salvation, which required orthodoxy of belief. The diminution of that urgency is the chief characteristic of seventeenth-century changes in papal attitudes.

The history of the papacy is unavoidably one of largely negative interventions in the spiritual history of Christendom, as successive popes condemned

The St Bartholomew's Day Massacre. German contemporary engraving.

propositions, attitudes, and movements. In contrast, a history of the Church in this period would deal with pastoral and missionary activity, with ancient and modern religious orders, monastic and mendicant, and with hospitals and education.

Two papal condemnations during the seventeenth and eighteenth centuries are notorious. Galileo Galilei's astronomical observations conflicted with a literal interpretation of certain passages of the Old Testament. He was warned in 1616 that his theories might be discussed only in hypothetical terms. Urban VIII encouraged him to return to his studies. Galileo's 1632 *Dialogue*, which stated that the earth went round the sun, was at first declared orthodox in Florence, but led to

inquisitorial proceedings. He was obliged to recant and spent the rest of his life under house arrest. The real importance of his trial, as all Europe recognized, was the implied papal claim to arbitrate between the accepted interpretation of scripture and the discoveries of empirical science.

A similarly fundamental stance ended in the condemnation by Benedict XIV in 1742 of the Jesuit position on 'Chinese rites'. In the first decade of the seventeenth century the missionary Matteo Ricci had made many converts in China. He had allowed them to continue certain rites, such as honouring their ancestors and Confucius, which he had regarded as merely civil and compatible with genuine Christianity. By 1636 there were 38,000 Chinese Christians, who heroically endured persecution. Disputes between members of the missionary orders and local hierarchies, between the missionary orders among themselves, and even between Portugese and other Jesuits about the extent of accommodation to indigenous rites, in Africa and South America as well as the far east, gradually drove the papacy to assert the importance of the strict Latin rite.

Between 1565 and 1721 the developing culture of the Renaissance had carried Christian doctrine with it, re-establishing the individual's responsibility for spiritual self-determination. Spiritual and secular sovereignties were autonomous in practice, although not yet in theory. The papacy had abandoned the belief of Julius II that its spiritual authority depended on the recognition of its temporal power, and now used its political influence chiefly to further its religious interests. Europe had moved from the Renaissance to the Enlightenment. More slowly, the papacy had been travelling the same route.

FURTHER READING

Jedin, Hubert (ed.), *History of the Church: vol. V, Reformation and Counter-Reformation*, London 1980; *vol. VI, The Church in the Age of Absolutism and Enlightenment*, London 1981

Krautheimer, Richard, *The Rome of Alexander VII*, Princeton 1985

Pastor, L. von, *The History of the Popes from the Close of the Middle Ages, 1891–1953*, 40 vols

Charles Bourbon visits Pope Benedict XIV at a coffee house in the Quirinale. Painting by Giovanni Paolo Pannini (c. 1691–1765).

CHAPTER SEVEN

THE EMERGENCE OF THE MODERN PAPACY

1721–1878

DR SHERIDAN GILLEY

PAPAL HISTORY FROM the pontificate of Innocent XIII to that of Pius IX divides neatly into two parts. The first runs to the French Revolution, and was the era in which absolutist governments throughout Europe made increasing encroachments on the privileges and powers of the Holy See. The Gallicanism patronized by Louis XIV, and embodied in the 'four articles' of 1682, was echoed in other absolutist states which found any authority but their own intolerable. Gallicans appealed over the head of a fallible pope to what they declared to be the only infallible tribunal, a future ecumenical council. Of more immediate consequence was the Gallican rejection of papal jurisdiction in the Church's daily affairs, in the name of secular monarchies which treated the Church as an obedient branch of the state bureaucracy, and drew on other dissenting elements within the Catholic tradition – Jansenism, and the reforming Catholicism of the Enlightenment – to assail the flagging Counter-Reformation. The principal victim of this campaign was not the papacy but its right

arm, the Society of Jesus, disbanded by Clement XIV in 1773; but the dissolution of the Jesuits was itself significant of how the popes were hemmed in by the secular powers throughout the century.

The French Revolution changed all that. The monarchies which had fallen out with Rome now shared with it a common enemy in the 'liberty, equality and fraternity' which applied Enlightenment doctrine not to kings but to peoples. Of course, matters were not quite so simple. Napoleon's destruction of ecclesiastical principalities everywhere, including the papal states, also removed or humiliated the main Catholic centres of opposition to Rome in the former Holy Roman Empire, and there were times and places when the democratic or revolutionary impulse – Belgium in 1830, Ireland and Poland more generally – coincided with the interests of Catholicism. In France, Félicité de Lamennais in the 1820s linked the popes with the popular cause.

Yet the restoration of the papal states, alone of the old ecclesiastical principalities, at the Congress of

Pope Pius VII (b. 1742–d. 1823). Portrait (1805)
by Jacques-Louis David (1748–1825)

Vienna in 1814–15 bound the papacy into the Austrian minister Metternich's conservative European order, even if the interdenominational character of the reactionary 'Holy Alliance' of Russia, Prussia and Austria prevented the Vatican from supporting it. The chief apologist for a reinvigorated papacy was the most famous of intellectual reactionaries, Count Joseph de Maistre, in his book *Du Pape* (1819). From 1830 the Risorgimento, the movement for a united Italy, turned increasingly against the papal states as the principal obstacle to the realization of its ideal, and greatly strengthened the opposition in the Church to what Pius IX denounced as 'progress, liberalism and modern civilization' in the *Syllabus of Errors* of 1864. The result was a rallying to Rome of papalist Catholics, some of them Protestant converts, and the decisive repudiation of Gallican theories at the first Vatican Council (1869–70). The occupation of the city of Rome itself by the new Italy in 1870 left the pope the so-called 'prisoner of the Vatican'. Yet the council had just declared him infallible and vastly enhanced his spiritual authority to compensate for the loss of his secular

Reverse of the portrait medal (1736) of Pope Clement XII (1730–40) showing the Trevi fountain, by Ottone Hamerani (1694–1761), in silver; portrait medal of Clement XI (1700–21) by Charles-Claude Dubut (d. 1742), in gilt metal.

dominion, as Europe began its slow de-Christianization, while European emigrants and missionaries won him new peoples throughout the world. The pontificate of Pius IX saw Rome emerge as a global rather than a European power, but a power of a rather different kind. It had survived the kings; it had yet to survive the peoples.

The loss of the papal temporal power was a blessing in disguise. Considered necessary for a thousand years to the papacy's independence from other governments, it had locked the pope into the European state system in which he was foremost an Italian prince. Innocent XIII, born Michelangelo de' Conti (1721–4), confronted very different conditions from those of the greatest member of his family, the medieval Innocent III, in whom the power of Rome

over princes had attained its apogee. The pope still had to maintain his own kingdom. At times in the middle ages, and continuously from the late fifteenth century, Italy had been a cockpit of conflict between the great Catholic powers, and as monarch of the papal states, Innocent XIII maintained a precarious balance between the Habsburg empire and the Bourbon kings of France and Spain, whose rivalries dominated the conclaves for papal elections, and divided the loyalties, often bought or pensioned, of the College of cardinals.

The College could not always escape the political realities of its world. Spain, France and the empire could exercise a veto against the candidacy of a cardinal, though the right was mostly used as a threat to spoil an aspirant's chances. In 1721, however, the emperor exercised his veto to exclude the secretary of state Cardinal Fabrizio Paolucci as a Bourbon sympathizer, while Conti himself promised France to raise the French first minister Guillaume Dubois to the cardinalate, in spite of Dubois' disgraceful private life. The new pope sanctioned the status quo by investing the Emperor Charles VI as king of Naples in 1722, but at the same time tried to regain the city of Comacchio, which was to be returned to his successor, and to assert his sovereignty over the north Italian duchy of Parma and Piacenza, a bone of contention throughout the eighteenth century. He continued Clement XI's support for James III, the Stuart Old Pretender to the thrones of Britain and Ireland, in a late piece of Counter-Reformation politics also doomed to failure.

Bound up with this power game was the complex of issues around Jansenism, Clement XI's Bull 'Unigenitus' of 1713 condemning the Jansenist Pasquier Quesnel's *Moral Reflections on the New Testament*, and the anti-Jansenist Society of Jesus. Innocent XIII was known as an anti-Jesuit from his days as nuncio in Lisbon, and in 1723 he compelled the Jesuits to obey Clement XI's bull condemning the Chinese rites which had made Catholicism more acceptable to the Chinese. The pope thought 'Unigenitus' inopportune, as it had polarized French Catholicism between an acquiescent majority – supported by the crown and the Jesuits – and a

Cardinal Melchior de Polignac visits St Peter's. Painting (1730) by Giovanni Paolo Panini (c. 1691–1765), oil on canvas.

ferocious Jansenist minority. But in 1722 the Roman inquisition condemned the request by seven French bishops for the withdrawal of 'Unigenitus', and in 1723 the Jansenist Church of Utrecht withdrew from the Roman obedience. These events set the seal on the conversion of the Jansenists into Gallicans, and gave the Gallicans another weapon against the Holy See. From a dispute over the theology of grace, the Jansenist controversy became one about papal infallibility and jurisdiction and the Jesuits. Jansenism

would only disappear with the *ancien régime* and the Church–state system which gave it significance.

Innocent XIII was overweight and ill, and reigned for only two and half years. He is remembered for instituting the feast of the Holy Name of Jesus in 1721. The papal conclave of 1724 saw a struggle between Habsburgs and Bourbons which resulted in the election of Pietro Francesco Orsini as Benedict XIII (1724–30). He had renounced his inheritance, the duchy of Gravina, to

Pope Clement XIII
(1758–69) with his nephew
Cardinal Carlo Rezzonico,
the cardinal's nephew
Ludovico and Ludovico's
wife Faustina Savorgan.
Painting (1758/62) by
Pietro Longhi (1702–85),
oil on canvas.

Pope Benedict XIV.
Marble statue (from 1769)
by P. Bracci in St Peter's,
Rome.

become first a Dominican, then a model shepherd of souls as metropolitan of Benevento. As pope, he was unique in his century in devoting himself entirely to Rome as its pastor, visiting the sick and dying, consecrating churches and altars and hearing confessions in St Peter's, and in 1725 assembling a provincial council. He enlarged the Trinità dei Pellegrini hospital to receive 2,000 convalescents from elsewhere, and employed the architect Filippo Raguzzini to design San Gallicano, a hospital for skin and venereal diseases. A stern disciplinarian on the model of the Counter-Reformation's prince of pastors, Carlo Borromeo, he abolished the Roman lottery. In confirming 'Unigenitus' he distinguished the Jansenist teaching on grace from that of Aquinas

and of his own Dominicans, and received the retraction in 1728 of the most eminent champion of Jansenism, Cardinal Louis-Antoine de Noailles. The pope's extension to the whole Catholic world in 1728 of the liturgy of St Gregory – Pope Gregory VII, Hildebrand, the great medieval upholder of the papal prerogative – was resisted in France, Sicily, Holland and the Empire.

Benedict was the last pope of the Counter-Reformation. He was loved for his private qualities; his Achilles heel was his favourite from Benevento, Niccolò Coscia, whom he raised to the cardinalate in 1725 against opposition from the existing college, and who plundered the papal administration to enrich himself and his cronies. The pope refused to hear any complaints against Coscia, moving unspotted through his corrupt administration 'like the Holy Sepulchre in the hands of the Turks'. Coscia was brought down by the pope's death in 1730. The new pope Clement XII, Lorenzo Corsini (1730–40), a Florentine nobleman from an immensely wealthy family, won popularity by bringing him to trial.

Clement was an able administrator who tried to restore the papal finances and reintroduced the Roman lottery, but he was seventy-eight on his election, went blind within two years and was frequently ill. His pontificate was overshadowed by the rivalry of the great powers, whose armies marched across the papal states with impunity, and who ignored his claim to Parma when it was awarded to the Bourbon Don Carlos. Spain especially treated the pope with contempt in 1736, by damaging buildings in Rome and conscripting for its armies even within the walls.

Clement's successor, Benedict XIV, the Bolognese Prospero Lorenzo Lambertini (1740–58), was the ablest pope of the century, and the most attractive personally. The eighteenth-century popes were, as Owen Chadwick remarks, 'mostly good-humoured men', but only in Benedict XIV did they rise above well-meaning competence. A mine of good-natured wit, he once returned a lampoon upon him to the author with improvements, and even when pope he chatted naturally with the least of his subjects in working-class Trastevere and the countryside around Castel Gandolfo. He achieved a surplus on the papal budget. He was also described as 'the greatest of canonists', having written the standard work on the procedures for canonization (1734–8), published treatises on the sacrifice of the mass and on diocesan synods (both in 1748) and revised the *Caeremoniale Episcoporum*, containing the ceremonial for use by a bishop (1752). An able administrator and pastoral bishop and archbishop, first of Ancona and then of Bologna, he was in a different mould from Benedict XIII. 'I like to leave the Vatican lightnings asleep,' he said, preferring compromise to confrontation with both the European powers and the spirit of the age.

His concordats with Naples and Sardinia

(1741) and Spain (1753) surrendered the right to nominate to benefices hitherto in the papal gift, and to grant various ecclesiastical immunities from state authority. He conferred on the Portuguese monarch John V, the father of four bastard children, the title of 'Most Faithful' in 1748 and, more reluctantly, benefices on the bastards. He was fortunate in the treaty of Aix-la-Chapelle of 1748, which gave Italy forty-eight years of peace. His temper as much as his learning won him the plaudits of Enlightenment

Pope Clement XIV (b. 1705–d. 1774).
Anonymous portrait, oil on canvas.

sceptics such as Voltaire and Hume. He corresponded with the great scholar Muratori and protected his work, *On a Well-Ordered Devotion*, from condemnation; in 1753 he reformed the *Index of Prohibited Books*. He also encouraged the new Catholic revivalism, so like its Wesleyan counterpart, approving the new Passionist order of St Paul of the Cross in 1741 and 1746, and St Alphonsus Liguori's Redemptorists in 1749; and in 1741 extending the devotion of the stations of the Cross in parish churches. In 1749 the missionary friar Leonard of Porto Maurizio, later to be canonized, created a Via Sacra for the stations of the Cross around the Colosseum, and preached before the pope in the great Roman mission for the jubilee of 1750. Benedict further protected the Colosseum by consecrating it as a church in 1756.

Pope Clement XIV. Marble bust (1771) by Christopher Hewetson (c. 1736–98).

The popes had always delighted in adorning their city, an interest enhanced by the Counter-Reformation's use of art and architecture for preaching and propaganda. The waning of these religious energies gave Rome a new role as the cultural capital of Europe, as a magical city, with its magnificent palaces and churches, massive ruins and air of pastoral peace and gentle decay, celebrated in the engravings of Giuseppe Vasi and Giovanni Battista Piranesi, a city for painters, poets and lovers, the Rome of Winckelmann, Goethe, Keats and the Brownings. The popes encouraged this cultivated tourism especially among Protestant northern Europeans, and showed a particular concern for the romantic theatrical backdrops of piazzas, streetscapes and façades. In 1723 Innocent XIII chose Francesco de Sanctis' plan for the Spanish steps, which were completed under Benedict XIII to mark the jubilee year. In 1726–7 Raguzzini built the piazza di San Ignazio in rococo style. Under Clement XII, Alessandro Galilei designed the façades of the Lateran basilica and San Giovanni de' Fiorentini, and on the Quirinal Ferdinando Fuga built the Secretariat of the Ciphers and the palace of the Consultà with its grand piazza. Clement also commissioned Nicola Salvi to design the Trevi fountain, leaving 40,000 scudi for its completion, and established the Capitoline museum with part of the Albani collection. Benedict XIV repaired the Acqua Vergine aqueduct, but regretted as a disaster Fuga's ambitious new façade for Santa Maria Maggiore.

One of Benedict's last acts, in 1758, was the appointment as apostolic visitor to the Portuguese Jesuits of Cardinal Saldanha, who accused the society of involvement in trade in defiance of canon law. Saldanha was the creature of the Portuguese first minister, Sebastião José de Carvalho e Mello, later Marquis of Pombal, who was bent on the destruction of the society, a matter which would dominate the next two pontificates.

Clement XIII, Carlo della Torre Rezzonico (1758–69), a Venetian, as a pastorally minded Bishop of Padua had spent his official revenues on the Church and the poor, but as pope was caught up in a series of ecclesiastical typhoons. In 1759 he condemned the materialist French Enlightenment as set forth in Diderot's *Encyclopédie* and Helvetius' *De l'Esprit*. In 1763 the auxiliary Bishop of Trier, Johann Nikolaus von Hontheim, under the pseudonym Justinus Febronius, published a work attacking the doctrines of the pope's infallibility and of his universal jurisdiction. The German equivalent of Gallicanism is called Febronianism after him. This confronted Clement with opposition to his own authority from Hontheim's patrons, the three archbishop-electors of the Holy Roman Empire. The term 'ultramontane' in its modern reference to supporters of the pope, originally those living north of the Alps, belongs to the 1760s. Clement's authorization of the feast of the Sacred Heart in 1765 recognized one of the Jesuits' favourite devotions in the hour of their martyrdom.

The society was the victim of new ideas as well as of the power of the ever more absolutist state. The Portuguese Pombal had absorbed, partly from French and British sources, ideas on economic renewal, in part by ruthlessly restricting ecclesiastical influence. The initial pretext for attacking the Jesuits was the Indian resistance in some of their Paraguay reductions (mission settlements) to a new boundary between Spanish and Portuguese territory. The Jesuits' offence was compounded by an attempt in 1758 on the life of King José I. The Jesuit holy man Gabriel Malagrida was strangled and burnt as a heretic in the king's presence, a number of other Jesuits were imprisoned and executed, and more than a thousand more were shipped to the papal states to become pensioners on papal charity.

The bankruptcy of the West Indian estates run by the Jesuit Antoine Lavalette and an attempt on the life of Louis XV were the prelude to an onslaught on the society in France, where the chief minister Choiseul, the royal mistress Madame de Pompadour, the Gallican and Jansenist enemies of 'Unigenitus' and the intellectual leaders of the anti-Christian Enlightenment rejoiced in the disbanding of the society in 1762–4. Alleged Jesuit involvement in the 'Hat and Cloak' riots in Madrid in 1766 against a government ordinance imposing French dress in the

Tomb of Pope Clement XIV. Work (1783–7) of Antonio Canova (1757–1822), marble, in the Basilica dei Santi Apostoli, Rome.

towns in place of the traditional Spanish cape and sombrero gave an opportunity in 1767 for the abolition of the society in the other great Bourbon state, Spain, and in its vast American dominions; 4,400 Jesuits were deported and dumped in Corsica, having been refused admission to the papal states. France acquired the island from Genoa in 1768 and moved the exiles to the Italian mainland, and hundreds of Jesuits, half dead of starvation, straggled through the horrified Italian towns and villages to Rome. Another Bourbon chief minister, Tanucci, expelled the Jesuits from Naples in 1767. This assault on the principal teaching and missionary order of the Catholic Church dissolved hundreds of schools, colleges, universities and missions, leaving the victory not by the power of ideas but by force of arms to the anti-Christian Enlightenment. The

dissolution also demonstrated the ascendancy of state over Church in its national divisions, though Clement XIII courageously protested against the persecution of the order, especially in his thunderous bull of 1765, 'Apostolicum pascendi'; all in vain.

Clement exacerbated the situation by issuing in 1768 a Monitorium denouncing the drastic restrictions on his rights over the Church in the Bourbon duchy of Parma, which until 1731 had been a papal fief, and by invoking the ancient bull 'In coena Domini', traditionally read in Rome on Maundy Thursday, in which the Holy See excommunicated a ragbag of enemies from Protestants to pirates. The pope thus united the Bourbon monarchs

in insisting on the withdrawal of the Monitorium against Parma, while France and Naples occupied the papal possessions of Avignon and the Venaissin, Benevento and Ponte Corvo. In January 1769 the Bourbon ambassadors in Rome demanded 'the total and irrevocable destruction of the Society of Jesus' which, Cardinal Negroni remarked, 'will open the pope's grave'. Clement died shortly afterwards.

The following conclave was dominated by the Bourbons' determination on the election of a pope who would dissolve the society; they are said to have excluded no fewer than twenty-three cardinals. The successful candidate, Clement XIV, the Franciscan Giovanni Vincenzo Antonio (in religion Lorenzo) Ganganelli (1769–74), had given a vague written

Façade of St John Lateran (begun 1732), by Alessandro Galilei (1691–1737). Engraving by Piranesi (1720–78).

assurance that it was in the pope's power to dissolve the society. Clement remained under heavy Bourbon pressure with the foreign occupation of his outlying dependencies, and promptly suppressed the annual reading of 'In coena Domini'. Spain was hottest for outright abolition, which was pressed from 1772 by its ambassador in Rome, Joseph Moñino, to whom the pope proposed a compromise abolishing the Jesuit General's power, dividing the society into its national components and allowing it to die off for want of novices. 'Toothache', replied Moñino, 'can only be cured by extraction', and pressed his cause by threats and bribery. The refusal of Austria to protect the order left it without defenders, and on 21 July 1773 the pope issued the brief 'Dominus ac Redemptor', suppressing the society on the grounds that it had been a cause of envy and division throughout the Christian world. Much the same could be said of its Master, Jesus Christ.

In some places, the order survived as an informal association; it was protected by Frederick the Great in Prussia and Catherine the Great in Russia, in their Catholic territories seized from Austria and Poland.

The great gainer from the dissolution was apparently the pope. He was free, having bought his enemies off. Among reform-minded Catholics and Gallicans and Jansenists, and among Protestants, he was declared the most enlightened monarch of his age; the British prime minister Gladstone would one day rank him with Pascal and Bossuet. He won back Avignon and the Venaissin, Benevento and Ponte Corvo. In the end, however, his surrender to the *Zeitgeist*, in its radical reforming and Enlightened aspect, was to prove disastrous both to Rome and to the princes who had wreaked the Jesuits' ruin. Rome faced further challenges from the Catholic states before they faced revolution from below. When in 1793 the Bourbon Louis XVI stood on the scaffold, when the Bourbon kings of Spain and Naples fled from the armies of revolutionary France, devout Catholics looked on the ruin of crowns and thrones and remembered the Society of Jesus.

In 1773, Clement XIV imprisoned the Jesuit general Lorenzo Ricci in Castel Sant' Angelo on a charge of theft. He died there in 1775, his saintly bearing throughout the whole disgraceful episode enabling the society to make a good death. The pope himself died in 1774. His corpse decayed so rapidly that the face could not be shown, and it was said that the Jesuits had poisoned him. His good works had been limited by the papacy's worsening finances, but he established in 1769 what was to become the

Vatican's Museo Pio-Clementino of classical antiquities. It was completed by his successor.

Austria and Portugal opposed the election of that successor, Giovanni Angelico Braschi (1775–99), who took the name of Pius VI, in honour of the last canonized pope, Pius V. He thereby reintroduced the most popular of modern papal names – during the next two centuries seven Piuses would rule the Church for nearly 130 years, and Pius VI's own pontificate of twenty-four years was the longest in history before that of Pius IX. A transitional figure, he faced the last great onslaught of the absolutist monarchs and the first challenge from the peoples, in the French revolution.

A strikingly handsome man, who had once engaged to marry and was ordained late, Pius had weaknesses: vanity of his fine form and features

Pope Pius VI. Engraving (1784) by Antonio Fiori.

which raised the cry from the Roman crowds of 'Com'è bello'; and his enrichment of his family, especially his nephew, created Duke Braschi, who profited even from the pope's most praiseworthy attempt to drain the Pontine marshes. His first difficulty was Emperor Joseph II, who, on the death of his pious mother Maria Theresa in 1780, embarked on a far-reaching programme of religious reform. Joseph was himself a *dévot* and has been misunderstood by Catholics and anticlericals misled by the forged Constantinople letters, allegedly from Joseph, which present the emperor as an enemy of the Church. But the Josephinist reform was inspired by the Gallican idea of an autonomous state Church, and by the Muratorian demand for a simplified and more 'scriptural' devotion. The emperor's first measures included the claim to nominate to the bishoprics in his duchy of Milan; the requirement that all papal documents entering Austria should be subject to a placet or permission, which had previously been needed only for some; the cutting of ties between religious orders and their Roman superiors; Austrian autonomy for marriage

dispensations; and an edict of toleration in 1781 for Lutheran, Calvinist and Orthodox Christians, extended to Jews in 1782. Plans were also announced for the suppression of contemplative monasteries and a reform of clerical training, all to be carried out regardless of views in Rome.

In 1782, the pope decided on a personal appeal to the emperor, and for the first time in centuries a ruling pontiff crossed the Alps. The journey was a personal triumph as through Italy, Austria and southern Germany vast crowds gathered for a blessing on their scapulars and rosaries, while the pope's benediction was ceaselessly demanded from the Hofburg balcony. The journey showed that the people would revere him when the princes abandoned him; but popular feeling had no influence on the imperial counsels, and the meetings with Joseph were politely fruitless. Joseph repaid the visit in 1783–4, when he won the right of nomination to the sees of Milan.

The subsequent dissolution of a third of the Austrian religious houses financed a major extension of the parochial system and, like the creation of new

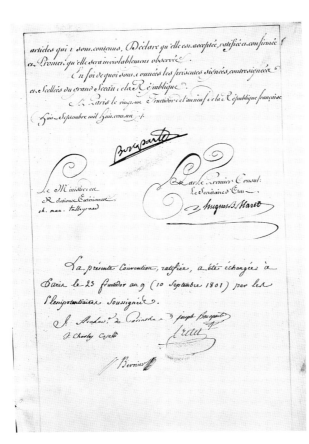

Ecclesiastical Arsenal: the partnership between the Jesuits and the Counter-Reformation. 'March, children: murder the foul villains.' 1800.

Right:
The last page of the concordat of 1801 between Pope Pius VII and Napoleon.

Left:
Pope Pius VII (b. 1742–d. 1823). Portrait (1819) by Sir Thomas Lawrence (1769–1830), oil on canvas.

Austrian dioceses, was of great benefit to the Church. But Joseph's 6,200 religious decrees attacked popular piety, on confraternities and saints' cults and reverence for the dead. Here was a gulf between the Catholicism of those who found the meaning of their religion in its rituals, and the book-based pietism of a semi-learned class. Yet monarchies in general and the Holy Roman Empire in particular owed their meaning to just such a world of expressive ritual. At the touch of the utilitarian reformer, those powers would fade and die.

A still more thoroughgoing reform was imposed in Tuscany by Joseph's brother, the Grand Duke Leopold and the Jansenist Bishop of Pistoia, Scipione de Ricci; his synod of Pistoia in 1786 included the amalgamation of all religions into a single order. In 1787 the townsfolk of Prato heard a rumour that Ricci intended withdrawing from public veneration their relic of the Virgin Mary's girdle. They rose in the 'Madonna riots' to tear out and burn the bishop's throne and coat of arms and to restore the votive statues which he had locked away. The Tuscan reforming programme faded in 1790, and Ricci submitted to Rome in 1805. The Josephinist reforms were also unpopular in the Austrian Netherlands, where they provoked a revolt of seminarians in 1786 and a revolution against Austrian rule in 1789. Parallel to Josephinism was the Febronian demand in the 'punctuation of Ems' in 1786 by the archbishop-electors of Trier, Mainz and Cologne and the Archbishop of Salzburg for a drastic reduction of papal power and influence in Germany. Thus their campaign reached a climax just as all these types of reform Catholicism – Jansenist, Gallican, Febronian, Josephinist – were about to be discredited by the French revolution.

The revolution at first looked like the final triumph of the Gallican idea. Rome watched with dismay as the revolutionaries in France abolished all payments to the Curia, sold the Church's properties, disbanded the contemplative orders and turned the clergy and bishops into elected and salaried state employees. In March 1791 Pius condemned the oath to the civil constitution imposed by the state on the priesthood in 1790, which divided the Church into

The entry in the Quirinale to carry off Pius VII into captivity, 6 July 1809. Engraving by B. Pirinelli (1781–1835).

The struggle between the State and the Church, 1871–89. The Black Sirens – Pius IX and the Jesuits as sirens, Bismarck as Odysseus. Wood engraving, from Kladderadatsch, Berlin, 1873.

an official constitutional body of those who had taken the oath, and the underground or exiled 'non-jurors' who had refused it. Avignon was occupied in reprisal for the papal ban, and some five to six thousand émigré ecclesiastics poured into Rome. Its independence was brief. In 1796, Bonaparte marched towards the city, and at the peace of Tolentino, the pope ceded to the French the legations of Bologna, Ferrara and Ravenna, as well as Avignon, and paid an indemnity of 30 million livres. Joseph Bonaparte became the French ambassador, but the death in a riot of the French General Duphot was the pretext for the occupation of Rome in 1798 by General Berthier, who set up a 'Roman republic' which lasted until 1799, when the French were expelled from Italy. The French plundered the treasures of the city and abducted the ailing octogenarian Pius to Siena, then to Florence, Parma and Valence, where he died as 'Jean Ange Braschi, exercising the profession of pontiff'. It looked like the end of the papacy.

There could be no conclave in Rome, but thirty-five cardinals met under imperial protection on the island of San Giorgio in Venice and elected the Benedictine Cardinal Barnaba Chiaramonti as Pius VII (1800–23). As Bishop of Imola, he had preached in 1797 a Christmas sermon which attempted a Catholic interpretation of liberty, equality and fraternity; the emperor disapproved the choice, and would not let him be enthroned in San Marco. In 1800 the pope set out for Rome with his pro-secretary of state, Cardinal Ercole Consalvi, just as France re-established her power in Italy at the battle of Marengo. Bonaparte was now, however, anxious for a deal with the Church, especially in France, and in 1801 he agreed on the restoration of the French Catholic Church through a concordat whereby Pius dissolved the old French hierarchy and appointed a new one. The Gallican Church re-established in 1802 was wholly subservient to the state, a point emphasized by Napoleon's issue of the Gallican 'Organic Articles'; but in order to use papal authority, Napoleon also had to grant it, and this unprecedented exercise of the papal prerogative was the turning point of its nineteenth-century recovery. A more favourable concordat was agreed for

northern Italy in 1803 and made effective by 1805.

In 1804, the pope came to Paris to preside at Napoleon's coronation as emperor. He anointed Bonaparte, who by prior arrangement crowned himself and his empress. The secularization of the last German prince-bishoprics and abbeys in 1803 heralded the dissolution of the Holy Roman Empire in 1806, the former Holy Roman Emperor having

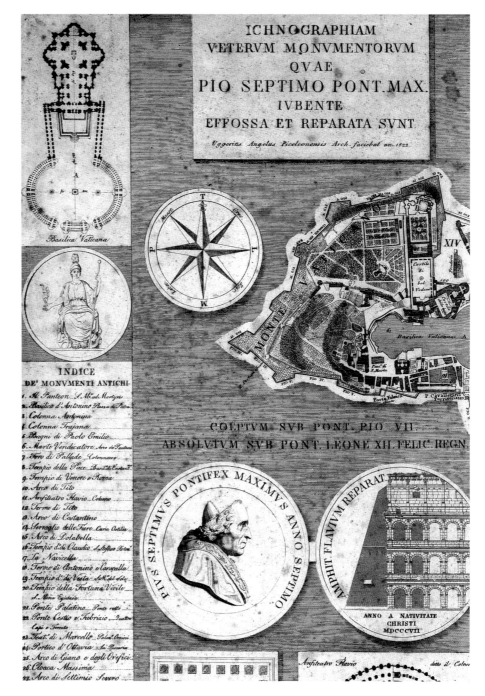

Plan of the Vatican city, showing buildings restored by Pius VII in Rome during his pontificate. Engraving (1822) by Angelo Uggeri.

Facing:
Coronation of Napoleon in the presence of Pope Pius VII (1804). Painting (1806–7) by Jacques-Louis David (1748–1825).

LA RELIGION ET LA CHARTE EXPULSANT LES JÉSUITES.

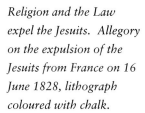

Religion and the Law expel the Jesuits. Allegory on the expulsion of the Jesuits from France on 16 June 1828, lithograph coloured with chalk.

become Emperor of Austria. These events weakened Catholic Germany and confirmed the rise of Protestant Prussia, but also destroyed the great electors who had attacked Rome in 1786, and humiliated proud Vienna.

The pope's authority was also enhanced by Napoleon's rough treatment of him. Pius refused to abandon his neutral status, so in 1808 French troops reoccupied Rome and in 1809 it was annexed to Napoleon's empire. Pius issued a general bull of excommunication of his enemies, and the French General Miollis had him arrested and sent with Cardinal Pacca first to Grenoble, then to Savona on the Italian Riviera. He refused to institute new bishops in France or its satellite states, and in 1812 he was bundled off incognito to Fontainebleau with such hasty brutality that he nearly died. After a six-day meeting with his illustrious prisoner in 1813, Napoleon got from him a concession allowing the investiture of the vacant French bishoprics, though Pius himself at once retracted it. He was held prisoner for five years, from 1809 to 1814, and reverted to the role of the monk who mended his own soutane. In 1814 the defeated emperor allowed

him to return to Rome, where he revived the Society of Jesus. Cardinal Consalvi negotiated the almost total restoration of the papal states at the Congress of Vienna, losing only Avignon and the Venaissin, before taking up the reigns of papal government. The papal archives and many of the artistic treasures looted by the French were also returned to Rome. The recovery in papal prestige was marked by concordats with Bavaria and Sardinia (1817), Naples (1818) and Prussia and the Upper Rhine Provinces (1821). The portrait of Pius by Sir Thomas Lawrence commissioned by the Prince Regent conveys the weariness of the man in the beauty of his wasted face and the long hands never raised except in blessing.

Consalvi's division of the papal states into four legations and thirteen delegations involved an element of lay participation and a compromise between Napoleonic and canon law, but the Romagna especially had been lay since 1800 and some of its more affluent citizens would never be happy again with rule by priests. The cardinals who supported Consalvi's reforms were outvoted in the conclave of 1823, and his enemy the conservative Annibale della Genga was elected as Leo XII (1823–9). He abolished lay participation in the higher levels of government, banned the waltz at carnival, and re-established the Jewish ghetto. Such conservatism drove opposition underground among the secret revolutionary brotherhood of carbonari or 'charcoal burners', and there was a reaction in the conclave of 1829, when Consalvi's disciple Cardinal Albani worked to secure the election of the moderate Francesco Xaverio Castiglione, Bishop of Frascati, who took the name of Pius VIII (1829–30). He attempted, unsuccessfully, to reach a compromise with the Prussian government which wanted him to authorize mixed marriages in the Catholic Rhineland provinces it had acquired in 1815. He also cultivated good relations with the 'July monarchy' established by the French revolution of 1830. Meanwhile a small but influential body of French Catholic ultra-montanes, led by Félicité de Lamennais, were demanding that the pope champion liberal reform. Pius was, however, already ill with a terrible neck abscess at his election, and after a pontificate of just over a year and a half, he died in November 1830.

Pope Gregory XVI on a steamboat excursion at Civitavecchia. Engraving (1835).

Pope Pius IX (b. 1792–d. 1878).

The conservative Leo XII had succeeded the moderate Pius VII and was followed by the moderate Pius VIII, in turn succeeded by the most conservative pope of the nineteenth century, the Camaldolese monk Bartolomeo (in religion Mauro) Cappellari who took the name of Gregory XVI (1831–46). Cappellari was a hale and vigorous old man, whose theology had always been strongly ultramontane: his best known work was called *The Triumph of the Holy See* (1799). On his election there was a rising in the Romagna which Austria crushed at the pope's request, leading to the liberal government of France, supported by England, to organize a memorandum signed by the Roman ambassadors of the powers demanding the introduction of laymen into his administration and other reforms. Gregory gave the rebels an amnesty which was followed by a further revolt and Austrian occupation, while the French occupied Ancona to keep pressure on the pope from the other side. The three greatest liberal Catholics of their generation, Lamennais, Lacordaire and the Comte de Montalembert, visited Rome in 1831–2 to persuade him of the value of a liberal Catholicism.

Lamennais was politely received, but his liberalism was anathematized in the encyclical 'Mirari vos' in August 1832 His apocalyptic tract, *Paroles d'un croyant* (1834), bitterly satirized the pope, who condemned the work in his encyclical 'Singulari nos' in 1834. Lamennais left the Church, but his followers did not, and their contribution to the Catholic revival was largely responsible for the Church's popularity in the French revolution of 1848. Gregory, however, continued intransigent: he urged his faithful Catholic Poles to obey the Tsar after their rising in 1831; and the secretary of state Cardinal Bernetti in 1832 created a civil guard, the 'centurions', whose unruly behaviour also contributed to the unpopularity of papal rule. The liberal conspiracy to kidnap three leading ecclesiastics (one of them the future Pius IX) in 1843 was repressed by another secretary of state, Lambruschini, with seven executions and over fifty condemnations to the galleys. Gregory's anti-liberalism was confirmed by the destruction of Spanish monasticism by anticlerical administrations from 1835, and the imprisonment of the Archbishop of Cologne in 1837 for his resistance to Prussian legislation on mixed marriages. Gregory's opposition to building railways in his states was taken by European liberals as symbolic of his hostility to change of any kind. More importantly, he made the papacy increasingly seem the main obstacle to Italian unity.

The Italian Catholic revival had produced such major figures as the theologian Rosmini and the novelist Manzoni, and liberals like Count Cesare Balbo who sought an accommodation between the Church and the spirit of the age. Thus the priest Vincenzo Gioberti, in his *Moral and Civil Primacy of the Italians* (1843), defended the ideal of a united Italy under a papal presidency. Gioberti influenced Giovanni Maria Mastai-Ferretti, like Pius VII the Cardinal-bishop of Imola and, following the nineteenth-century convention by which a conservative pope was followed by a liberal one, the conclave of 1846 elected him pope, under the name of Pius IX, Pio Nono (1846–78), the longest ruling pope in history. Pius had pleaded for the rebels in 1831 and given a safe conduct to the young carbonaro Louis Napoleon. He now announced the release of a thousand political prisoners, an amnesty for hundreds of political exiles, and the appointment of a consultative lay council. When a dove alighted on his coach it seemed to liberals as if heaven had come to earth.

The papacy was the weak point in Metternich's congress system, and the election of a liberal pope led on to the 1848 revolutions. Charles Albert of Piedmont-Savoy went into battle to expel Austria from Italy in 1848, and the excitable Roman revolutionary clubs put pressure on Pius through great public demonstrations to join the Piedmontese crusade against Austrian rule. The papal minister, Count Pellegrino Rossi, and the papal chamberlain, Monsignor Palma, were assassinated, and Rome came under a committee of public safety which made the pope a prisoner. He fled by night in a closed carriage to Gaeta, carrying the Blessed Sacrament in a ciborium previously borne into exile by Pius VI. An elected assembly in Rome in February 1849 declared a Roman republic, under the leadership of a soldier of fortune, Giuseppe Garibaldi, soon to be joined by the visionary journalist Giuseppe Mazzini, for whom the new republican Rome, as the symbol of a universal regenerate humanity, would supersede the

Pope Pius IX. Portrait in oil.

former Romes of the universal empire and papacy.

The victory of Austria over Piedmont at Novara in 1849 restored Austrian rule in northern Italy, while a French army overthrew the Roman republic and reinstated the papal power. Pius was henceforth the most resolute of the public enemies of liberalism, a course confirmed by the attacks upon the religious orders and ecclesiastical jurisdiction in Piedmont in the 1850s by the chief minister, Count Camillo di Cavour. The victory of France over Austria in 1859 brought about the union, in 1861, of most of Italy under the anticlerical government of King Victor Emmanuel II, ruling in Turin. This new Italy included the papal legations, which voted overwhelmingly in suspect plebiscites for union with Piedmont.

Rome itself was protected by a French force until 1870, but the pope's predicament had an enormous impact on ultramontane European Catholics, some of whom volunteered to fight for him. The mystical and visionary elements in Romanticism contributed to a major Catholic revival, while new apparitions of the Virgin, to St Catherine Labouré in 1830, at La Salette in 1846 and

*The election of the pope
with Castel Sant' Angelo in
the background. Painting
by Antonio Joli (1700–77).*

at Lourdes in 1858 were, after some initial hesitation, given official encouragement. Our Lady of Lourdes confirmed to a peasant girl, Bernadette, the dogma of the Immaculate Conception, which was defined by Pius in 1854 and commemorated by a monument in Rome. The spread of Marian pietism went with what one convert from the Church of England, Frederick William Faber, called 'devotion to the pope'. The greatest propagandist of this new populist ultramontanism in its political aspect was a French journalist, Louis Veuillot, while its high priest was an ex-Anglican archdeacon, Henry Edward Manning. It created a popular culture through the new means of industry and communication, in mass-produced newspapers, books, pictures and devotional objects, with the pope's portrait in

Catholic presbyteries, schools and homes. This underlies Cardinal Wiseman's comparison, in his hymn 'God bless our pope', of ultramontane loyalty with the electric telegraph. It was in this triumphalist mood that the pope negotiated concordats with Spain (1851 and 1859) and Austria (1855), restored the episcopal hierarchies of England and Wales (1850) and Holland (1853), and vastly extended the Catholic hierarchy in the mission fields in Africa and Asia pioneered by the French, and in the United States and the British Empire as the Church grew through European and especially Irish emigration.

Pius himself was a great admirer of English technology, and commissioned an English screw steamship called the *Immaculate Conception*. Ideological liberalism was something else, and the persecution of the Church by anticlerical liberals called from him in 1864 the encyclical 'Quanta cura' and its accompanying *Syllabus of Errors*, a list of the eighty great errors of the age. These errors were largely taken from previous papal responses to attacks upon the Church in its Latin heartland, and need to be read carefully in context, but they did not properly distinguish between the northern European liberalism which gave a new freedom to the Church to open churches and monasteries, and the Latin liberalism which wanted to close them down. The astute Bishop Dupanloup of Orleans suggested that the Syllabus described an ideal world in which everyone was Catholic, not the real world in which the Church must compromise. Meanwhile, great international gatherings of priests and bishops in Rome, for the canonizaton of the Japanese martyrs in 1862 and for the eighteenth centenary of St Peter's martyrdom in 1867, provided the preliminary to Pio Nono's decision to call an ecumenical council for 1869.

It was this council which set the seal on the triumph of the Holy See within the Church by declaring the pope infallible in matters of faith and morals, a decisive repudiation of all the forms of Gallicanism which had so haunted Rome for centuries. The decree on papal jurisdiction over the whole Church was also far reaching, and the withdrawal of the European states from involvement in religious matters during the next half century made it realizable. But the outbreak in 1870 of the Franco-Prussian war caused the departure of the French garrison from Rome and its occupation by Italy, and so with the loss of French protection, the council dispersed with its business incomplete, while the pope retreated from his city as 'the prisoner of the Vatican' to rule his new empire of the spirit.

European reaction to Vatican I was generally hostile. Italy remained largely estranged for a generation, though one of Pio Nono's last acts was to pardon his despoiler Victor Emmanuel II so that he could die with the rites of the Church. Austria repudiated its concordat, while in the new predominantly Protestant German Reich formed in 1871 after the Prussian defeat of France in 1870, Otto von Bismarck launched a persecution of

Catholicism called the *Kulturkampf* from which German Catholicism emerged strengthened and renewed. Some middle-class Catholics who rejected the Vatican decrees went off to found or join the Old Catholic Churches in union with Utrecht. In France, ultramontanism provoked anticlericalism, leading to the separation of Church and state in 1905. Pio Nono was the maker of the modern papacy. His strategy of opposition to modernity had its losses and gains. The true reward or cost is known to God alone.

FURTHER READING

Chadwick, Owen, *The Popes and European Revolution*, Oxford 1981

Gross, Hanns, *Rome in the Age of Enlightenment: the post-Tridentine syndrome and the ancien regime*, Cambridge 1990

Hales, E. E. Y., *The Catholic Church in the Modern World*, London 1958; *Pio Nono: a study in European politics and religion in the 19th century*, London 1954; *Revolution and Papacy, 1769–1846*, London 1960

Heimann, Mary, *Catholic Devotion in Victorian England*, Oxford 1995

Heyer, Friedrich, *The Catholic Church from 1648 to 1870*, London 1969

I am very grateful for Dr Mary Heimann's many improvements and suggestions for this essay.

Dedication page of Historia calchographica septemdecim annorum M. Iubilaei by Giuseppe Bianchini of Verona, priest of the Roman Oratory, published in Rome in 1750. The author dedicated the book to Pope Benedict XIV for his jubilee year, and this shows the medallions of the popes who had proclaimed previous jubilee years. The medallions are set into the façade of St Peter's, Rome.

THE PAPACY IN THE TWENTIETH CENTURY

1878–THE PRESENT DAY

MICHAEL J. WALSH

WHEN PIUS IX DIED thirty-seven cardinals were present in Rome. On 8 February, the day after his death, they met to discuss where the conclave should be held which would elect a successor. The majority were in favour of holding the election outside the city, preferably in Spain, but by the following day they had changed their minds. As Cardinal Di Pietro reminded them, the government of Italy had promised not to interfere, and no other country had invited them. So they stayed, and on 20 February chose Cardinal Gioacchimo Vincenzo Pecci, who took the name Leo XIII. All conclaves since then have been held in the Vatican.

This time cardinals travelled to Rome by rail and by steamship in a way hitherto impossible. When the electoral college had gathered all but three of the world's sixty-four cardinals were present. Though national boundaries had been different when they were born, the majority could be described as Italians. Nevertheless there was a substantial minority of other nationalities, including two Englishmen. Among those who did not arrive in time were the Archbishops of Dublin and of New York.

The new pope would no longer be ruler of the papal states, so for once the conclave was free from pressure from the great powers. Pecci was chosen on the third ballot. He was almost sixty-eight, his health not good. His early career had been spent in the service of the papal states, then as a papal diplomat in Belgium. He was appointed Archbishop of Perugia in 1846, and cardinal seven years later. Absorbed in episcopal life in Perugia, he was not particularly well known in Rome, at least partly because Cardinal Antonelli, Pius IX's secretary of state, did not trust him. Pius himself brought him to Rome after Antonelli's death, however, and made him *camerlengo*, the cardinal whose tasks included organizing the conclave. He did this with such efficiency that the electors were impressed – and, after active lobbying by the English Cardinal Manning among others, selected him. Pecci's choice of the name Leo XIII, in honour of Leo XII whom he greatly admired, was understood as a rejection of the policies of his recent predecessors.

Pope Leo XIII (1878–1903) showed himself much readier
than his long-lived predecessor to come to terms with the
modern world. Painted photo, 1890.

Salve

S. Tomaso d'Aquino

Madonna del Rosario

Religio

Fama

LEO XIII.
Pontifex maximus

Lazzaretto Pontificio

Abside Lateranense

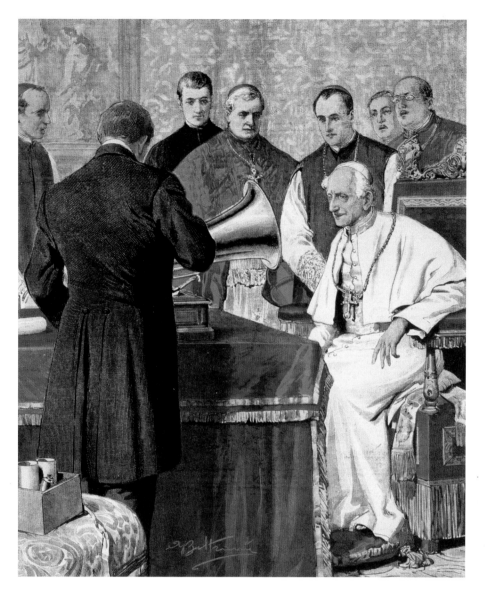

Pope Leo XIII speaks words of blessing on phonograph, 1903. He was within six months of his death after what was one of the longest pontificates in the Church's history.

'the workers' charter', even though the overall tone was conservative.

Leo was aware that the Church had to reach an understanding with the countries of Europe – and elsewhere – if Catholics were to live in harmony in these states. There was little chance of an accommodation with the new kingdom of Italy, but his diplomatic skills brought a fairly swift end to the campaign against the Church in Germany – which in any case Bismarck was by this time himself eager to resolve. The rather sharper confrontation in Switzerland took a while longer and some restrictions, such as those on the Jesuits, lasted well into the twentieth century. In French affairs he was considerably less successful. Here the battle between Church and state was ostensibly over control of the education system, but that masked an even greater hostility towards the republic on the part of Catholics working for the restoration of a Catholic monarchy. Pope Leo urged French Catholics to become reconciled to the republic, a call they received unenthusiastically. The government ignored it and, in the reign of Leo's successor, was to pass even more draconian legislation against the Church: although freedom of worship was guaranteed, all property was seized. The law of 9 December 1905 provided for some of this property – churches, presbyteries, seminaries – to be invested in 'religious associations', a solution accepted by the Protestant and Jewish communities in France, but rejected by Pius.

If this diplomatic initiative of Leo's was a failure, that should not obscure his successes. Possibly more important in the long term was the encouragement he gave to Catholic scholars, in particular to return to the study of the great medieval theologian Thomas Aquinas, and also to the study of scripture – though towards the end of his pontificate, alarmed by the path biblical scholars were taking, he founded the Biblical Commission to keep an eye on their activities. They were, very largely, applying methods of historical research to the texts of the scriptures. One of Leo's most important acts was to lay open the Vatican archives to those who wished to examine them. The Church has nothing to fear from

It is not that he was strikingly more liberal than they. The centralizing tendencies in the Church continued unabated – encouraged, indeed, by a series of jubilee celebrations which brought crowds of pilgrims into the city. Starting in the first year of his pontificate, he published a series of encyclicals on political issues which displayed an intransigent attitude toward the modern world. But in 1891 came the encyclical 'Rerum novarum' which condemned the excesses of industrial society, and insisted labourers be paid a just wage and be allowed to form 'associations' in defence of their rights. 'Rerum novarum' has, somewhat romantically, been called

Among Roman Catholics Pope Leo XIII is particularly remembered for writing Rerum Novarum, *an encyclical letter sometimes hailed as 'the charter of the working classes'.*

history, he declared. It was, as Professor Owen Chadwick remarked, 'one of the most liberal acts in an illiberal century'. His successor was to prove much less amenable.

Leo XIII had been born into the minor nobility; Giuseppe Melchior Sarto was the son of a postman and a seamstress. Although he was a similar age to Leo on his election, his route to the papacy had been entirely different. He had worked his way, as Pecci had never done, from country curate to Bishop of Mantua. Leo had simultaneously appointed him patriarch of Venice and cardinal in 1893. He had

been an outstandingly successful pastoral bishop, and, as the Italian cardinals had observed, was able to mediate between the Italian government and the Church: the stand-off between the two was now an embarrassment that had to be resolved.

Pope Leo died on 7 July 1903. The conclave met on 1 August: this time the American Cardinal James Gibbons, Archbishop of Baltimore, arrived in time. There were twenty-four foreign cardinals in attendance, well outnumbered by thirty-eight Italians. One of the foreigners, Cardinal Jan Puzyna, made conclave history on the second day by abruptly ruling out, on behalf of the Austro-Hungarian emperor, Leo's secretary of state Mariano Rampolla. Puzyna was Archbishop of Cracow, then part of the empire, and the emperor had many reasons to oppose Rampolla.

Through the machinations of the English Cardinal Vaughan, in the bull 'Apostolicae curae' of 1896, Leo had condemned Anglican orders as 'absolutely null and utterly void', but in other ways he had been sympathetic to a rapprochement between the Churches of England and Rome. More importantly, however, he had been eager to establish links with the Churches of the east, and improve relationships with both Russia and the Balkan states. The Austrian emperor saw Rampolla's pro-Slav and, for that matter, his pro-French, policy as unfriendly towards his devotedly Catholic monarchy, and several other cardinals agreed.

It had seemed likely that Rampolla would have been elected: he was well in front at the first ballot, before Puzyna exercised the emperor's veto. Even after the veto there remained a protest vote for him

and, although support gradually shifted to Sarto, at the conclusive ballot on 4 August Rampolla still received ten votes. Sarto, however, was elected with fifty votes. His choice of the name Pius X indicated a return to the policies of Leo's predecessor, the pope who had so roundly condemned the errors of liberalism. Rampolla was not confirmed in office as secretary of state. Instead Pius X chose Cardinal Rafael Merry del Val, the London-born and partly English-educated son of a Spanish nobleman and diplomat, who had been secretary to the conclave. It was the first time such an office had been entrusted to a non-Italian, though his extensive travels and knowledge of languages made him an obvious choice. As for the ban exercised against Rampolla, the following January Pius X abolished the right of veto.

The new pope soon set up a commission to codify the law of the Church, something resented by many in the Curia (which, incidentally, he reorganized and made more efficient) because the notion of having a 'code' of canon law seemed to them too reminiscent of the *Code Napoléon*, and therefore of the detested French revolution. He was concerned about the standard of worship in Catholic Churches, and in particular about that of music: he attempted to restore congregational singing. He is particularly remembered for urging the frequent, even daily, reception of the Eucharist, and for encouraging children to receive communion as soon as they reached the age of reason. He was renowned for the simplicity of his personal life, and for impatience with public ceremonial. He took the side of the poor and the oppressed, and was outstandingly generous in charitable giving. For all these things and more he came to be regarded by the Catholic world at large, but especially by the people of Rome, as something of a saint, a reputation enhanced even during his lifetime by reports of miracles. Less than a decade after his death the first steps were taken in the process which led in 1954 to his canonization. Yet despite all the benefits his pontificate brought to the Church, his reign is overshadowed by the disaster of the campaign against modernism.

Pope Pius XI (1922–39), seen here in a formal pose, had been an enthusiastic mountaineer before his election.

condemning sixty-five propositions concerned with theology and exegesis; the following September Pius' encyclical 'Pascendi' described, named, and condemned the 'modernist' approach to the Bible and to doctrine. Then, in November, the pope decreed that all the decisions of the Pontifical Biblical Commission, to which exegetical problems had to be referred, were to be accepted by all Catholics – not only those which had already been issued, but all that would be issued in future. They were to be accepted as if they were the word of the pope himself. These decisions have since all been repealed.

Even worse was the persecution that followed. It briefly caught up even the future Pope John XXIII. An oath was introduced, to be taken by all professors and parish priests; networks of informers were established to check on the orthodoxy of teachers and preachers. This system of spies was known to Pius X, who did nothing to stop it; Merry del Val was also deeply implicated. At the same time encouragement was given to right-wing political and cultural movements. Catholics, though urged to take an active part in the life of their nations through Catholic Action, were to do so only under the strict guidance of the bishops. It was an extraordinarily severe, and remarkably effective, effort to reduce the influence of modern scholarship on the teachings of the Church. When Benedict XV was elected to succeed Pius X he made it clear from his very first encyclical that the campaign of terror had to stop. And so it did, thanks to the demotion of Merry del Val, to the pope's own hostility to what had been happening, and most of all, perhaps, to the outbreak of the first world war.

It is sometimes said that the war hastened Pius' death, yet international politics had never been a major consideration in his pontificate. France had seemed to go irrevocably down an anticlerical path, and the Vatican gave support to the ardently nationalistic Action Française – though five of its leader's writings and the movement's journal were condemned before the end of the pontificate. In Italy he permitted bishops to lift in individual cases the ban on Catholics taking part in politics, imposed by Pius IX in 1868. But this action was inspired more by

The Church had confronted the challenge of the modern world in the time of Pius IX, who had rejected it in the *Syllabus of Errors*. Leo XIII had been much more sympathetic to the scholarship of his day, especially historical scholarship, though alarmed by the impact of history on the study of scripture. By December 1903 Pius X had placed on the *Index of Forbidden Books* five works by the French exegete Loisy. More condemnations followed, both of scripture scholars and theologians. Even historians were not exempt. In July 1907 the Holy Office issued a decree, 'Lamentabili',

a fear of socialism than by any liberal sentiment. He did not share his predecessor's interest in the Christians of the east, and considered it of the utmost importance that the Austro-Hungarian Empire should hold sway in the Balkans as a Catholic bulwark against Russian, and therefore orthodox, expansion. Though he may have expected the events in Sarajevo to have only local significance, it nevertheless seems that Merry del Val gave the Vatican's support to Austrian demands on the Serbs. Only a very few months earlier the Holy See had signed a concordat with Serbia.

Once the war had broken out the pope declared himself ready to mediate, but it was left to his successor to be a real force for peace. Pius X died on the night of 19–20 August. As the cardinals gathered in Rome the armies were already marching. It was imperative, therefore, that the electors should choose someone with diplomatic skills, and there were also those in the conclave which met on 31 August who wanted an end to the persecution of modernism. In Giacomo della Chiesa, elected on the tenth ballot on 3 September 1914, they got their ideal candidate.

But only just. The papal electors need not necessarily choose a cardinal, but six centuries had passed since someone who was not of that rank had been selected: della Chiesa had been created a cardinal less than four months earlier. His see, Bologna, where he had been enormously successful in very difficult circumstances, was in normal circumstances a cardinatial one. But he had been sent there to exile him from the Curia, where he had been a supporter of Leo's secretary of state, Mariano Rampolla.

A formal photograph to mark the signing of the Lateran Pacts in 1929: Mussolini is seated on the right of the photo, Cardinal Gasparri on the left.

Vatican to handle relations with the east, and also an institute, run by the Jesuits, to study the history, theology, spirituality and law of the eastern Christian communities. The law was important, for in 1917 the codification of the western Church's rules and regulations, begun under Pius X , was completed and published as the *Codex Iuris Canonici*, the code of canon law.

The code had been the responsibility of the remarkable Cardinal Pietro Gasparri, whom Benedict chose to be his secretary of state, and who was closely associated with the pope in his efforts, sadly fruitless, to hasten the end of the war. The pope established a missing persons' bureau to link prisoners of war and their families at home (which he was forced to close when it was denounced as a front for espionage); he instructed the clergy to visit and to comfort prisoners of war, and distributed aid to countries devastated in the conflict. He gave away so much of the Vatican's wealth that a loan had to be raised to pay for his burial.

His most important wartime initiative was the seven-point peace plan which proposed disarmament and international arbitration to settle disputes. He sent a note containing his suggestions to the warring parties at the beginning of August 1917. Austria and Great Britain were sympathetic; Germany was opposed, and so was the United States, which had joined in the war only the previous April. The rejection of his plan disappointed the pope: he had attempted neutrality in the conflict, but each side believed he favoured the other.

There was, indeed, a sense in which he favoured France. The French had been less than enthusiastic about the peace plan, but he was determined that diplomatic relations should be restored between the Holy See and the Quai d'Orsay, a *rapprochement* marked in 1920 with the canonization of Joan of Arc. He posed problems for the colonial powers, however, in 1919 by an encyclical calling for the better education of indigenous clergy in missionary territories, instructing the congregation in charge of the Church's missionary activity to establish regional seminaries for training local priests.

Left:
Pope Pius XI photographed at the opening of the reorganized Vatican library in 1933: he had served as a librarian first in Milan and then at the Vatican.

The new pope took the name of Benedict to pay tribute to the last pope to be elected from the see of Bologna. But it also marked a distinct break with the pontificate which had just ended. Merry del Val was moved aside and put in charge of the Holy Office, shackled by the new pope's first encyclical of 1 November 1914 which made it clear that the persecution of 'modernists' had to stop. He encouraged Christian unity – the octave of prayer for unity was promulgated to the whole Catholic Church in 1916, and the Malines conversations between Anglicans and Catholics began in the closing month of his pontificate. He was also interested, as Leo had been and Pius X had not, in the eastern Churches, establishing in 1917 a special department in the

In the resolution of 'the Roman question', the status of the Vatican within the kingdom of Italy, he appeared to make no progress. But there was a secret meeting between Gasparri and Benito Mussolini which paved the way for the Lateran pacts. Negotiations were concluded in the pontificate of Benedict's successor.

Benedict died unexpectedly on 22 January 1922. The conclave started on 2 February with seven of the sixty cardinals missing. The Americans did not arrive in time, and one of the new pope's first acts was to extend the time permitted between the death of a pontiff and the opening of the conclave. In 1914 it had taken ten ballots to elect della Chiesa; now it took fourteen to choose Achille Ratti. He was papabile from the beginning of the conclave, but at first it looked as though the favoured candidate was Merry del Val, who won most support in the first ballot. Finally, however, it became a contest among Ratti, Gasparri and the patriarch of Venice, Cardinal Pietro la Fontaine. In the documents gathered for a possible canonization of Merry del Val there is the testimony that he had been a man of enormous ambition, and during the conclave had broken the rules seriously enough to incur excommunication. If true, it can only have been either for breaking conclave secrecy, of which there is no evidence, or because he canvassed for his own election. When it became clear that he was not going to be elected, his supporters threw their votes behind Ratti to prevent Gasparri becoming pope. That tactic succeeded, but the newly elected Pius XI confirmed Gasparri as his secretary of state. No clearer sign could have been given that he intended, despite his choice of name, to continue his predecessor's policies.

He had, indeed, been a close collaborator with Benedict XV. Born in 1857, the son of a factory owner, he studied in Rome and went to teach in the major seminary in Milan, and then to the great Ambrosian library as a member of staff. He moved to the Vatican library and became its head in 1914. Benedict appreciated his many talents – which included mountaineering – and sent him to the newly created Polish republic in 1918, first as apostolic visitor and then with the rank of papal nuncio. Six

months before his election he became simultaneously a cardinal and Archbishop of Milan. The choice by the cardinals of Ratti, a relative newcomer to their ranks, has to be seen as an endorsement of the pontificate of Benedict XV, even though the election was so hard fought and he had been chosen by a compromise.

It soon became evident that the new pope's policies were similar to his predecessor's. Immediately after his election he gave his blessing to the world silently – but from the balcony of St Peter's looking out across Rome. This practice had ceased since the fall of Rome in 1870. The gesture indicated a readiness on Pius' part to reach an understanding

Pope Pius XII (1939–58), pictured here shortly after his election, was the last pope of modern times to come from an aristocratic background. Photo, 1939.

'Jews and Jesuits cannot shoot at us', says the slogan on the lorry. Many Jesuits were active in the campaign against Nazism. Undated German photograph.

with the kingdom of Italy. The secret meeting between Gasparri and Mussolini now bore fruit. Negotiations began in earnest – though still in secrecy – in August 1926, with Francesco Pacelli, brother of the future Pius XII and the Vatican's legal advisor, representing the Holy See. Mussolini and Gasparri signed the Lateran pacts on 11 February 1929, definitively putting an end to the 'Roman question'.

There were three agreements. The central one was a treaty between Italy and the Holy See, the governing authority of the Church. It recognized the Holy See's independence and sovereignty; it created an independent state, the Vatican City, within which the Holy See would reside and over which it would exercise sovereignty; and it guaranteed to keep open lines of communication between the Vatican and the rest of the world – telephone, postal and rail links: Italy even undertook to build a railway station in the Vatican. It thus became the smallest independent state in the world, only a third of the size of the principality of Monaco. It wisely undertook to remain neutral in any international conflict.

The second part was a concordat which regulated relations between Church and state in Italy, and the third was a financial settlement through which Italy undertook to compensate the Holy See for the loss of the papal states. The financial compensation was modest – Pius waived larger claims because of Italy's financial difficulties – but enough to provide funds for a long time to come.

The signing was greeted with satisfaction on all sides, but Mussolini had misunderstood its implications. He believed that the Church in Italy was now subordinated to the state. On this he was rapidly proved wrong – partly by the pope's refusal to support the Spanish bishops in their distress at the overthrow of the monarchy in their country in the spring of 1931, but more particularly by the activities of Catholic Action.

Catholic Action typified Pius' vision of the Church. He was a man of conservative theological views (displayed in his encyclical on marriage, 'Casti connubii', of December 1930), with an authoritarian cast of mind. He described Catholic Action as 'the participation of the laity in the apostolate of the hierarchy', thereby bringing all activity by lay people in the mission of the Church under the close supervision of their bishops. That at least was the theory. In Italy, however, where the Catholic and democratic Popular Party had been disbanded, those

The future Pope Pius XII
is saluted by a German
soldier when, as papal
nuncio (ambassador) to
Germany he leaves the
presidential palace in
Berlin, 1929.

of its leaders who had not gone into exile used Catholic Action as a means to continue the battle against the fascist state. In May 1931 Mussolini dissolved Catholic Action's youth organizations. Pius protested vigorously in an encyclical attacking fascism directly, and the youth groups survived though their political activity was curtailed.

The pope's attack on fascism was a surprise because only shortly before, in 'Quadragesimo anno', written to mark the fortieth anniversary of 'Rerum novarum', he had appeared to support it in a number of paragraphs which were, as is now known, added by Pius himself to the draft written for him by a Jesuit sociologist. In the aftermath of the economic crash of 1929, it is not surprising that the pope again stressed the importance of workers coming together to defend their interests – though not crossing denominational boundaries in doing so. The encyclical is famous for enunciating the 'principle of subsidiarity', insisting that a higher authority should not take over responsibility for activities which could perfectly well be done by people lower down the scale of command. This sensible principle is hardly one that the Church has applied to itself.

Pius' unwillingness to countenance inter-denominational trade unions reflects his unwillingness to permit Catholics to take part in the burgeoning ecumenical dialogue. Although the Malines conversations begun late in his predecessor's pontificate continued into his own, and though he encouraged links with the Orthodox Church and even sent a Jesuit missionary bishop into the Soviet Union (with disastrous consequences), he was really trying to bring dissidents back to the fold. After the 1925 'Life and Work' ecumenical conference in Stockholm his attitude hardened against what he regarded as a too liberal interpretation of doctrine. In his encyclical 'Mortalium animos' of January 1928, and under the influence of a conservative group of cardinals led by Merry del Val, he effectively forbade Catholic participation in ecumenical initiatives. In contrast he fostered links with the eastern-rite (uniate) Churches in communion with Rome, and encouraged the work of the Oriental Institute. He

also encouraged the development of an indigenous clergy, insisting against much opposition that missionary territories be handed over as soon as possible to locally born bishops.

Despite his early career as an academic, Pius XI emerged as a man of action rather than a theoretician. This may have been why, shortly after the signing of the Lateran pacts, he replaced Cardinal Gasparri with Cardinal Eugenio Pacelli as secretary of state. Pacelli's career had been almost entirely in the papal diplomatic service, and for over a decade he had been in Germany as nuncio, first in Bavaria and later in Berlin. He was therefore out of touch with the workings of the Vatican, and Pius may well have thought that he could more readily manipulate such a relatively inexperienced functionary. Whatever the reason for the appointment, it was providential. In the years leading up to the second world war Germany was the major problem occupying the Vatican, and Pius could scarcely have had an advisor more informed about German affairs than Pacelli.

Hitler had come to power in January 1933; at Easter that year he was asking for a concordat with the Holy See. It was the period of concordats: Pius XI signed a dozen of them during his pontificate, believing them to be the best way to preserve religious schooling and ecclesiastical control over marriage, as well as the freedom of the Church to exercise its mission. In such circumstances, and especially after one had been agreed with Austria, the Holy See could not reasonably refuse Hitler, whose government was prepared to accept everything the Holy See proposed. It was signed on 20 July: earlier concordats with individual German states remained in force. From then on Pacelli's battle was a continuous, losing, one to ensure that Germany fulfilled its obligations. Pius' anger eventually expressed itself in 'Mit brennender Sorge' ('With burning anxiety') of 14 March 1937. The encyclical was smuggled into Germany and dramatically read from pulpits, a condemnation of the whole ideology of racism and the overriding power of the state, though Nazism was not mentioned by name. Within a week another encyclical was published, 'Divini Redemptoris', explicitly condemning communism.

Pius XI died on 10 February 1939. As he had stipulated, the college of cardinals waited for the arrival of the Americans, and the conclave opened on 1 March. Pacelli was elected pope the following day after only three ballots, taking the name of Pius XII. There was a story that he had been chosen unanimously, the only contrary vote being his own, but it is probable that several votes went to the saintly Cardinal dalla Costa, Archbishop of Florence. Even so, the swiftness of the decision needs explaining. Pacelli had travelled widely as secretary of state, visiting the United States and Germany: with the second world war looming the electors must have felt the need to appoint someone with knowledge of the situation. Pius XI had been ill during the last two years of his life, and Pacelli had played an increasingly prominent role in running the Church.

The new pope assumed office shortly before the war broke out, and he was to govern the Church for nearly two decades. Yet the war years dominate any discussion of his pontificate. The Vatican has itself published twelve volumes of *Actes et documents du Sainte-Siège relatifs à la seconde guerre mondiale* which have fuelled, rather than resolved, the controversy surrounding the 'silence' of Pius XII on the massacre of European Jewry. They demonstrate two things: first that the Holy See knew what was going on, and second that individual prelates did as much as they possibly could – including the pope himself in Rome. But he never spoke out publicly against the atrocities. He may well have thought diplomatic means would prove more successful than overt condemnation. There were condemnations, but couched in such coded language that they could easily be overlooked. He may also have thought that public criticism would only bring even greater suffering. He had seen that happen to the Catholic Church in Germany after 'Mit brennender Sorge', and again in Holland after the Dutch bishops had spoken out against the persecution of the Jews.

Whatever reasons lay behind his silence, they were undoubtedly his own. Rarely has a pontiff been so clearly his own man, acting for almost all his pontificate without a secretary of state. He was a

The future Pope John XXIII, photographed here in 1905 just after finishing his studies and just before taking up his post as secretary to the Bishop of Bergamo.

Facing:
Pope John XXIII (1958–63) established a new, outgoing, friendly image of the papacy in contrast to the remoteness of his predecessor. Photo, 1962

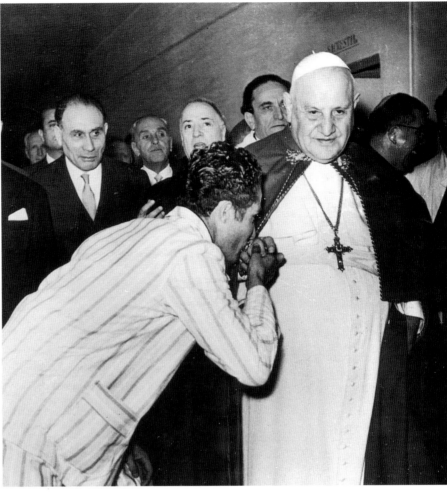

Pope John XXIII visited Rome's gaol at Christmas 1958, declaring that as the prisoners could not come to him, he would go to them.

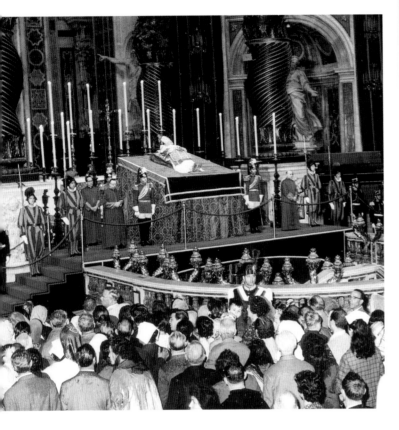

The death of Pope John XXIII brought messages of condolence from around the world, demonstrating how much he had succeeded in changing attitudes to Roman Catholicism during his pontificate.

man of high intelligence and of principle – and also of a remarkably deep spirituality which in practice somewhat separated him from those he governed. For many he became, and has remained, the ideal of what a pope should be. But in pursuit of that role he also became what has been described as 'the oracle of God'. He spoke frequently and at length on all the problems of the day, among which, in the immediate postwar years, was the problem of communism. He looked sympathetically on right-wing regimes in Spain, Portugal and Latin America. He avoided being uncritically pro-American – he condemned nuclear weapons, for instance – but was heavily dependent on the financial support of American Catholics.

Doctrinally, his pontificate is a puzzle. One of the most significant encyclicals of modern times was his 'Divino afflante spiritu' of 1943, in which he encouraged the study of scripture. This to some extent laid the ghost of the Biblical Commission's decisions under Pius X, and prepared the way for the theological scholarship which, in turn, paved the way for the second Vatican council. Yet, apparently fearful of what he had unleashed, in 'Humani generis' of 1950 he suppressed some of the teachings of the Church's most important theologians. Yet there were other encyclicals which showed Pius in a more progressive light, in particular 'Mediator Dei' on Church liturgy. This encyclical was followed by a number of minor practical measures which, however, did two things of long-term significance. First, the liturgical reforms made it easier for lay people to participate in the Church's worship; and second, they demonstrated that the liturgy was not after all immutable. Pius was also much more open than his predecessor to relations with other Churches.

Pius XII died on 9 October 1958. He had

created few cardinals during his pontificate. There were only fifty-one electors in the conclave which opened on the 25th of the same month, and lasted, with eleven ballots, until the 28th, when Angelo Giuseppe Roncalli was chosen, taking the title John XXIII. At the time he was seen as a surprise choice, even a stopgap until someone more appropriate emerged. It now seems, however, that Roncalli, who had spent most of his life in the papal diplomatic service – including, crucially, in Paris at the end of the war – before being appointed patriarch of Venice in 1953, had expected that the cardinals might very well elect him. He received only the barest minimum of votes (two-thirds plus one) for election. Next in line was the Armenian Cardinal Agagianian. The prospect of choosing a non-Italian had therefore been seriously considered long before the election of the Polish John Paul II. The Archbishop of Milan, Giovanni Battista Montini, received a few votes even though he was not yet a cardinal: it was one of John XXIII's first acts to raise him to that rank.

John XXIII was, on his election, only five years younger than Pius XII had been when he died, yet no pontiff in modern times has so transformed the face of Catholicism. He did this in part by his own simplicity, generosity and charm. More importantly, he did it by calling the second Vatican Council on 25 July 1959. This act is often treated as if it were a sudden decision. In fact John had thought it over carefully, as indeed his predecessor had done before deciding against it. But whereas every other council of the whole Church ('ecumenical' councils) had met to discuss doctrinal issues, the pope's intention was to have a gathering of all the bishops to bring the Church up to date: *aggiornamento* was the term used. In a speech, the exact meaning of which is much disputed, he said that the purpose of the council was to put into modern language the age-old teachings of Christianity. What occurred was an updating of the whole outlook of the Church, which was afterwards to show itself in changes in the liturgy (a simpler form of mass, the vernacular instead of Latin); in a greater openness not only to other Christian denominations, but also to those of other faiths, especially the Jews; and an assertion of collegiality, the notion that all the

bishops of the Church jointly share responsibility for its wellbeing and governance.

John's pontificate was short: he died on 3 June 1963, when he had been pope only a little over four and a half years. Yet he made an enormous impact both on the Church and on those outside. He was much more open to ecumenical contacts than had been his predecessors; the Archbishop of Canterbury was only one of many leaders of other Churches who visited him. He received the editor of the Moscow

newspaper *Izvestia* and his wife, the daughter of Nikita Khrushchev – thus beginning in a small way what was to become a major theme of his successor's papacy, the Vatican's *Ostpolitik*. When he was awarded the Balzan prize for his work for international understanding, the patriarch of Moscow sent congratulations and John replied, the first time a pope and the Moscow patriarch had engaged in a friendly exchange. He produced eight encyclicals, but will be remembered in particular for two, 'Mater et magistra' (1961) and 'Pacem in terris' (1963). In the former, for the first time, a pope discussed development aid and acknowledged a major role for the state in the organization of society, particularly in social welfare. In the latter he laid stress on peace and human rights. When he died expressions of sympathy were widespread and sincere; they came from Jewish, Muslim and

In January 1964 Pope Paul VI visited Jerusalem where he met the ecumenical patriarch Athanagoras I. A Roman Catholic pontiff had not met an Orthodox patriarch since 1439.

Pope John Paul II (1978–) kissing the ground at the airport at Vilnius, Lithuania, 1993. His visit to the Lithuanian capital was his first to any country formerly part of the Soviet Union.

Buddhist leaders as well as from Christians, and at the United Nations flags were flown at half-mast.

There was an obvious successor in Cardinal Montini, Archbishop of Milan. Even so there was a battle between the conservative faction who regretted the council, and those cardinals who were vigorous in its support: Montini had already let it be known that he belonged among the latter. In his last sermon before he left Milan for Rome he quoted John 21:18 and the words 'another will gird you and carry you where you do not wish to go'. He was in tears as he preached. To those who heard him the implication was clear – he did not expect to return to his diocese. But Montini was not the only candidate, and those who opposed the council were more united. Eventually votes swung his way. He was elected on 21 June, on the sixth ballot. His majority was only just enough: it seems that up to two dozen of the eighty electors who entered the Sistine chapel did not give him their backing.

Montini chose the name Paul to recall the adventurous spirit of the apostle Paul, but in reality

he was hesitant and in some ways unsure of himself. He was conscious that many of the cardinals of the Curia had not wanted him, and that made him rather timorous, trying to take the conservatives with him – or with the council, which was still going on during the early years of his pontificate. He was personally convinced of the values of ecumenical relations, but uneasy about Vatican II's document on ecumenism. He was even more concerned about the doctrine of collegiality and tried to water it down. Yet in both these areas he took important steps in the years after the council. He received two Anglican primates, and travelled to Istanbul to meet the Orthodox patriarch, who also visited Rome. The mutual act of excommunication of 1054 was finally lifted. He established regular meetings of the synod of bishops, consisting of elected representatives from episcopal conferences around the world, to debate matters of importance to the whole Church.

Paul's pontificate has been overshadowed by the encyclical 'Humanae vitae' of 1968, banning Catholics from using artificial means of

Pope John Paul II's reaching out to those of other faiths was dramatically exemplified by the World Peace Day gathering in Assisi on 27 October 1986.

contraception. A commission set up to advise the pope came down very firmly in favour of the legitimacy of contraception, and Paul's actions seemed to contradict the new openness the council was supposed to initiate. The ban was ignored by large numbers of Catholics, calling papal authority into question. He never again wrote an encyclical.

He did, however, write many other documents of considerable significance. 'Populorum Progressio', an encyclical published the year before 'Humanae vitae', spoke of 'development as the new name for peace', and even recognized that under certain circumstances armed revolution might be justifiable. 'Octagesimo adveniens' broke with the tradition that solutions were arrived at deductively, insisting that different answers had to be found for situations in different countries – he had just come back from a trip to the far east, where he had seen the problems for himself. But perhaps his most abiding memorial

will be 'Evangelii nuntiandi' ('On proclaiming the gospel'), which linked the Church's missionary activity with urgent social concern. In words which resonated with the liberation theologians in Latin America, he saw evangelization as a liberation not only from sin but from every kind of oppression, social, political or economic.

Ecumenical relations appeared to flourish, especially those with the Anglicans; after four centuries the *Index of Forbidden Books* was abolished; relations with at least some of the countries in the Soviet bloc continued to improve; a new eucharistic liturgy was introduced. But there were also some crises which he bequeathed to the Church at his death on 6 August 1978. The controversy over birth control was not resolved. One archbishop, Marcel Lefèbvre, was threatening schism with a number of followers because of the changes the council had introduced; liturgical reforms were unpopular with many; there was a major financial scandal involving the Vatican Bank. But more personally distressing was the assassination of Aldo Moro, one of Italy's leading politicians and a friend since his days in the Curia when together they had battled against fascism.

The election of Paul's successor was swiftly achieved. One hundred and eleven cardinals met in conclave on 25 August. The following day Albino Luciani was chosen with 101 votes on the fourth ballot. He was God's candidate, said Cardinal Hume. Luciani's choice of title was to combine those of John and Paul – no other pope had ever had two names. He had risen through the ranks, both as an academic and as a pastor. His family had been socialist and, though he had moved to the right, especially while patriarch of Venice, he was able to establish good relations with members of the communist party when need be. He was a humble man, rejecting the ceremonial of a papal coronation. At a press conference – itself a novelty – he admitted that, had he not entered the priesthood, he might well have become a journalist. On the morning of 28 September he was found dead in his bed. Rumour immediately suggested he had been murdered, perhaps to stop him investigating the Vatican Bank affair or because officials had

Pope John Paul II frequently preached to the crowds below him from this window in the Vatican's papal apartments. Photo, 1994.

discovered he was about to reverse the teaching on birth control. More confusion was created by concealing the fact that he had been found by a nun, bringing him an early-morning cup of coffee.

The conclave began on 14 October. The name 'conclave' comes from Latin, meaning 'with a key': it was to be the last of its kind because John Paul I's successor changed the rules so that the electors would no longer be locked into a small area of the Vatican palace, but have more comfortable accommodation elsewhere, coming into the Sistine chapel to vote. It was also an historic gathering because for the first time the non-Europeans outnumbered the cardinals from Europe. There were eight ballots. The battle seems at first to have been between the Cardinal of Genoa, Giuseppe Siri, representing the conservative members of the Sacred College, and the Cardinal of Florence, Giovanni Benelli; the first seen as the conservative successor to Pius XII, the second as the liberal successor to Paul VI. It became clear that the election would be long, since neither side was prepared to yield. At this point the Cardinal of Vienna, the highly respected Franz König, emerged as something of a campaign manager for the Polish Karol Wojtyla, Archbishop of Cracow. Wojtyla, like John Paul I, had risen through the ranks both academically (he had doctorates in theology and philosophy) and pastorally. He spoke many languages. He had experience of communism, fitting him to carry on the Ostpolitik as well as to deal with the growing communist party in Italy. He was also wrongly thought by many to be a liberal. Voting quite suddenly swung his way, and he appears to have been elected by approximately 100 votes out of 111. He took the name John Paul II.

'I speak to you in your - no, our - language', he said when he went out on to the balcony of St Peter's for the traditional blessing. Once over the shock of the first non-Italian pope since 1522, the crowd cheered vigorously. In his younger days he had been both actor and play-wright: to some the verbal stumble seemed contrived. Yet it demonstrated his remarkable rapport with his audience which, coupled with his travels to every part of the world, made him an

unprecedentedly international figure. He was welcomed in every country in the world with a substantial Catholic population - and in many where Catholics are a tiny minority. The Holy See's diplomatic representation has doubled in size; presidents and prime ministers have been eager to be seen in his presence; his most enthusiastic biographer credits him as having worked with the CIA to bring down communism in eastern Europe.

He had, of course, a personal acquaintance with the problems of eastern Europe, and constantly insisted on the integration of the former eastern bloc into a single European community. His dealings with the eastern Churches, however, were less than happy. Even the eastern-rite Churches in communion with Rome were dissatisfied - though they had been at least as dissatisfied under Paul VI. Relations with the Orthodox Churches, which Paul VI had so diligently cultivated, have deteriorated sharply with the revival of the uniates after the collapse of the Soviet Union, and especially when John Paul established Latin-rite bishoprics in Russia.

He did not have the same degree of interest as

Regular trips to make the papacy better known, such as this to the Philippines in 1981, were a feature of John Paul II's pontificate.

had Pope Paul in the Anglican communion, and regarded with horror the decision of the Church of England to ordain women to the priesthood. He reiterated his opposition to women priests, and wrote to Catholic bishops to forbid any further debate on the topic. He did not succeed, any more than by a simple prohibition he could prevent Catholics from practising contraception. But he tried both by exhortation and, on the international scene, by diplomacy: the Cairo conference on population and development held by the United Nations in September 1994 found the Vatican's representatives in curious alliance with Islamic fundamentalists. In contrast, his social teaching has generally been hailed as progressive, both by what he has said to the poor- and to dictators – around the world, and by what he has written. His encyclical 'Sollicitudo rei socialis' (1987) raised an outcry, particularly in the United States, for implying a 'moral equivalence' between the ideologies of capitalism and communism. It was a view from which he retreated, apparently being readier to sympathize with the capitalist system, though without ever abandoning a passion for justice.

He held a high view of the authority of the papacy, one common before the Vatican Council of the 1960s, but which many Catholics believed to have been superseded by the declarations of that council. His flair for exploiting the media went hand in hand with deeply conservative theological convictions. The ultra-reactionary Archbishop Lefèbvre clearly thought he had a better chance of remaining in the Church under John Paul II than under Paul VI, though efforts to keep him in the fold ultimately failed. Cardinal Joseph Ratzinger, the outstanding conservative theologian of his generation (elected Pope Benedict XVI on 19th April 2005), was chosen to be the guardian of orthodoxy as head of the Congregation for the Doctrine of the Faith.

He published many encyclicals – well written, well argued and too long, including important ones on social issues. In 'Veritatis splendor' (1993) on ethics he seemed on the point of claiming infallibility for his teaching, but finally did not do so. Theologians have been restive, especially after being told to conform to Vatican thinking. A number of them were summoned before Ratzinger's congregation to explain their views. Hans Küng had his authority to teach as a Catholic professor withdrawn. Leonardo Boff was silenced, and eventually forced to resign the priesthood. In France a progressive bishop was summarily removed from office. Only once did he appear to have had a major change of heart. In 1984 an instruction from the Congregation for the Doctrine of the Faith was harshly critical of liberation theology; two years later another was more sympathetic.

On 13 May 1981, in St Peter's Square, Mehmet Ali Agca attempted to assassinate John Paul II. It is still not clear whether he was a lone Turkish terrorist, or whether the KGB lay behind it, alarmed at the pope's influence on the countries of the eastern bloc. The pope was rushed to the Gemelli clinic, where a room – now a suite – is kept for such emergencies. He changed the rules for the conclave, and, it is reported, wrote his resignation, to be used were he ever to be impeded from fulfilling his office. As it happened, Pope John Paul II died on April 2nd 2005, aged 84, in his private apartment. His health had deteriorated severely over the past weeks, but he continued to draw enormous crowds to his last few public appearances, where he was seen to be suffering great pain and was unable to speak after an emergency tracheotomy. Thousands of pilgrims gathered in St Peter's square and in his native Krakow, keeping vigil until the news finally came. On the evidence of past successions, Joseph Ratzinger, elected Pope Benedict XVI on 19th April 2005, will probably be quite unlike the man he replaced.

FURTHER READING

Aubert, Roger, *et al.*, *The Christian Centuries V: The Church in a Secularised Society*, London 1978

Chadwick, Owen, *Catholicism and. History: The Opening of the Vatican Archives*, Cambridge 1978

Hebblethwaite, Peter, *John XXIII*, London 1984; *Paul VI*, London 1993

Holmes, J. D., *Papacy in the Modern World*, London 1981

Jedin, Hubert (ed.), *History of the Church: vol. IX The Church in the Industrial Age; vol. X, The Church in the Modern Age*, London 1981

Walsh, M. J., *John Paul II*, London 1994

Facing:
Families were a common theme of the moral teaching of John Paul II, and he promoted gatherings such as this in the Vatican, 1994.

BISHOPS OF ROME

IN THE CONTEXT OF WORLD EVENTS

The list of popes is taken from that published in the Vatican's official yearbook, the *Annuario Pontificio*. Their dates, however, are mainly taken from J. N. D. Kelly's *Oxford Dictionary of the Popes* (Oxford 1986). It does not include antipopes or claimants of the Avignon or Pisan obediences during the Great Schism.

1	St Peter	?	67?	That Peter was in Rome is not now much disputed; it is, however, anachronistic to refer to him as 'Bishop' of Rome	43	Roman invasion of Britain
2	St Linus	67	76	Probably an historical person, but still not technically a bishop	45	Start of St Paul's journeys
3	St Anacletus	76	88	His name indicates that he was a Greek, possibly a slave	64	Nero's persecution of Christians
4	St Clement	88	97	A leading Christian spokesman in Rome, but still not a bishop		
5	St Evaristus	97	105	Again a Greek, but otherwise nothing is known of him	70	Fall of Jerusalem to Romans
6	St Alexander I	105	115	Nothing for certain is known of him, except that he was from Rome		
7	St Sixtus I	115	125	Also Roman, but possibly of Greek ancestry		
8	St Telesphorus	125	136	A Greek, probably, and almost certainly a martyr		
9	St Hyginus	136	140	It is claimed that he was from Athens, and formerly a philosopher		
10	St Pius I	140	155	The first leader of the Roman Church reasonably identifiable as a bishop		
11	St Anicetus	155	166	From Syria; it was probably Anicetus who erected the first memorial to St Peter on the Vatican hill	161	Marcus Aurelius emperor (d. 180)
12	St Soter	166	175	During his pontificate the annual celebration of the feast of Easter was introduced at Rome		
13	St Eleutherus	175	189	The first Bishop of Rome whose date of death can be fixed with any certainty		
14	St Victor	189	199	From Africa. He attempted to standardize the date on which Easter was celebrated according to the practice of the Church at Rome		
15	St Zephyrinus	199	217	Presented as a somewhat weak man, at a time when the Church was faced with many heresies		
16	St Callistus I	217	222	A freed slave, with a chequered career, who had been curator of the catacomb which still bears his name		
17	St Urban I	222	230	Little is known about him, except that he may have been faced with the first antipope of history, St Hippolytus		
18	St Pontianus	230	28 Sep 235	The first pope to abdicate – on being exiled to Sardinia (where he died) because of his leadership of the Church in Rome		
19	St Anterus	21 Nov 235	3 Jan 236	His short reign appears to indicate he died a martyr, but this is unlikely		
20	St Fabian	10 Jan 236	20 Jan 250	An able administrator, and a man held in great respect by his contemporaries; he was one of the first to die in the persecution of the Emperor Decius	250	Decius' persecution of Christians
21	St Cornelius	Mar 251	Jun 253	His election was delayed by the persecution, and contested by the rigorist Novatian		
22	St Lucius I	25 Jun 253	5 Mar 254	Banished on his election, he made his way back to Rome, but otherwise little is known of him		
23	St Stephen I	12 May 254	2 Aug 257	A powerful man, proud of the see of Rome's prerogatives		
24	St Sixtus II	Aug 257	6 Aug 258	Restored friendly relations with other Churches, damaged by his predecessor; martyred in the persecution of Valerian	258	Martyrdom of St Cyprian
25	St Dionysius	22 Jul 260	26 Dec 268	Reorganized the Church in the aftermath of Valerian's persecution		
26	St Felix I	3 Jan 269	30 Dec 274	Very little indeed is known about this pope		
27	St Eutychian	4 Jan 275	7 Dec 283	Again, little is known of his activities	276	Death of Mani, founder of Manichaeanism
28	St Caius	17 Dec 283	22 Apr 296	His name may possibly have been Gaius		
29	St Marcellinus	30 Jun 296	25 Oct 304	May have at first apostatized during the persecution of Diocletian, and perhaps was deposed, though later believed to have been a martyr	303	Persecution of Diocletian
30	St Marcellus	Nov/Dec 306	16 Jan 308	Possibly for a time himself an apostate, he treated other apostates harshly		
31	St Eusebius	18 Apr 310	21 Oct 310	Clashes between rival Christian parties in Rome led to exile, where he died		
32	St Miltiades	2 Jul 311	10 Jan 314	Pope when Constantine brought peace to the Church – received from him the palace of the Empress Fausta, the Lateran, henceforth to be the headquarters of the Bishop of Rome	312	Battle of Milvian Bridge
					313	'Edict' of Milan
					325	Council of Nicaea
33	St Sylvester I	31 Jan 314	31 Dec 335	Pope throughout the period of Constantine, but very little is known about him	331	Constantinople effective capital of empire
34	St Marcus	18 Jan 336	7 Oct 336	During his short reign the official listing of Rome's bishops was begun		
35	St Julius I	6 Feb 337	12 Apr 352	A vigorous defender of orthodoxy, a founder of churches in Rome, and responsible for reorganizing the work of the bishop's officials		
36	Liberius	17 May 352	24 Sep 366	Builder of the church which eventually became Santa Maria Maggiore; he was exiled for a time for his defence of orthodoxy, and Felix elected; he is the first Bishop of Rome not to be regarded as a saint		

#	Pope	Elected	Ended	Notes		Date	Event
37	St Damasus I	1 Oct 366	11 Dec 384	A follower of Felix; his election was marred by riots between Felix's supporters and Liberius'; a vigorous promoter of the authority of the pope			
38	St Siricius	Dec 384	26 Nov 399	Continued Damasus' policy of promoting the 'apostolic see' as lawgiver for western Christendom		387	Baptism of St Augustine (born 354)
39	St Anastasius I	27 Nov 399	19 Dec 401	In his short reign managed to repair some of the friendly relations damaged by his predecessor		401	Visigoth invasion of Italy
40	St Innocent I	11 Dec 401	12 Mar 417	The son of Anastasius; the most powerful advocate so far of the supreme teaching authority of the Roman see		410	Alaric's sack of Rome
41	St Zosimus	18 Mar 417	26 Dec 418	Possibly of Jewish origin; his heavy-handed style aroused opposition in Rome			
42	St Boniface	28 Dec 418	4 Sep 422	Had to deal with the unrest left by his predecessor		430	Death of Augustine
43	St Celestine I	10 Sep 422	27 Jul 432	The major battle over the nature of Christ came to a head in his reign		432	Start of St Patrick's mission to Ireland
44	St Sixtus III	31 Jul 432	19 Aug 440	Worked hard to reconcile the opposing parties in the christological dispute		436	Last Roman troops leave Britain
45	St Leo I	Sep 440	10 Nov 461	Is named 'the Great'; by his influence he vastly extended the power of the papacy; he persuaded Attila the Hun not to attack Rome; and is a Doctor of the Church			
46	St Hilarus	19 Nov 461	29 Feb 468	A close associate of Leo, whose policies he vigorously continued		451	Council of Chaledon
47	St Simplicius	3 Mar 468	10 Mar 483	His reign saw the end of any pretence of there being an emperor in the west		455	Rome sacked by Vandals
48	St Felix III	13 Mar 483	1 Mar 492	The first pope formally to announce his election to the emperor in the east; most of his time was spent on eastern affairs (Felix II, 355–65, was declared to be an antipope, and is not included)		479	Death of Romulus Augustus, last Roman emperor in the west
49	St Gelasius I	1 Mar 492	21 Nov 496	Established friendly relations with the 'barbarian' ruler of Italy; he formulated the theory of the 'two powers', civil and spiritual, but insisted on the primacy of the spiritual over the civil ('temporal')		496	Baptism of Clovis, king of the Franks
50	Anastasius II	24 Nov 496	19 Nov 498	Only the second pope not to be regarded as a saint; he was (wrongly) thought to have supported heretical opinions			
51	St Symmachus	22 Nov 498	19 Jul 514	His pontificate was marred by a schism in the Roman Church; he built a residence for the pope and his staff at St Peter's			
52	St Hormisdas	20 Jul 514	6 Aug 523	A rich man, and a supporter of Symmachus, he made great efforts to restore unity to the Roman Church			
53	St John I	13 Aug 523	18 May 526	Forced by Theodoric, the Gothic king of Italy, to travel to Constantinople to win concessions for Arians from the emperor; he was not wholly successful, and would have been imprisoned by Theodoric had he not died of old age			
54	St Felix IV	12 Jul 526	22 Sep 530	Moved definitively to side with Theodoric and his heirs		527	Justinian I emperor (d. 565)
55	Boniface II	22 Sep 530	17 Oct 532	Nominated by Felix because he was pro-Goth – he was of German ancestry		532	Founding of Santa Sophia in Constantinople
56	John II	2 Jan 533	8 May 535	The first pope to change his name			
57	St Agapetus	13 May 535	22 Apr 536	Sent, fruitlessly, by the Gothic king of Italy to persuade the emperor not to invade Italy; he had to pawn church plate to pay for his passage, and then died in Constantinople		534	Toledo capitol of Visigoth Spain
58	St Silverius	8 Jun 536	deposed1, 11 Mar 537, died 2 Dec 537	He was deposed after being accused of pro-Goth sentiments by the emperor's commander-in-chief Belisarius; probably died from the treatment he received; is regarded therefore as a martyr			
59	Vigilius	29 Mar 537	7 Jun 555	Belisarius imposed Vigilius on the Roman Church, but his theological orthodoxy was suspect, and he was twice imprisoned by the emperor; he died in Syracuse, Sicily, on his way back from Constantinople		546	Rome captured by Totila, king of the Ostrogoths
60	Pelagius I	16 Apr 556	3 Mar 561	Imposed on Rome by the emperor, but because he was thought to be implicated in the death of Vigilius, it was six months before he could be consecrated; however, his efficient administration of Rome, and relief of poverty, won him support		550	Rome taken by Totila again
61	John III	17 Jul 561	13 Jul 574	A pope of pro-eastern sentiments; otherwise little is known of his reign, partly at least because of the invasion of Italy by the Lombards		563	Foundation of St Columba's monastry of Iona
62	Benedict I	2 Jun 575	30 Jul 575	The delay in his consecration was caused by problems of communicating with Constantinople; he died during a siege of Rome by the Lombards		570	Birth of Muhammad (d. 632)
63	Pelagius II	26 Nov 579	7 Feb 590	He made the first – unsuccessful – appeal for the support of the Franks			
64	St Gregory I	3 Sep 590	12 Mar 604	One of the greatest popes, he had been prefect of Rome before becoming a monk; after his election he took charge of the temporal, as much as of the spiritual, governance of the city; he sent Augustine to England		596	Augustine sent by Gregory to convert English (arrived 597)
65	Sabinian	13 Sep 604	22 Feb 606	Peace with the Lombards, brokered by Gregory, collapsed in this reign			
66	Boniface III	19 Feb 607	12 Nov 607	Re-established good relations with Constantinople			
67	St Boniface IV	15 Sep 608	8 May 615	Kept friendly links with the emperor; turned the Pantheon into a church		614	Fall of Jerusalem to Persians
68	St Deusdedit (or Adeodatus I)	19 Oct 615	8 Nov 618	An elderly man, and the first priest to be elected pope for almost a century			
69	Boniface V	23 Dec 619	25 Oct 625	A kindly, generous man, but also a good administrator			
70	Honorius I	27 Oct 625	12 Oct 638	An efficient administrator of the papal estates and a vigorous bishop, he unfortunately became involved in theological controversy and adopted a view later condemned as heretical		637	Fall of Jerusalem to Arabs
71	Severinus	28 May 640	2 Aug 640	Became entangled in the controversy over the nature of Christ's will, though probably adhering to the opposite view to that of his predecessor			
72	John IV	24 Dec 640	12 Oct 642	From Dalmatia; attempted to clear Honorius of charge of heresy			

73	Theodore I	24 Nov 642	14 May 649	A Greek, and the son of a bishop, he had been born in Jerusalem, and had come to Rome probably as a refugee from the Arab invasions	645	Arrival of Nestorian missionaries in China
74	St Martin I	5 Jul 649	deposed 17 Jun 653, died 655	Accepted election without waiting for the emperor's permission, and opposed his religious policies; was arrested, taken to Constantinople and mistreated; he was deposed, and died in exile		
75	St Eugenius I	10 Aug 654	2 Jun 657	Elected while Martin was still alive, he attempted to restore good relations with Constantinople, but his conciliatory policy only made matters worse		
76	St Vitalian	30 Jul 657	27 Jan 672	More successful in improving relations with the emperor; he had a particular interest in Christianity in England. Established a singing school in Rome	664	Synod of Whitby
77	Adeodatus II	11 Apr 672	17 Jun 676	Little is known about him, though he was remembered as a generous man		
78	Donus	2 Nov 676	11 Apr 678	Again little is known, though in his reign Constantinople made efforts to improve relations with Rome		
79	St Agatho	27 Jun 678	10 Jan 681	Called a council which succeeded in reconciling the theological differences between Rome and Constantinople during his reign, though in the process Honorius I was condemned as a heretic		
80	St Leo II	17 Aug 682	3 Jul 683	A graduate of the papal choir school; his election probably occurred soon after Agatho's death, but consecration was delayed pending imperial ratification		
81	St Benedict II	26 Jun 684	8 May 685	Again, ratification was delayed by nearly a year, but the emperor agreed that in future his representative in Italy could give approval		
82	John V	23 Jul 685	2 Aug 686	From Antioch – perhaps a refugee – he played an important part in the papal administration before his election, but was ill for most of his pontificate		
83	Conon	21 Oct 686	21 Sep 687	Again elderly and ill – and also naive – he was the son of a general, and a compromise candidate between the papal militia and the Roman clergy		
84	St Sergius I	15 Dec 687	9 Sep 701	Chosen after a violently contested election, he proved an able administrator and a promoter of papal authority in the west; in the east he clashed with Emperor Justinian II, but was supported by the imperial troops in Italy	700	Arab conquest of North Africa complete
85	John VI	30 Oct 701	11 Jan 705	Events in Italy demonstrated that John VI had more support than the emperor in Constantinople, but John's reign was also marked by the growing power of the Lombards		
86	John VII	1 Mar 705	18 Oct 707	Son of a Byzantine official, he established friendly links with the Lombards but temporized over relations with Constantinople		
87	Sisinnius	15 Jan 708	4 Feb 708	Crippled with gout, he was pope for only four months, including the period before his election was ratified by Constantinople		
88	Constantine	25 Mar 708	9 Apr 715	Made a triumphant journey to Constantinople, where he was reconciled with Emperor Justinian – who was, however, overthrown shortly afterwards	712	Arab capture of Seville
89	St Gregory II	19 May 715	11 Feb 731	An able politician, he managed to establish friendly relations with the Lombards, and to resist excessive imperial demands in Italy; he rejected the iconoclasm of the Byzantine Emperor Leo the Isaurian	720 / 726	Arab capture of Narbonne / 'Peter's Pence' begun by Ine, king of Wessex
90	St Gregory III	18 Mar 731	28 Nov 741	Elected by acclaim on the death of his predecessor, he was the last pope to seek imperial ratification for his election; threatened by the Lombards, and with the emperor no longer able to help, Gregory turned for support to the Franks	732	Northward advance of Arabs stopped by Charles Martel
91	St Zacharias	3 Dec 741	15 Mar 752	Last of the Greek popes, and a consummate politician; he made peace with the Lombards, reached a *modus vivendi* with Constantinople, and was instrumental in transferring authority from the Merovingian to the Carolingian dynasty, an act of immense importance for the future of the papacy		
92	Stephen II (III)	26 Mar 752	26 Apr 757	He was aided by the Franks to recover from the Lombards territory to which the papacy laid claim (another man was elected just before him as Stephen II, but died two days later still unconsecrated)		
93	St Paul I	20 May 757	28 Jun 767	Brother of the previous pope, he continued his policy towards the Franks, and defended the incipient papal states with their help	759	Franks recapture Narbonne from the Arabs
94	Stephen III (IV)	7 Aug 768	24 Jan 772	Tried, somewhat ineffectually, to play the Lombard king against the Franks	771	Charlemagne crowned king of the Franks
95	Hadrian I	1 Feb 772	25 Dec 795	Sought, and received, assistance of Charlemagne against the Lombards, and recovered much of Italy for the papal states; also a considerable reformer in religious matters, both in Rome and among the Franks	778	Battle of Roncesvalles
96	Leo III	26 Dec 795	12 Jun 816	A controversial figure in Rome, he was supported by Charlemagne, who was crowned Roman Emperor by Leo in St Peter's on Christmas Day 800	806	Iona sacked by Norsemen
97	Stephen IV (V)	22 Jun 816	24 Jan 817	He crowned Charlemagne's successor as emperor at Rheims		
98	St Paschal I	24 Jan 817	11 Feb 824	A firm but unpopular pope who resented the authority exercised in Rome by the Frankish emperor		
99	Eugenius II	Jun 824	Aug 827	A pro-Frankish pope, who recognized the temporal sovereignty of the Franks over Rome; a vigorous opponent of iconoclasm	827	Arab invasion of Sicily and Sardinia
100	Valentine	Aug 827	Sep 827	Died after scarcely a month in office		
101	Gregory IV	827	25 Jan 844	Attempted to release the papacy from quite so much dominance by the Franks; also had to prepare fortifications around Rome against the Saracens		

102	Sergius II	Jan 844	27 Jan 847	Consecrated without ratification by Frankish emperor, who was annoyed and marched on Rome to reimpose his authority; he was regarded as an unscrupulous pope, and the sack of St Peter's and St Paul's by the Saracens was looked upon as his divine punishment.
103	St Leo IV	10 Apr 847	17 Jul 855	Built defences against Saracen attack, won back a measure of independence of the Franks, and instituted a number of reforms in the Church
104	Benedict III	29 Sep 855	17 Apr 857	A pious man; consecrated without Frankish consent, but efforts to replace him failed
105	Nicholas I	24 Apr 858	13 Nov 867	Known as 'the Great', he was a vigorous defender of papal authority both in the east and in the west, and of the independence of the Roman see
106	Hadrian II	14 Dec 867	Nov 872	In his reign the apostles of the Slavs, SS Cyril and Methodius, who evangelized the Slavs, visited Rome
107	John VIII	14 Dec 872	16 Dec 882	Preoccupied with defending Italy against the Saracens, to do which he had to cultivate alliances with both the Franks and Constantinople
108	Marinus I	16 Dec 882	15 May 884	Tried to improve relations with Constantinople whose Patriarch, Photius, had excommunicated Nicholas I in 867, and had been excommunicated in turn by Hadrian II
109	St Hadrian III	17 May 884	Sep 884	Continued the policy of friendship to Constantinople; a harsh man, possibly murdered
110	Stephen V (VI)	Sep 885	14 Sep 891	Turned from the Franks to the Duke of Spoleto to defend papal interests, crowning him emperor
111	Formosus	6 Oct 891	4 Apr 896	A bishop before his election, the first pope to be so; turned to the east Franks against the Spoletans, crowning their king, Arnulf, emperor; his corpse was exhumed nine months after his death by his successor-but-one and at a mock trial accused of abandoning his earlier bishopric
112	Boniface VI	11? Apr 896	26? Apr 896	Died of gout; he was unfrocked for immorality at the time of his election
113	Stephen VI (VII)	May 896	Aug 897	Switched back to the Spoletans for support; deposed and thrown into prison for his brutality, he was strangled in gaol
114	Romanus	Aug 897	Nov 897	A supporter of Formosus, he was deposed, though apparently not assassinated
115	Theodore II	Nov 897	Nov 897	Gave Formosus' body an honourable burial; reigned twenty days (see also Sergius III, no. 119)
116	John IX	Jan 898	Jan 900	Had the support of Lambert of Spoleto until Lambert's early death; a good, reforming pope
117	Benedict IV	May 900	Aug 903	There was no satisfactory military power protecting Rome, which fell into chaos; Benedict personally was a good man
118	Leo V	Aug 903	deposed 904, died Sep 904	Unusually, not a member of the Roman clergy; was deposed, and murdered in prison
119	Sergius III	29 Jan 904	14 Apr 911	Had been elected in Dec 897, but deposed almost immediately; in 904 took Rome by force
120	Anastasius III	Jun? 911	Aug? 913	Dominated, as his predecessor had been, by the Theophylact family
121	Lando	Aug? 913	Mar? 914	Son of a wealthy Lombard family, but little otherwise known of him
122	John X	Mar? 914	May 928	Something of a reformer, and was particularly proud of his part in the sea battle which defeated the Saracens; was deposed, probably for being too independent
123	Leo VI	May 928	Dec 928	A stopgap election, until a member of the Theophylact family was old enough
124	Stephen VII (VIII)	Dec 928	Feb 931	Another stopgap; virtually nothing is known about him
125	John XI	Mar 931	Dec 936	Almost certainly the illegitimate son of Pope Sergius; supported the reforms of monasticism which began at Cluny
126	Leo VII	3 Jan 936	13 Jul 939	Odo of Cluny came to Rome and undertook reform of the city's abbeys
127	Stephen VIII (IX)	14 Jul 939	Oct 942	Died in prison of his injuries, having fallen foul of the ruler of Rome, Alberic
128	Marinus II	30 Oct 942	May 946	Dominated by Alberic — even the papal coins bore Alberic's name
129	Agapitus II	10 May 946	Dec 955	Managed to re-establish links with the kings of France and of Germany
130	John XII	16 Dec 955	deposed 963, died 14 May 964-	Alberic's illegitimate son, and only 18 when he became pope as Alberic had insisted, he instituted the Holy Roman Empire, but promptly fell out with the emperor and was eventually forced to flee Rome; reputed to have suffered a stroke, from which he later died, while in bed with a married woman
131	Leo VIII	4 Dec 963	deposed 964, died 1 Mar 965	Illicitly elected when John XII was deposed by the Emperor Otto, he took over at John's death even though a layman
132	Benedict V	22 May 964	deposed 965 died 23 Jun 966	Also illicitly elected during his predecessor's pontificate, took over after his death, but was himself then deposed. He died, with a reputation for holiness, two years later
133	John XIII	1 Oct 965	6 Sep 972	Imposed against the will of the Romans by the Emperor Otto, he could govern only with imperial support
134	Benedict VI	10 Jan 973	Jul 974	Another pontificate which depended on imperial goodwill; murdered on the orders of an antipope
135	Benedict VII	Oct 974	10 Jul 983	Though close to the emperor, he was a vigorously reforming pope
136	John XIV	Dec 983	20 Aug 984	Again the emperor's choice, but after Otto II's death was thrown into gaol
137	John XV	Aug 985	Mar 996	Unpopular in Rome, he was active in the wider Church and was the first pope formally to carry out a canonization
138	Gregory V	3 May 996	18 Feb 999	A German, appointed by Otto III to whom he was related; an energetic, reforming pope

846	Rome sacked by Arabs
849	Alfred the Great born
851	Canterbury Cathedral founded
871	Alfred the Great king of England (d. 899)
880	Italy reconquered from Arabs by Byzantines
900	Start of Christian reconquest of Spain
910	Foundation of the abbey of Cluny
982	Eric the Red and Vikings colonize Greeland
987	Hugh Capet (d. 996) king of France
988	Baptism of Vladimir; start of Russian Christianity

#	Pope	Start	End	Notes
139	Silvester II	2 Apr 999	12 May 1003	The first Frenchman, and one of the most cultured men, to become pope
140	John XVII	16 May 1003	6 Nov 1003	Practically nothing is known of this short reign
141	John XVIII	25 Dec 1003	Jul 1009	Improved relations with Constantinople; may have been deposed
142	Sergius IV	31 Jul 1009	12 May 1012	The son of a shoemaker, though little else is known about him
143	Benedict VIII	17 May 1012	9 Apr 1024	Although elected (while still a layman) in a disputed contest which he won by force of arms, he was a reformer of the Church as well as a powerful ruler who regained control of the papal estates in Italy
144	John XIX	19 Apr 1024	20 Oct 1032	Also a layman on his appointment; although under the thumb of the emperor, he was apparently greatly respected in the Church at large
145	Benedict IX	21 Oct 1032	finally deposed 16 Jul 1048 died 1055 or 1056	A layman on election, with a scandalous life, but proved to be an adequate pope; he was deposed three times
146	Silvester III	20 Jan 1045	abdicated 10 Mar 1045, died 1063	Included in the list of official popes, but was appointed while Benedict was still claiming papacy
147	Gregory VI	1 May 1045	deposed 20 Dec 1046, died 1047	Benedict IX supposedly sold the papacy to a member of Gregory's family; he was later deposed and replaced by Benedict himself
148	Clement II	24 Dec 1046	9 Oct 1047	Imposed by Emperor Henry III, he was a reforming pope with a particular campaign to stamp out simony
149	Damasus II	17 Jul 1048	9 Aug 1048	Delay in his appointment was a result of the intervention of Benedict IX
150	St Leo IX	12 Feb 1049	19 Apr 1054	Again a campaigner against simony, he travelled Europe promoting reform
151	Victor II	13 Apr 1055	28 Jul 1057	A vigorous reformer against simony and clerical concubinage; deposed several bishops
152	Stephen IX (X)	2 Aug 1057	29 Mar 1058	Was, and continued to be, Abbot of Monte Cassino, whose funds he used to defend southern Italy from the Normans
153	Nicholas II	6 Dec 1058	26 Jul 1061	Published election decree declaring that the choice of pope was to be in the hands of the cardinals
154	Alexander II	30 Sep 1061	21 Apr 1073	Supported Normans against English, and French against Moslems; forbade attendance at masses celebrated by married priests
155	St Gregory VII	22 Apr 1073	25 May 1085	Probably the greatest of the 11th-century reformers, with exalted view of powers of the papacy which brought him into collision with the emperor; he was forced to leave Rome, and died in exile
156	Bl Victor III	24 May 1086	16 Sep 1087	Abbot of Monte Cassino, he was elected in May 1086 but forced out of Rome to Monte Cassino, and was only able to recover the papacy on 9 May 1087
157	Bl Urban II	12 May 1088	29 Jul 1099	Most notable event of his reign was his proclamation of the first crusade, which was intended not only to recover the Holy Land, but to improve relations with the eastern Church
158	Paschal II	13 Aug 1099	21 Jan 1118	Campaigned for the abolition of lay investiture of bishops, without success in Germany, but more successfully in England and France
159	Gelasius II	24 Jan 1118	29 Jan 1119	Opposed by a faction in Rome and by the emperor, he had to flee the city and eventually died in France
160	Callistus II	2 Feb 1119	14 Dec 1124	He managed to bring a settlement to the investiture contest with the Concordat of Worms
161	Honorius II	21 Dec 1124	13 Feb 1130	Launched a campaign for the spiritual renewal of the Church
162	Innocent II	14 Feb 1130	24 Sep 1143	His election was irregular, but he gradually won support from across Europe for himself and for the reforms he continued in the spirit of Gregory VII
163	Celestine II	26 Sep 1143	8 Mar 1144	One of the more learned popes
164	Lucius II	12 Mar 1144	15 Feb 1145	Died of injuries received when trying to regain control of Rome from the commune by armed force
165	Bl Eugenius III	15 Feb 1145	8 Jul 1153	A Cistercian monk, he retained the dress, and way of life, of a monk even after his election, and quickly gained a reputation for sanctity
166	Anastasius IV	8 Jul 1153	3 Dec 1154	He was able to reach a *modus vivendi* with the Roman commune
167	Hadrian IV	4 Dec 1154	1 Sep 1159	Nicholas Breakspear – the only Englishman so far to be elected pope
168	Alexander III	7 Sep 1159	30 Aug 1181	During his pontificate the requirement of a two-thirds majority in papal elections was introduced, which is still in force
169	Lucius III	1 Sep 1181	25 Nov 1185	For most of his reign he was forced to live outside Rome. However, he proved an effective pope, thanks in part to generally good relations with Emperor Frederick Barbarossa
170	Urban III	25 Nov 1185	26 Oct 1187	He reversed Lucius' policy of good relations with Emperor Frederick, was unable to live in Rome
171	Gregory VIII	21 Oct 1187	17 Dec 1187	Friendly with Frederick, was on his way to Rome when he died
172	Clement III	19 Dec 1187	Mar 1191	Resolved conflicts both with the emperor and with the people of Rome, to which he returned
173	Celestine III	30 Mar 1191	8 Jan 1198	He was 85 on his election, and wanted to abdicate some months before he died, but was prevented from doing so by the cardinals

1014	Battle of Contarf, defeat of Danes in Ireland
1040	Macbeth king of Scotland (d. 1057)
1053	Foundation of Norman kingdom in southern Italy
1065	Consecration of Westminster Abbey
1066	William of Normandy's invasion of England
1086	Foundation of Carthusian order
1095	First crusade proclaimed
1098	Foundation of Citeaux, first Cistercian monastery
1099	Jerusalem captured by crusaders
1119	Foundation of University of Bologna
1145	Second crusade proclaimed
1150	Foundation of the University of Paris
1155	Birth of Genghis Khan
1167	Oxford University founded
1170	Murder of Thomas Becket
1174	'Leaning Tower' of Pisa begun
1187	Saladin defeats Christians at Battle of Hittin
1189	Third crusade proclaimed
1202	Fourth crusade proclaimed
1206	Genghis Khan Mongol ruler
1209	Francis of Assisi's first rule
1211	Genghis Khan invades China
1215	Dominican order founded; Magna Carta

174	Innocent III	8 Jan 1198	16 Jul 1216	The greatest of medieval popes as lawgiver, reformer and administrator	1217	Fifth crusade proclaimed
175	Honorius III	18 Jul 1216	18 Mar 1227	Great advocate of the crusade (the fifth) called for by his predecessor, and also for crusades against heretics in France and Moslems in Spain	1228	Sixth crusade proclaimed
176	Gregory IX	19 Mar 1227	22 Aug 1241	Made heresy punishable by death, and created the papal inquisition, entrusting it to the Dominican order		
177	Celestine IV	25 Oct 1241	10 Nov 1241	The cardinals were locked up to force them to reach a decision: they hoped to be able to vote free from external pressure in the next ballot, and deliberately chose a sick man as pope		
178	Innocent IV	25 Jun 1243	7 Dec 1254	The long delay in electing him was occasioned by the cardinals trying to free two of their number from imprisonment by the emperor	1248	Seventh crusade proclaimed
179	Alexander IV	12 Dec 1254	25 Mar 1261	He was humiliated in Rome, and spent most of his pontificate in Viterbo	1259	Kublai Khan first Mongol ruler of China
180	Urban IV	29 Aug 1261	2 Oct 1264	He had been a diplomat, and patriarch of Jerusalem, before his election; much more capable than his predecessor		
181	Clement IV	5 Feb 1265	29 Nov 1268	Continued Urban's policy of keeping the empire at bay	1265	Birth of Dante (d. 1321)
182	Bl Gregory X	1 Sep 1271	10 Jan 1276	Elected after two and a half years only when the mob threatened to lock the cardinals in, and starve them until they decided upon a candidate	1270	Eighth crusade proclaimed
183	Bl Innocent V	21 Jan 1276	22 Jun 1276	The first Dominican to become pope	1274	Death of Thomas Aquinas (b.c.1225)
184	Hadrian V	11 Jul 1276	18 Aug 1276	Although elected pope, he still had not been ordained priest when he died	1275	Marco Polo in service of Kublai Khan
185	John XXI	8 Sep 1276	20 May 1277	Died of injuries received when his study fell in on him (there was never a John XX)		
186	Nicholas III	25 Nov 1277	22 Aug 1280	He was the first pope to make the Vatican palace his main residence		
187	Martin IV	22 Feb 1281	28 Mar 1285	Very sympathetic to French interests, and so supportive of the friars that he annoyed the diocesan clergy	1282	'Sicilian Vespers' (massacre of the Normans)
88	Honorius IV	2 Apr 1285	3 Apr 1287	Also sympathetic to the French; but attempted, with little success, a rapprochement with the empire		
189	Nicholas IV	22 Feb 1288	4 Apr 1292	The first Franciscan to become pope	1292	Conquest of Acre by Mamelukes; last Christian presence in Holy Land
190	St Celestine V	5 Jul 1294	abdicated 13 Dec 1294, died May 1296	An 85-year-old hermit elected against his will, he abdicated after less than six months	1302	Bull 'Unam sanctum': zenith of papal claims
191	Boniface VIII	24 Dec 1294	11 Oct 1303	One of the most powerful and ambitious of popes, his ambitions frustrated because of a disastrous clash with the king of France; he called the first 'Holy Year' in 1300		
192	Bl Benedict XI	22 Oct 1303	7 Jul 1304	Attempted a policy of appeasement towards France		
193	Clement V	5 Jun 1305	20 Apr 1314	A Frenchman, and dominated by France, he asserted the papacy's control over the (German) empire	1314	Execution of Master of the Templars in Paris
194	John XXII	7 Aug 1316	4 Dec 1334	Another Frenchman, he effectively settled the papacy at Avignon; a very able administrator	1324	Death of Marco Polo
195	Benedict XII	20 Dec 1334	25 Apr 1342	Very much a reformer, he considered returning to Rome, and refurbished St Peter's and the Lateran, but also began work on the Palace of the Popes at Avignon	1327	Death of Meister Eckhart
196	Clement VI	7 May 1342	6 Dec 1352	A fifth Frenchman in succession, he spent lavishly in Avignon and depleted the papal treasury which his two predecessors had built up	1346	Battle of Crécy
197	Innocent VI	18 Dec 1352	12 Sept 1362	A rigorous reformer, he was preoccupied by efforts to pacify the papal states to prepare for a return to Rome – which he was unable to achieve	1349	Death of William Ockham (b. 1290)
198	Bl Urban V	28 Sep 1362	19 Dec 1370	Though French, in 1367 he returned the papal curia to Rome; but he left the financial administration in Avignon		
199	Gregory XI	30 Dec 1370	27 Mar 1378	Again French, and elected in Avignon, he did not arrive in Rome until Jan 1377		
200	Urban VI	8 Apr 1378	15 Oct 1389	First papal election in Rome since that of Benedict XI – and he was an Italian – but he alienated his cardinals, who declared him deposed and elected another pope, thus beginning the Great Schism	1384	Death of John Wyclif (b. c. 1328)
201	Boniface IX	2 Nov 1389	1 Oct 1404	A highly capable pope who strengthened his own position while making little or no attempt to resolve the schism		
202	Innocent VII	17 Oct 1404	6 Nov 1406	Made some, but very ineffectual, effort to end the schism, but was himself not particularly popular in Rome		
203	Gregory XII	30 Nov 1406	4 Jul 1415	Deposed in 1409 at the Council of Pisa in an effort to end the schism (though all it did was to create a third claimant to the papacy), he did not abdicate until the Council of Constance, and died in Oct 1417	1411	John Hus excommunicated
204	Martin V	11 Nov 1417	20 Feb 1431	Elected after the death of Gregory; his succession effectively ended the schism; though constrained by Constance to reform the Church and accept conciliar government, Martin attempted fairly successfully to regain authority for the papacy	1415	Battle of Agincourt; execution of John Hus
205	Eugenius IV	3 Mar 1431	23 Feb 1447	His reign was dominated by a final effort to assert the supremacy of a council over a pope, from which struggle Eugenius emerged victorious; he also negotiated a (short-lived) reunion with the Greek Orthodox Church	1431	Execution of Joan of Arc
206	Nicholas V	6 Mar 1447	24 Mar 1455	Won back the friendship of the Romans largely lost by his predecessor, and greatly enhanced the beauty of the city, as well as attracting scholars there	1450	Guttenberg's commercial printing venture
207	Callistus III	8 Apr 1455	6 Aug 1458	Wanted to organize a crusade to reconquer Constantinople – his efforts to raise money to do so alienated several of the nations of Europe	1453	Fall of Constantinople to the Turks
208	Pius II	19 Aug 1458	15 Aug 1464	The father of several illegitimate children before his ordination, he lived a blameless life afterwards; he was renowned both as a scholar and as a diplomat	1458	Turkish sack of Acropolis

209	Paul II	30 Aug 1464	26 Jul 1471	In reaction to Pius, definitely not a humanist, though he continued his predecessor's efforts to halt the Turkish advance	1469	Ferdinand of Aragon marries Isabella of Castile
210	Sixtus IV	9 Aug 1471	12 Aug 1484	Though he came from a poor family and was a Franciscan, as pope he added greatly to the wealth of his relations; he was a great patron of the arts		
211	Innocent VII	29 Aug 1484	25 July 1492	Affable but wholly ineffectual both within the Church and in his foreign policy	1492	First voyage of Columbus
212	Alexander VI	11 Aug 1492	18 Aug 1503	The most notorious of Renaissance pope because of his profligate life, he promoted the careers of his children, especially Cesare Borgia, and created the brother of his current mistress a cardinal; he was also a patron of the arts	1493	Bull 'Inter cetera divina'; to divide New World between Spain/Portugal
213	Pius III	22 Sep 1503	18 Oct 1503	Chosen as a compromise candidate because of his age	1498	Erasmus teaching : Oxford
214	Julius II	1 Nov 1503	21 Feb 1513	A sworn enemy of the Borgia family, he tried to win back the papal states which Alexander VI had alienated, himself in full armour leading the papal troops in battle; he commissioned a new St Peter's, to pay for which he authorized the sale of indulgences	1506	Rebuilding of St Peter's begins
215	Leo X	11 Mar 1513	1 Dec 1521	He encouraged the sale of indulgences, and did not take seriously Luther's revolt	1517	Luther's ninety-five thesis
216	Hadrian VI	9 Dec 1522	14 Sep 1523	A devout man, the last non-Italian (from Utrecht) before the present pope	1520	Luther excommunicated
217	Clement VII	19 Nov 1523	25 Sep 1534	Tried to keep a balance between France and the Empire, but Rome was sacked by imperial troops, and he himself held prisoner for a while; the pope of Henry VIII's divorce from Catherine of Aragon	1521	Pope givesHenry VIII title 'Defender of the Faith'
					1527	Sack of Rome by imperial troops
218	Paul III	13 Oct 1534	10 Nov 1549	The pope who called the great reforming Council of Trent; also a patron of Michelangelo, whom he commissioned to paint 'The Last Judgement' in the Sistine Chapel	1535	Execution of Thomas Moore and John Fisher
219	Julius III	8 Feb 1550	23 Mar 1555	Also a patron of the arts, and in some respects a reforming pope, he reconvened the Council of Trent	1540	Jesuits formally established by papal bull
220	Marcellus II	9 Apr 1555	1 May 1555	Was expected to be a highly cultivated, reforming pope, but died three weeks after his election	1556	Archbishop Thomas Cranmer burnt at the stake
221	Paul IV	23 May 1555	18 Aug 1559	A vigorous, even fanatical, opponent of anything that seemed unorthodox in doctrine, he published the first *Index of Forbidden Books*	1558	English loss of Calais
222	Pius IV	25 Dec 1559	9 Dec 1565	He reconvened the Council of Trent, bringing it to a successful conclusion		
223	St Pius V	7 Jan 1566	1 May 1572	A rigorist in moral matters and personally very devout, he promoted the reforms of Trent; he also excommunicated, and claimed to depose Queen Elizabeth I of England	1571	Battle of Lepanto
224	Gregory XIII	14 May 1572	10 Apr 1585	A reformer, though in a more gentle mode than his predecessor, he promoted in particular better education for the clergy; he was in general a patron of learning, and sponsored the reform of the calendar which is named after him. Calendar reformed in much of Europe, but not in England.	1572	St Bartholomew's Day massacre in Paris
					1582	Reform of calendar in much of Europe
225	Sixtus V	24 Apr 1585	27 Aug 1590	Ruthless in bringing law and order to the papal states, he also brought the papal finances under control, and reorganized the administration of the Catholic Church into the style which it still has today	1588	Defeat of Spanish Armada
					1600	Giordano Bruno executed as a heretic
226	Urban VII	15 Sep 1590	27 Sep 1590	Taken ill just after his election, he died before he was crowned	1607	First English settlement on American mainland
227	Gregory XIV	5 Dec 1590	16 Oct 1591	A pious man, but ineffectual, he left much of the running of the papacy to his 29-year-old nephew, whom he made a cardinal, and who was equally useless		
228	Innocent IX	29 Oct 1591	30 Dec 1591	Elected as a stopgap, he made efforts to improve the papacy's finances	1611	Authorized version of the Bible published
229	Clement VIII	30 Jan 1592	5 Mar 1605	Devout and conscientious, he was also somewhat indecisive, though completely committed to reform; revised versions of the Roman liturgy were published during his pontificate	1616	Death of Shakespeare (b.1564) and Cervantes (b. 1547)
230	Leo XI	1 Apr 1605	27 Apr 1605	His career had shown him a reformer, but he died too soon to pursue a programme of reform as pope	1618	Beginning of the Thirty Year's War
231	Paul V	16 May 1605	28 Jan 1621	Also a reformer, though one with a high, and somewhat outmoded, view of papal supremacy	1620	Plymouth colony in Massachussetts founded by Pilgrim Fathers
232	Gregory XV	9 Feb 1621	8 Jul 1623	He was the first pope to have been educated by the Jesuits, and was committed to reform; one aspect of Church life he reformed (in great detail) was the method of electing popes; he also founded a congregation to promote missionary work	1633	Galileo forced to reject theories of Copernicus by Roman Inqusition
233	Urban VIII	6 Aug 1623	29 Jul 1644	He founded a college to train missionaries, which is still named after him, and settled the procedures for canonizing saints; he also completed, and consecrated, St Peter's, after more than a century in building; he condemned Galileo, though the astronomer was a personal friend	1642	Start of English Civil War
234	Innocent X	15 Sep 1644	1 Jan 1655	His pontificate saw the first condemnation of the 'Chinese Rites' adopted by Jesuit missionaries to China, and of the doctrines of Jansenism	1649	King Charles I beheaded
235	Alexander VII	7 Apr 1655	22 May 1667	A deeply spiritual, learned and cultured man, though no great politician, he commissioned Bernini to surround the piazza in front of St Peter's with colonnades; he repeated the condemnation of Jansenism, though he relaxed the prohibition on the Chinese Rites	1658	Death of Oliver Cromwell
					1660	Restoration of the monarchy in England
236	Clement IX	20 Jun 1667	9 Dec 1669	He improved relations between the papacy and France, at a low ebb during previous pontificates, but only at the cost of allowing Louis XIV to control appointments to bishoprics	1665	Great Plague
					1666	Great Fire of London
237	Clement X	29 Apr 1670	22 Jul 1676	He was outmanoeuvred by Louis XIV, but financially assisted Jan Sobieski in his campaign to halt the Turkish advance	1673	Defeat of Turks by Polish army under Jan Sobieski

238	Bl Innocent XI	21 Sep 1676	12 Aug 1689	A devout man with high moral standards for others as well as himself, he stood up to Louis XIV and formed a 'Holy League' against Turkey	1682	French claim to Louisiana
239	Alexander VIII	6 Oct 1689	1 Feb 1691	Attempted to improve relations with France, though finally without success, and reiterated the condemnation of Jansenism; he improved the standard of life of the population of the papal states, and was generally popular	1688	'Glorious Revolution', James II flees England
240	Innocent XII	12 Jul 1691	27 Sep 1700	Another devout man who consciously modelled himself on Innocent XI, he continued to improve conditions in the papal states, and improved relations with France	1689	Dutch foundation of Natal in southern Africa
241	Clement XI	23 Nov 1700	19 Mar 1721	He was ordained priest only shortly before the conclave, and accepted the papacy with reluctance; he definitively condemned Jansenism, and was an energetic supporter of missionary activity – though he also finally condemned the Chinese Rites	1703	Foundation of St Petersberg
242	Innocent XIII	8 May 1721	7 Mar 1724	When he learned that the Jesuits were not observing the condemnation of Chinese Rites, he considered suppressing the order		
243	Benedict XIII	29 May 1724	21 Feb 1730	A Dominican of devout life, he was concerned with the religious discipline of the Church and left more secular matters to others – with disastrous results	1729	Foundation of Baltimore
244	Clement XII	12 Jul 1730	6 Feb 1740	Bedridden and blind for much of his pontificate, and ineffectual as a politician, he tried without much success to improve the situation in the papal states, but certainly improved Rome itself; he also showed considerable interest in the eastern-rite Churches, especially the Maronites	1738	John Wesley's conversion
245	Benedict XIV	7 Aug 1740	3 May 1758	One of the most sympathetic of all popes, he established good relations with many of the states of Europe, improved the finances of the papal states, reformed the liturgy, and revised the Index along more scholarly lines	1746	'Young Pretender' defeated at Culloden
246	Clement XIII	6 Jul 1758	2 Feb 1769	Had to withstand efforts to have the Jesuit order suppressed	1759	British victory at Quebec
247	Clement XIV	19 May 1769	22 Sep 1774	His election was dominated by the efforts of France, Spain and Portugal to ensure that the new pope would suppress the Jesuits – he did so	1771	*Encyclopeaedia Britannica*
248	Pius VI	15 Feb 1775	29 Aug 1799	Sympathetic to the Jesuits, he was unable to do anything to help the order; his pontificate was dominated by Austrian efforts to control the Church, then by the effects of the French revolution, and finally by Napoleon, who had him arrested and brought to France, where he died after one of the longest papacies in history	1773	Boston Tea Party
					1775	American Revolution starts
					1780	Gordon riots in London
					1783	Independence of USA
					1789	Storming the Bastille
249	Pius VII	14 Mar 1800	20 Jul 1823	A reign again dominated by Napoleon, who arrested Pius and brought him back to France after the papal states had been annexed; he was a prisoner from 1809 to 1814, a fact which won him much sympathy with the result that, after Napoleon's defeat, the papal states were restored; Pius also reinstated the Jesuits	1791	Death of John Wesley
					1793	Execution of Louis XVI
					1805	The Battle of Trafalgar
					1813	Napoleon's retreat from Moscow
250	Leo XII	28 Sep 1823	10 Feb 1829	A generally conservative figure, especially in his treatment of the papal states, pursuing a policy which made him very unpopular	1822	Battle of Waterloo
251	Pius VIII	31 Mar 1829	30 Nov 1830	Something of a reformer, particularly in the papal states	1829	Emancipation of Catholics in Britain
252	Gregory XVI	2 Feb 1831	1 Jun 1846	An austere monk, he was uncompromisingly conservative in his treatment of the papal states and of Catholic doctrine	1837	Accession of Queen Victoria
253	Pius IX	16 Jun 1846	7 Feb 1878	When elected Pius had a reputation as something of a liberal, but he became increasingly conservative, both religiously and politically; in his pontificate the papal states finally disappeared with the fall of Rome in 1870 to Italian troops; this happened while the first Vatican Council was in session, which approved the declaration of papal infallibility	1848	'The Year of Revolutions';
					1861	American Civil War began
					1883	Death of Karl Marx
					1899	Start of the Boer War
					1914	Outbreak of first world war
254	Leo XIII	20 Feb 1878	20 Jul 1903	An old man when elected, he lived to the age of 93; he made considerable efforts to bring the Church into line with modern scholarship	1918	End of the first world war
255	St Pius X	4 Aug 1903	20 Aug 1914	Though personally very devout, and eager to encourage devotion in others, an intransigent opponent of much contemporary scholarship, condemned under the name of 'modernism'	1926	General strike in Britain
					1929	Vatican City state established by Lateran pacts
256	Benedict XV	3 Sep 1914	22 Jan 1922	Much of his pontificate was dominated by the first world war, and afterwards by his efforts towards reconciliation among nations	1933	Adolf Hitler chancellor of Germany
257	Pius XI	6 Feb 1922	10 Feb 1939	His pontificate saw the establishment of the independent Vatican City state, but his reign was overshadowed by the rise of fascism, first in Italy and then in Germany	1939	Start of second world war
258	Pius XII	2 Mar 1939	9 Oct 1958	The 'silence' of Pius over the persecution of Jews has coloured his reputation which, doctrinally, was progressive until the 1950s	1945	End of second world war
259	John XXIII	28 Oct 1958	3 Jun 1963	One of the most popular of popes, he summoned the second Vatican Council to bring the Church up to date	1947	Independence for India and Pakistan
260	Paul VI	21 Jun 1963	6 Aug 1978	He had the task of implementing the decisions of the council, something which he approached rather hesitantly; in his social outlook, however, he was very progressive	1950	Start of Korean war
261	John Paul I	26 Aug 1978	28 Sep 1978	His sudden death occasioned rumours that he had been poisoned because he was either going to expose scandals in the Church, or reverse the teaching on birth control; he died, of course, a natural death	1956	Suez crisis; Russian invasion of Hungary
262	John Paul II	16 Oct 1978	2 Apr 2005	A Pole, the first non-Italian in over four centuries, and one of the papacy's most charismatic, as well as most controversial, figures	1980	Jerusalem proclaimed capital of Israel
263	Benedict XVI	19 Apr 2005		Formerly Dean of the College of Cardinals, Joseph Ratzinger was a close friend of John Paul II		

INTO THE NEXT MILLENNIUM

PAUL JOHNSON

AT THE END OF THIS survey of two thousand years of papal history, it is necessary to ask three questions. The first is: will the papacy survive? Will there still be popes at the end of the third millennium? We can answer this with confidence: yes, there are likely to be popes as long as the human race endures. The papacy is not only the oldest institution of its kind in the world, it has also succeeded in adjusting itself to modernity. It has put its relationship with the Italian state on a sensible footing. It has official, and usually cordial, relations with most of the world's powers, great and small. It has an experienced and, in most respects, highly efficient diplomatic service. It is remarkably well informed, and it has its own extensive press and broadcasting services for putting its point of view.

The Vatican state is not large, but it is not insignificant either. The City State itself employs about 1,300 people, mostly lay people recruited in Italy. The Holy See is larger and far more international, with (in the mid–1990s) 719 clergy, 261 religious men, 110 nuns, 1,115 laymen and 278 laywomen. It can and does function as a small government with administrative links all over the world, and it pays its way. There have been difficulties and even scandals in Vatican finances in recent decades, but they are now managed far more openly and in accordance with modern accounting procedures. The papacy is not rich. Despite the mythology, it never has been, and never will be. But its means are adequate and are now soundly looked after. One reform which has been carried through successfully in recent years is the rationalizing of the Vatican's matchless art collection. The linked series of museums, galleries and libraries employs 250 people and is now self-supporting from the entrance fees charged its 2.6 million annual visitors, from cassettes, reproductions and the profits of its gift shops. The royalties earned by the museum and library from printing and licensing deals enable them to spend about $5 million annually on maintaining, repairing, cleaning and exhibiting their treasures. The popes, in fact, having been among the greatest of art collectors and patrons, are now celebrated for the care and the wisdom with which they look after the Vatican's possessions. And, under the late pope, immense trouble was taken to improve, regularize and order the liturgical ceremonies at St Peter's which, by general agreement, had never been better conducted and sung. In all externals, therefore, the future of the papacy seems secure and serene.

The second question is: what function does the papacy perform for the world today? That is more difficult to answer, because its work is so many-sided. But the Holy Roman Catholic and Apostolic Church is the largest of all religious communities on earth, and the most widespread. The papacy is its living heart, its organizing principle, and its directing mind. That is a huge task in itself. But the papacy is also in a wider sense one of the world's most pervasive international institutions. It speaks for humanity at prayer. When the Second Vatican Council – the twenty-first in the history of the papacy, going back to Nicaea in 325 AD – assembled in 1962, more than 2,500 bishops, archbishops, patriarchs and other dignitaries of the Church came to Rome from all over the world, representing communities big and small. The Vicar Apostolic or Holar, in Iceland, had a flock of only 806; the Cardinal-archbishop of Chicago had nearly 2,120,000 Catholics under his care. Those present deliberated on behalf of close to a billion Catholic believers, and not even the United Nations in full session was more representative of all peoples and races and cultures. To gather together, in peace and fruitful discussion, leaders of so many people united in their religious faith, was a noble work in itself. Of course, an ecumenical council is not an everyday affair, and we do not know when the next will be held. But much of the routine work the papacy performs, in private and without ostentation, resembles the tasks which a council undertakes in so public and spectacular a fashion – informing the world, receiving messages from the world, concerting with the world. The daily task of the papacy is one of enlightening, ordering and harmonizing. It is a global spiritual empire, in which the final bell for vespers and sleep never sounds.

Finally, we must ask: will the papacy ever change? The answer is that the papacy has been, and is still, changing all the time. It is an organic institution, which has deep roots in the past and the ability to refresh and renew itself with every year that passes. The changes which have taken place in the papacy since the pontificate of John XXIII, during which the Second Vatican Council opened, have been

without precedent and are still being absorbed, adapted and modified. There have been commensurate changes under the late pope, John Paul II, who turned the papacy into a great engine of pastoral solicitude, reaching out constantly to the entire world. These changes will continue, and possibly accelerate and intensify. The world is changing and the Catholic Church is changing too. The biggest areas of numerical growth in the Church are now Africa, Latin America and parts of Asia. We must expect their influence to increase accordingly, as the once-predominant (and still important) role of Europe declines. The papacy will become more international. Popes will be elected from Asia, Africa and the Americas. And popes will continue, from time to time, to call ecumenical councils, which will reflect these shifts in the Church's centre of gravity, and will introduce the changes in organizing, worship and interpretation of doctrine which will be needed.

But while such changes will be constant, if sometimes almost imperceptible – the time-scale of the papacy is geological in its slow processes – the great certitudes of the Catholic and Apostolic faith will be maintained. The papacy changes, the popes come and go, but the faith remains, as Jesus Christ gave it to his apostles, led by Peter, and as Peter and his successors have given it to the world for two thousand years. The popes stand for continuity, and they stand for certitude. What they teach is in all essentials what they taught in the first century AD, when they were hunted men living in the catacombs. That, to most believers, is the central attraction of the Catholic Church, and the chief virtue of the papacy which rules it. At the dawning of the third millennium, the continuing ability of the papacy to combine changes in externals and means, with perpetuity in fundamentals and ends, is its strength and its appeal. So the centuries stretch ahead, and the papacy, from its setting in the Eternal City, looks towards them with confidence.

INDEX

PICTURE CREDITS